"In an age where AI is amplifying human capabilities, this book makes a timely contribution by demystifying how groups can generate novel insights. It shows how hybrid intelligence can be orchestrated with structure and vision. It is a practical blueprint for collaborative problem-solving."

Dr. Alan Dennis, *Professor of Information Systems, Indiana University*

"Kevin facilitated a strategy workshop for our global professional association using many of the methods explained in *Hybrid Intelligence: Merging Collective and Artificial Intelligence to Solve Complex Problems*. It was the most insightful strategy session we've ever conducted."

Patrick Farrey, *CEO, SPE*

"As a researcher specializing in computer-supported collaborative learning and the author of *Group Cognition: Computer Support for Building Collaborative Knowledge*, I can tell you that Kevin's book is a worthy read. He does a remarkable job of explaining the sociological and technological configurations that support collaborative knowledge building."

Dr. Gerry Stahl, *Professor Emeritus, Drexel University*

"I have been engaged in research on Group Support Systems for 35 years. I see great promise in the path to the future of team collaboration that Kevin Holt sketches out in this book. And he does so in a very interesting way: He engages in a discussion with the great scholars of the field, with ChatGPT and with his own past as a facilitator. Thus we can see at work what he tells us: AI will fundamentally change the way teams collaborate. I recommend this book for all visionaries, practitioners, and researchers of team collaboration."

Dr. Gerhard Schwabe, *Professor of Informatics, University of Zurich*

"Kevin is a pioneer of computer-supported meetings. In *Hybrid Intelligence: Merging Collective and Artificial Intelligence to Solve Complex Problems*, he charts how collective and artificial intelligence can be combined. I highly recommend this book."

Dr. Wolfram Hoegel, *Co-Founder, XLeap*

"The best solutions come from harnessing diverse perspectives—whether human or AI. Kevin's book dives deep into how collective and artificial intelligence can work together to solve complex problems, a concept we live every day at IdeaS decision-making, innovation, and the futu ust-read."

CEO, IdeaScale

"I'm happy to endorse *Hybrid Intelligence: Merging Collective and Artificial Intelligence to Solve Complex Problems*. This future-forward treatment of group thinking is a critically important read for leaders who want to survive and thrive in a world that is growing progressively more complex."

Woody Wade, *Author of* Scenario Planning: A Field Guide to the Future

"Some two decades ago, Kevin started facilitating computer-supported planning meetings for our global hotel industry conferences. He was ahead of his time then. And he's ahead of his time now. Merging collective and artificial intelligence has amazing potential to generate breakthrough ideas."

Jim Burba, *Co-Founder, Burba Hotel Network*

Hybrid Intelligence

Uniquely aimed at teams that think together to solve problems and make decisions, this book explains how to enhance the collective intelligence of a team-size group and combine it with the artificial intelligence of generative AI to create a hybrid intelligence that is smarter than either one on its own.

Boards, committees, and other team-size groups of 5–20 people are the primary problem-solving and decision-making units within organizations, and they form the bridges between organizations, industries, and nations that collaborate on projects. So how can leaders exponentially improve their teams' capabilities? Assemble the right *people*, arm them with the right *processes*, and execute those processes on the right *platforms*—then add generative AI to enhance those practices. This book describes and synthesizes various ways of increasing a group's collective intelligence through people, process, and platform practices, and goes on to explain how to augment the practices with generative AI, including how to ask it questions and what questions to ask to obtain superior answers. The resulting upsurge in team capability enables organizations to survive and thrive in a world that is growing progressively more competitive and complex.

This book will become the definitive resource for leaders and managers of commercial, government, and nonprofit organizations who want to learn how to significantly improve their teams' problem-solving and decision-making ability by increasing their collective intelligence and combining it with the artificial intelligence of generative AI.

Kevin Holt, the founder of Co.Innovation Consulting, is a Phoenix-based consultant who has been facilitating strategy and problem-solving workshops since 2001. His unique approach combines computer-supported meeting technology, generative AI, and specialized software tools. He has facilitated workshops throughout the United States and in London, Geneva, Singapore, and Delhi, as well as online. Kevin is the author of

Differentiation Strategy: Winning Customers by Being Different, published by Routledge in June 2022. Before he started facilitating meetings, he held officer-level real estate positions with national hotel companies, owned a small retail business, and operated a hotel development consulting practice. Kevin received a BS degree from the University of Wisconsin–Madison and an MBA from Arizona State University.

Hybrid Intelligence

Merging Collective and Artificial Intelligence to Solve Complex Problems

Kevin Holt

Routledge
Taylor & Francis Group
NEW YORK AND LONDON

Designed cover image: Getty

First published 2026
by Routledge
605 Third Avenue, New York, NY 10158

and by Routledge
4 Park Square, Milton Park, Abingdon, Oxon, OX14 4RN

Routledge is an imprint of the Taylor & Francis Group, an informa business

ISBN: 978-1-041-10303-5 (hbk)
ISBN: 978-1-041-10302-8 (pbk)
ISBN: 978-1-003-65440-7 (ebk)

DOI: 10.4324/9781003654407

Typeset in Sabon
by Apex CoVantage, LLC

For Hattie, Nora, Ruthie, Lucy, Mae, and Hayes

Contents

Introduction

This book explains how to enhance the *collective intelligence* of a group of people and combine it with the *artificial intelligence* of generative AI to create a *hybrid intelligence* that is smarter than either intelligence alone.

The focus of this book is boards, committees, and other team-size groups gathered in a meeting room (physical or virtual) who are *thinking together* to solve a problem. Imagine, for example, a board of directors in a boardroom thinking about how to prevent a hostile takeover, or a group of engineers on a video conference call pondering the best design for a mechanical part, or a management team in a meeting room planning a product launch. This book is *not* about sports teams, surgical teams, or other teams where the members are *acting together* to win a game, repair a heart, or perform some other physical task. Nor is it about the networks, crowds, swarms, and other large groups that are frequently the focus of books on collective intelligence.[1]

Why focus on small problem-solving groups? Three reasons. First is the essential role they play in the organizations to which they belong. As Geoff Mulgan, a professor at University College London, former CEO of Nesta, and author of *Big Mind: How Collective Intelligence Can Change Our World*, explains, "Most organizations still depend on the board or committee, usually made up of between five and twenty people, for the most crucial decisions. This remains the supreme decision-making body in organizations as varied as Ford and the Politburo, Green-peace, and Google."[2] Others note that teams are the means by which organizations collaborate with one another, "Teams form the bridges between organizations, industries, and nations that 'collaborate' on massive projects. . . . The team as organizing instrument is tailored to address specific problems and challenges ranging from pharmaceutical research on personalized medicine to [the] assembly of deep-sea, oil-drilling rigs or [the] launch of a rocket to the planet Mars."[3]

The second reason relates to the first. The reason small teams play such an essential role in and between organizations, explains computer scientist

DOI: 10.4324/9781003654407-1

Gerry Stahl, is the fact that they are the fundamental units of knowledge building. "Collaborative knowledge building," he elaborates, "involves the construction or further development of some kind of knowledge artifact . . . [which] might be developing a theory, model, diagnosis, conceptual map, mathematical proof, or presentation. . . . In effective collaborative knowledge building, the group must engage in *thinking together* (italics mine) about a problem or task and produce a knowledge artifact . . . that integrates their different perspectives on the topic and represents a shared group result that they have negotiated."[4]

The third reason I chose to focus on small problem-solving groups is a selfish one. As Max Bennett, author of *A Brief History of Intelligence: Evolution, AI, and the Five Breakthroughs That Made Our Brains*, put it, "I wrote this book because I wanted to read this book."[5] I wrote this book for the same reason. I wrote it to clarify and expand my thinking about the best ways to facilitate a meeting. I started facilitating meetings in 2001 when I became enamored of electronic brainstorming, a collaboration technology developed at the University of Arizona. This led me to the idea of combining behavioral, procedural, and technological interventions—more easily remembered as *people*, *process*, and *platform* practices—to increase the collective intelligence of a small group. In the past year, I've come to realize the *extraordinary* potential of adding generative AI to the mix. I've italicized extraordinary to convey that I mean *extraordinarily extraordinary*. Like so extraordinary that it prompted Henry Kissinger (former Harvard professor and Secretary of State), Eric Schmidt (former CEO of Google), and Daniel Hutttenlocher (inaugural dean of the College of Computing at MIT) to co-author a multi-page opinion piece in the *Wall Street Journal* titled "ChatGPT Heralds an Intellectual Revolution."[6]

This book explains the people, process, and platform *practices* you can use to increase the collective intelligence of a small problem-solving group, with considerable attention paid to the way artificial intelligence can be used to augment the practices. But before that, it explains the *theory* that underlies the practices, which is to say, the meaning and nature of collective intelligence, artificial intelligence, problem-solving, thinking, and thinking together. I've included the theory because I'm a big believer in an idea arguably attributed to the philosopher Immanual Kant: *Theory without practice is empty; practice without theory is blind.*

At times, you might think I've veered too far into the theoretical weeds: *Semantic pointers? Are you kidding me? And cognitive linguistics? Give me a break! What could these things possibly have to do with making my team smarter?* Keep an open mind and read on, for in nearly every case I provide practical applications of the concepts, like using semantic pointers and cognitive linguistics to get better answers out of the kind of generative AI known as large language models (LLMs), such as ChatGPT.

Or you might consider parts of the book too practical, too pedestrian: *Whiteboards? Floorplans? Tables? Seating arrangements? Managing the conversation? These are things better left to a meeting facilitator or low-level person. Surely, they don't warrant the attention of* CEOs *and senior managers.* Well, I beg to differ. And so too, I suspect, would some significant CEOs. Like Apple's Steve Jobs, who loved whiteboards for brainstorming and designed meeting spaces to foster deep focus and collaboration.[7] And Tesla's Elon Musk who, like Jobs, is a whiteboard devotee and obsessed with making meeting spaces more functional. And Amazon's Jeff Bezos who, like Musk, insists on meeting rooms that are designed for work, not luxury, and who uses the *Two-Pizza Rule* to limit the size of meetings—if the meeting can't be fed with two pizzas, it's too big.[8] And General Stanley McChrystal, who concerned himself with the tiniest details of the way the Joint Operations Center in Iraq was set up, including the U-shaped seating configuration that enabled the Task Force commander and key leaders to see and communicate with each other as they worked.[9] And Alan Mulally, the CEO responsible for the near-miraculous turnaround of Ford Motor Company, who prohibited mobile phones, side discussions, and jokes at other's expense in his weekly meetings.[10]

I've written this book for leaders who want to get serious about increasing the collective intelligence of their teams. It's for CEOs who understand the value of people like Julia Rozovsky, the researcher at Google who played a key role in Project Aristotle, the internal Google study that identified *psychological safety* as the most critical factor in high-performing teams and Laszlo Bock, the former senior vice president at Google, who advocated for using *data-driven approaches* to understand and optimize team performance.[11] It's for leaders who want to emulate Ed Catmull, the co-founder and former president of Pixar Animation Studios, and Ray Dalio, the founder and CEO of the hedge fund Bridgewater Associates, both of whom recognize the value of *constructive dissent* and have gone to great lengths to institutionalize it in their organizations. And it's for managers who appreciate the way Demis Hassabis, co-founder and CEO of DeepMind, who along with John Jumper, the lead research scientist, assembled the *cognitively diverse* multi-disciplinary AlphaFold team that revolutionized protein structure prediction, solving one of biology's grand challenges.

Despite the extraordinary success of CEOs and managers who have attended to the minutia of *meetings*—as Jobs, Musk, Bezos, McChrystal, Mulally, Rozovsky, Bock, Catmull, Dalio, Hassabis, and Jumper have done—most leaders pay scant attention to *this way we think together.*

Just ask Geoff Mulgan, who observes, "Oddly, the vast majority of meetings in business, academia, and politics ignore almost everything that is known about what makes meetings work."[12] James Surowiecki, the author of *The Wisdom of Crowds*, elaborates on Mulgan's observation, "In fact, few organizations have figured out how to make groups work consistently well. For all the lip service paid, particularly in corporate America, to the importance of teams and the need to make meetings more productive, it's still unusual for a small group to be more than just the sum of its parts. Much of the time, far from adding value to their members, groups seem to subtract from it."[13]

In a world where generative AI is equalizing intelligence, making a team more than the sum of its parts has become a critical thing to do. Traditionally, management teams have outperformed others by being collectively more intelligent, by being smarter than their peers. Generative AI changes that by enabling less intelligent teams to be as smart as top performing teams. Azeem Azhar, a British futurist who specializes in technology, explains, "For most of history, hiring a dozen PhDs meant a massive budget and months of lead time. Today, a few keystrokes in a chatbot summon that brainpower in seconds. As intelligence becomes cheaper and faster, the basic assumption underpinning our institutions—that human insight is scarce and expensive—no longer holds.... The question facing individuals and organizations alike is: What will you do when intelligence itself is suddenly ubiquitous and practically free?"[14] My answer is that organizations—their CEOs, in particular—must get serious about attending to the people, process, and platform practices that make a team more than the sum of its parts. Then go a step further by using generative AI to augment the practices. That's what this book is about.[15]

I explain the theory (foundational knowledge) that underlies these practices in Chapter 1, where I ask and answer the following questions: *What is collective intelligence? What is artificial intelligence? What is a problem? What is thinking? Where is thinking? How do groups think together? What makes a group smarter than its smartest member?* You'll be in far better position to practice the practice once you know the answers to these questions.

In Chapter 2, I explain that the central driver of a group's collective intelligence is the cognitive diversity of its members. But the benefits of this diversity are fully realized only when the group members know how to speak, listen and converse, abstain from dysfunctional meeting behaviors, and employ a collaboration strategy.

Chapter 3 addresses three types of processes—meeting, group, and problem-solving processes, including task-specific problem-solving methods. Meeting processes have to do with the agenda and facilitator's guide used to design the meeting. Group processes are about ways for the group members to interact with each other to exchange and synthesize their unique perspectives. Problem-solving processes include methods for identifying the causes of the problem and generating ways to act on the causes. In sum, the meeting process specifies the group processes that will be used to implement the problem-solving processes.

The meeting rooms and analog and digital tools used to execute the processes are explained in Chapter 4, where I talk about *what* questions to ask generative AI and *how* to ask them (prompt engineering). I also emphasize the extraordinary potential of pairing generative AI and electronic brainstorming technology and the value of using dialogue mapping tools to track the elements of a conversation.

Chapter 5 ends this book where others begin, by explaining why this age, more than any other, demands that we learn to do a better job of thinking together, which is to say, by explaining why we need to learn how to increase our *collective intelligence* and combine it with *artificial intelligence* to create a *hybrid intelligence* that is smarter than the two intelligences alone.

One last thing. You'll find that throughout this book I've asked ChatGPT-4o questions about the topic I'm explaining or describing. In each case, the use of ChatGPT is referenced with an endnote and the question and answer are set off by a box. I've asked the questions for four reasons. First, to capture what ChatGPT knows about the topic. Second, to discover how generative AI can be used to augment the people, process, and platform practices. Third, to show you the kinds of questions you can ask generative AI and the surprising depth and utility of its answers. And fourth, to help you understand that your mindset needs to shift from *knowing the answers* to *knowing the questions*. AI is many orders of magnitude smarter than you are, so it's almost always going to have better answers than you do.[16] But it doesn't know the questions to ask itself. That's your role. You need to understand that with the advent of AI, your role is shifting from being the *knower* to being the *questioner*. Most important is to understand the role hybrid intelligence can play in creating the *ingenious questions* that enable your organization to solve problems others cannot.

Now, let's take our first step into the future of thinking together.

Notes

1 See, for example, James Surowiecki, *The Wisdom of Crowds: Why the Many Are Smarter Than the Few and How Collective Wisdom Shapes Business, Economies, Societies, and Nations* (New York, NY: Anchor Books, 2004); Peter A. Gloor, *Swarm Creativity: Competitive Advantage Through Collaborative Innovation Networks* (Oxford, UK: Oxford University Press, 2006).

2 Geoff Mulgan, *Big Mind: How Collective Intelligence Can Change Our World* (Princeton, NJ: Princeton University Press, 2018), 131.
3 Michael Beyerlein, Soo Jeoung Han, and Ambika Prasad, "A Multilevel Model of Collaboration and Creativity," in Roni Reiter-Palmon (Ed.), *Team Creativity and Innovation* (Oxford, UK: Oxford University Press, 2018), 196.
4 Gerry Stahl, *Group Cognition: Computer Support for Building Collaborative Knowledge* (Cambridge, MA: The MIT Press, 2006), 3.
5 Max Bennett, *A Brief History of Intelligence: Evolution, AI, and the Five Breakthroughs That Made Our Brains* (New York, NY: Mariner Books, 2023), 11.
6 Henry Kissinger, Eric Schmidt, and Daniel Huttenlocher, "ChatGPT Heralds an Intellectual Revolution," *The Wall Street Journal*, February 25–26, 2023, A13, A15.
7 Walter Isaacson, *Steve Jobs* (New York, NY: Simon & Schuster, 2011).
8 Nick Sonnenberg, "How Jeff Bezos Used the 2-Pizza Rule to Put an End to Useless Meetings at Amazon," *Inc.*, October 26, 2022, https://www.inc.com/nicholas-sonnenberg/jeff-bezos-2-pizza-rule-meetings-at-amazon.html
9 Stanley McChrystal, Tantum Collins, David Silverman, and Chris Fussell, *Team of Teams: New Rules of Engagement in a Complex World* (New York, NY: Penguin Publishing Group, 2015), 161.
10 Stanley McChrystal, Tantum Collins, David Silverman, and Chris Fussell, *Team of Teams: New Rules of Engagement in a Complex World* (New York, NY: Penguin Publishing Group, 2015), 194.
11 Google's Project Aristotle (named after Aristotle's quote "The whole is greater than the sum of its parts") was a major research initiative that aimed to discover what makes teams effective. The study analyzed 180 teams over two years and found that the most successful teams had five key dynamics, with psychological safety being the most important.
12 Geoff Mulgan, *Big Mind: How Collective Intelligence Can Change Our World* (Princeton, NJ: Princeton University Press, 2018), 131.
13 James Surowiecki, *The Wisdom of Crowds: Why the Many Are Smarter Than the Few and How Collective Wisdom Shapes Business, Economies, Societies, and Nations* (New York, NY: Anchor Books, 2004), 177.
14 Azeem Azhar, "AI Will Upend a Basic Assumption About How Companies Are Organized," *Bloomberg*, February 28, 2025, https://www.bloomberg.com/news/articles/2025-02-28/how-ai-reasoning-models-will-change-companies-and-the-economy?cmpid=BBD030125_WKNDNL&utm_medium=email&utm_source=newsletter&utm_term=250301&utm_campaign=weekendnl
15 See Figure 5.2 for a visual summary.
16 As I explain later, that's not entirely correct. You will always know more about your specific circumstance than it does. And there is the possibility of hallucination and misaligned objectives.

Chapter 1

Prelude

Problems, Intelligence, and Thinking Together

I said in the introduction that this book explains how to enhance the *collective intelligence* of a group and combine it with the *artificial intelligence* of generative AI to create a *hybrid intelligence* that is smarter than either of the intelligences alone. I also said that the focus of this book is small groups (teams) that are *thinking together* to solve a *problem*. Before you learn *how* to enhance collective intelligence and combine it with artificial intelligence, it will help you to understand *what* these terms mean. And you will have a better understanding of these terms if you understand the definition of a problem and the what, where, and how of thinking and thinking together. So in this chapter I ask and answer the following questions:

- What is collective intelligence?
- What is artificial intelligence?
- What is a problem?
- What is thinking?
- Where is thinking?
- How do groups think together?
- What makes a group smarter than its smartest member?

What Is Collective Intelligence?

In the *Handbook of Collective Intelligence*, Thomas Malone, a management professor at MIT, and Michael Berstein, a computer science professor at Stanford University, observe that there are almost as many definitions of collective intelligence as there are people who have written about it. After reviewing a representative list of the definitions, they opt for a simple one: *groups of individuals acting collectively in ways that seem intelligent.*[1] But they purposely refrain from defining intelligence because, they say, "There are so many ways to define it, and we do not want to prematurely constrain what we believe to be an emerging area of study."[2]

DOI: 10.4324/9781003654407-2

Thus, Malone and Bernstein get us only part way to a definition. Fortunately, the neurophysiologist William Calvin picks up where they left off. According to the psychologist Jean Piaget, Calvin explains, "intelligence is what you use when you don't know what to do."[3] John Holt, the educator who pioneered the home schooling movement, defines it similarly, "Intelligence is not the measure of how much we know how to do, but of how we behave when we don't know what to do."[4] Calvin adds that intelligence "also involves a creative aspect whereby you invent something new 'on the fly'. . . . various answers occur to your brain, some better than others."[5] Both of Calvin's perspectives on intelligence, he says, "[capture] the element of novelty, the coping and groping ability needed when there is no 'right answer,' when business as usual isn't likely to suffice."[6]

Elsewhere, in the 1,000-page *Handbook of Intelligence*, intelligence is considered in near endless ways. The psychologist Robert Sternberg, the book's editor, notes that the common theme in all these viewpoints is that intelligence is expressed in terms of adaptive, goal-directed behavior.[7] Adaptive behavior is behavior that "confronts and meets successfully the challenges that are encountered" and goal-directed behavior is "behavior that is ultimately purposive." In other words, intelligence is manifested in behavior that overcomes one or more challenges to achieve a goal.

Calvin's coping and groping when you don't know what to do and Sternberg's surmounting challenges to achieve a goal, when combined, sound a lot like problem-solving to me. So let's say that *an individual exhibits intelligence when the individual solves a problem* and that *a group exhibits collective intelligence when it acts collectively to solve a problem.* An important distinction, as next explained, is that groups are oftentimes able to solve a problem that a lone individual is unable to solve or at least do a better job of solving a problem than a lone individual.

Michael Schrage, a prolific author and research associate at the MIT Media Lab, explains that groups of people with complementary skills can often "create a shared understanding that none [of the people in the group] had previously possessed or could have come to on their own."[8] Another way of putting this is to say that a collectively intelligent group is oftentimes able to create a solution that none of the group members previously possessed or could have come to on their own. Intellectual Ventures (IV) provides an excellent example. As described on their website, the company's engineers, lab scientists, lawyers, and technologists work to create and license impactful inventions. The physicist Leonard Mlodinow explains that one of IV's inventions, the Photonic Fence, uses a laser to kill up to ten mosquitos per second (36,000 per hour), thereby decreasing the incidence of malaria in Africa.[9] The invention, he explains, required the complementary knowledge of three experts—a *mosquito expert's* knowledge of the size, shape, and wingbeat frequency of the species and gender of malarial mosquitos[10] and where and when to target them; an *optics expert's* knowledge of a technology that enables the identification of a mosquito's species and gender; and a *laser expert's* knowledge of which type of laser to use and how to aim it at the targeted mosquitos. Absent any of this complementary knowledge, the Photonic Fence could not have been invented.

Not all problems require a group to solve them. But it's often the case that a group can create a solution that is better than any of the solutions created by its individual members. Consider, for example, that an experienced landscape architect could independently design a functional and aesthetically pleasing park. But a group consisting of a landscape architect, an urban planner, an environmental scientist, several community members (diverse in age, abilities, and cultural backgrounds), a local artist, a local historian, a public safety expert, and an accessibility expert would almost certainly create a better design than the lone architect.

The park and Photonic Fence are products of *group synergy*. The psychologist James Larson defines synergy as "a gain in performance that is attributable in some way to group interaction. More specifically, a group is said to exhibit synergy when it is able to accomplish collectively something that could not reasonably have been achieved by any simple combination of individual member efforts. Synergy is thus an emergent phenomenon rooted in group interaction."[11] Let's take a closer look at emergent phenomena and group interaction as they pertain to problem-solving.

Paul Thagard, a cognitive scientist, explains, "An emergent property [quality, behavior, ability] belongs to the whole but not to any of its parts and is not the aggregate of the property of the parts because it results from the interactions of the parts."[12] He gives the example of a bicycle (the whole) that has the emergent ability to transport people, an ability that is enabled by the interaction of its parts, not by any of the parts individually, nor by piling (aggregating) the parts in a heap on the sidewalk. The ability to transport people is enabled by a relation structure (the whole bike) in which the parts interact with each other in a particular way—the pedals turn the front sprocket, which drives the chain, which turns the rear sprocket, which turns the rear wheel, and so on.

In the case of a problem-solving group, the emergent property is the group's ability to create a solution that a lone person couldn't create (the Photonic Fence) or a solution that is superior to a lone person's solution (a better park). The parts are the individual group members. The interaction consists of conversing or otherwise communicating with each other in ways that enable them to contribute and combine the knowledge that comprises the solution, including equal turn taking, respectful discourse, technological support, and the other ways detailed in this book. In other words, in ways that enable them to think together.

With the foregoing in hand (or head), we can complete our definition of collective intelligence: *A group exhibits collective intelligence when it interacts to solve a problem in a synergistic way, which is to say, in a way that enables the group to create a solution that none of its members previously possessed or could have come to on their own.* But this definition, while complete, raises the question of what a group is doing when it interacts to solve a problem.

Problem-solving is fundamentally about generating alternative solutions and choosing one of them as best, which means that a group exhibits collective intelligence when it generates solutions that none of its members could have generated alone, then chooses one of them as best. Generating the solutions is mostly about *group reasoning*, whereas choosing one of the solutions is mostly about *group judgment*, though each involves some of both. Group reasoning is the inference-based process by which a group uses if-then logic and structured discourse to reach a conclusion.[13] Group judgment involves voting (i.e., aggregating judgments) to select one of the solutions as best.

The distinction between group reasoning and group judgment is important because collective intelligence is sometimes equated with group judgment alone. This usually happens when people refer to collective intelligence as the *wisdom of crowds* effect, which is the phenomenon where the aggregated judgments of a diverse group of individuals tend to be more accurate than the judgment of any single expert. The classic example is the group that generates a more accurate guess of the number of jelly beans in a jar by adding up the individual guesses (judgments) and dividing by the total number of guesses. In our case, the group is better able to guess (judge) the best solution by using some means of voting to aggregate their judgments. We'll talk about different means of voting in Chapter 4.

What Is Artificial Intelligence?

The excitement (and money) being showered on artificial intelligence is driven by its extraordinary potential to augment human intelligence, including the collective intelligence of the small problem-solving groups that are the focus of this book. There are three types of artificial intelligence—discriminative, predictive, and generative:

- *Discriminative AI*: Discriminative AI distinguishes things, which is to say, it makes distinctions. Examples are spam filters that classify emails as spam or not, and image classifiers that classify an image as a dog or a cat.
- *Predictive AI*: Predictive AI refers to systems that use historical data to forecast outcomes or trends. Examples are recommendation engines (e.g., recommend a Netflix movie based on the movies you've watched

in the past) and predictive maintenance models that anticipate equipment failures based on historical failure rates.
- *Generative AI*: Generative AI generates text, images, videos, music, and computer code. The large language models (LLMs) that generate text belong to this category of AI. Multimodal generative AI models can generate more than one type of output (e.g., text, images).

Here, I'm going to focus on LLMs, which I'll alternatively refer to as LLMs and generative AI models. The major LLMs are *ChatGPT* (created by OpenAI), *Gemini* (created by Google), and *Claude* (created by Anthropic). For a detailed, yet understandable, explanation of the way that generative AI models work, see Timothy B. Lee and Sean Trott's article titled "A jargon-free explanation of how AI large language models work."[14] A much simpler explanation is this. The LLMs have read every book, magazine article, newspaper article, Wikipedia article, journal article, conference proceeding, blog post, social media post, user feedback post, website, newsletter, annual report, think tank report, government document, historical document, legal document, piece of computer code, and any other item that is freely available on the internet (i.e., not located behind a paywall). LLMs don't memorize the content word-for-word. Instead, they use it to learn how to predict the part of a word (token), word, sentence, paragraph, page, and larger piece of text that is most likely to follow some other piece of text. This is sometimes referred to as *next-token maximum likelihood prediction*. For example, ask yourself the most likely way to complete this: "It's a nice day. We should go for a ____." Based on everything you've heard and read in your life, you probably predicted that the next word is "walk." This is essentially what LLMs do. Based on the tens, or even hundreds, of billions of documents the LLM has read, it predicts the most likely answer to the question you ask it.

Not only has AI read many more things than you have, it can see patterns in the things that you can't. *Pattern* is one of those words that people use without explaining what it means, so before I explain how AI can see patterns that you can't, I'm going to explain what I mean by a pattern. A pattern is a *reliable repetition*. It's reliable in the sense that it always repeats or usually repeats. A carpet or wallpaper pattern is the reliable repetition of a shape or set of shapes. A numeric pattern is a reliable repetition of a number or set of numbers, such as the reliable repetition of 123 in the sequence of numbers 123123123123. And you can expect the word "walk" to reliably repeat when you encounter the string of words "It's a nice day. We should go for a ____." Another sort of pattern is the correlation between two things in the world, such as the correlation of smoke and fire, dark clouds and rain, birds and feathers, and McDonald's restaurants and hamburgers. More complex patterns involve the correlation of three or more things, such as the correlation of dogs, fur, and four legs and the correlation of companies, profits, and smart management teams. These two- and three-dimensional correlations are patterns because they reliably repeat in the world.

High-dimensional patterns are patterns in which many things—say, tens, hundreds, or thousands of things—are correlated. These are the sorts of patterns that AI can detect that we humans cannot. To help you (and me) understand how much more adept AI is at detecting patterns, I gave ChatGPT the following instruction.[15] Before you read its response, keep in mind the distinction between a *variable* and the *value of the variable*, which is another thing writers, including ChatGPT in this case, rarely point out. When someone refers to the correlation of two variables (e.g., store revenue and surrounding population), they're usually referring to the correlation of the values of the variables.

Prompt

First read the following text: "AI makes predictions by identifying patterns extracted from data. The patterns that AI detects are often so high dimensional that humans cannot make sense of them." Then explain what a high-dimensional pattern is; include a business example. Then explain why humans cannot make sense of high-dimensional patterns."

ChatGPT's Response

What Is a High-Dimensional Pattern?
A high-dimensional pattern is a complex relationship between multiple variables that AI can detect but is difficult or impossible for humans to intuitively grasp. Unlike simple patterns in two or three dimensions (which humans can visualize, like a trend in a scatter plot), high-dimensional patterns involve interactions across many factors simultaneously—often in ways that are nonlinear and counterintuitive.

Business Example: AI-Driven Market Expansion Strategy
Imagine a retail company trying to decide where to open a new store. Traditionally, business executives might consider a few key factors, such as population density, average income, and foot traffic. However, an AI system can analyze hundreds of variables simultaneously, detecting a high-dimensional pattern that drives optimal store placement.

The AI might uncover that a successful new store location is influenced by unexpected [surprising] interactions between:

- Demographic Factors—Not just population size, but age distribution, employment types, and cultural shopping preferences.
- Competitor Presence—A competitor closing a store in an area might signal an opportunity rather than a risk, depending on why they left.
- Real Estate Market—Rent prices alone don't dictate profitability—success might depend on how property values correlate with consumer spending in the area.
- Consumer Behavior Data—GPS tracking data, online searches for similar products, and purchase history can reveal hidden demand.
- Local Infrastructure—Proximity to public transport, walkability scores, and even traffic congestion patterns can influence store visits.
- Economic Trends—The AI might find that regions with high numbers of remote workers have different spending habits than those dominated by office-based professionals.

For example, AI could detect a non-obvious pattern, such as: *A mid-income neighborhood near a major bus route is a high-potential location for expansion—but only if social media engagement with the company's brand is above a certain threshold and nearby gym memberships are increasing.*

Why Can't Humans Make Sense of High-Dimensional Patterns?

1. Limited Cognitive Capacity—Humans can only track a few variables at once, whereas AI can analyze thousands in real-time.
2. No Intuition for High-Dimensional Spaces—Our brains evolved to recognize patterns in three-dimensional space, not in hundreds of interdependent variables.
3. Complex, Nonlinear Interactions—AI-detected patterns don't follow simple logic (e.g., "if X is high, Y increases"). Instead, they often involve conditional relationships (e.g., "X is high only if Y and Z are in specific ranges, but not if W is also present").
4. Hidden Correlations—AI can detect subtle, counterintuitive relationships between factors that humans wouldn't even think to compare.

Conclusion

A high-dimensional pattern captures intricate relationships among numerous variables, allowing AI to make superior strategic decisions. However, because human cognition is optimized for lower-dimensional thinking, we struggle to understand these patterns or intuitively interpret why AI makes certain recommendations.

So we low-dimensional humans are unable to understand the way that generative AI's high-dimensional thinking arrives at its answers. That wouldn't necessarily be a problem if generative AI's answers were always right. But the fact is its answers are sometimes wrong (factually incorrect or nonsensical), a phenomenon that computer scientists refer to as *hallucination*.[16] Researchers Lu Hong, Anusha Kallapur, and Scott Page explain that AI's added value depends on producing *surprises*, that is, different choices or predictions than humans.[17] An example is the surprising, non-obvious pattern in the foregoing example that store profitability is correlated with gym memberships. But a surprising answer raises the question of whether the AI is hallucinating. It also raises the possibility that the objectives of the humans and the AI are *misaligned*. In the foregoing example, the human's objective is to find a store location that optimizes traditionally accepted business factors, like population and income, whereas the AI's objective is to find a location with the highest statistical profitability, which includes gym memberships and social media. Hong and his colleagues refer to this as an *inferential trilemma*: Was the AI correct? Did it hallucinate? Was it misaligned?

The possibility of hallucination and misalignment is no small matter when it comes to major (strategic) decisions, so it's important for organizations to develop ways to confirm that generative AI's surprising answers are factually correct. One way is to have a cognitively diverse team use processes and platforms described in this book to evaluate the surprise from a range of perspectives. A second way is to have AI explain why it responded the way it did. A third way is to test AI's conclusion by doing a pilot test or running a simple, affordable experiment.[18] And a fourth way is to clarify the criteria of an optimal answer to make sure that the AI is optimizing for the right objective. Even better is to combine or layer these ways of examining a surprising answer, say, for example, by having a cognitively diverse team evaluate the surprise by having the AI explain its answer, then running a simple experiment. The key is to approach surprising answers to strategic questions with a sort of structured skepticism—trust the AI's answers when justified but challenge them when necessary.

Generative AI can be used for a variety of purposes, including creating content (text, images, music, video, and computer code), summarizing documents, rewriting documents, analyzing data, exploring hypothetical scenarios, explaining concepts, translating from one language to another, translating text to speech and speech to text, identifying trends or anomalies, forecasting, aggregating and presenting knowledge, answering questions, generating ideas, and proposing solutions. For the most part, this book focuses on the last three abilities.

Prompt engineering is the technical term for the art and science of crafting effective questions and instructions (*prompts*) for generative AI to respond to. It has emerged as a critical skill in the age of AI because generative AI's output is only as good as its input, the prompts. Crafting well-thought-out prompts ensures relevant outputs (responses aligned with your goals), creative exploration (novel ideas, solutions, and insights), and efficiency (reduces the need for iterative corrections). I'll explain the mechanics of writing prompts in Chapter 4.

Prompt engineering addresses *how* to ask generative AI for answers, but it doesn't say *what* to ask. Knowing what questions to ask generative AI is even more important than knowing how to ask them. Why? The key reason, as business professor Jeff Dyer and his colleagues explain, is that "Questions hold the potential to cultivate creative insights. Einstein knew this long ago, as he often repeated the phrase, 'If I only had the right question . . . If I only had the right question . . .' No wonder he finally concluded that 'the formulation of a problem is often more important than its solution' and that raising new questions to solve a problem 'requires creative imagination.'"[19]

Along the same lines, in connection with the massive amount of astronomy data made openly available to amateur astronomers by the Sloan Digital Sky Survey (SDSS), Michael Nielsen, a pioneer of quantum computing, notes that now anyone "can come along and ask fundamental questions [of the SDSS data] that no one had ever thought to ask before. . . . Confronted by such a wealth of data, in many ways we are not so much knowledge-limited as we are question-limited. We're limited by our ability to ask the most ingenious and outrageous and creative questions."[20] What Nielsen has to say about the SDSS can just as well be said about generative AI. When it comes to the massive amount of knowledge contained in generative AI models, we are not so much knowledge-limited as we are question-limited. Our ability to take advantage of generative AI is limited by our ability to ask insightful questions.

You might well wonder why generative AI models aren't able to generate Einstein's "right questions" or Nielsen's "ingenious questions." In fact, generative AI can generate very useful questions. However, it will only generate the questions if you ask it to. And it will only generate *useful* questions if you tell it the purpose of the questions and, even better, provide it with a lot of background information (context). But even if you do all that, there's a limit to generative AI's ability to ask insightful questions, a limit that humans do not have. Later in this chapter I explain that we produce new knowledge (what we don't know) from old knowledge (what we do know). Generative AI does the same thing. It produces new knowledge from what it knows from having read everything on the internet. And while it knows a whole lot more than you do, it doesn't know everything you know. It's never seen, heard, felt, tasted, or touched what you have, and it's never felt the emotions you've felt. Which means that it doesn't know the specifics of your particular problem. For example, it doesn't know the specifics of the employee turnover problem at your company, or the homelessness problem in your community, or whatever other problem you're facing.

Consider the example of peer-to-peer services like Airbnb and Uber. Before any of these services existed, AI would never have thought of the question, "What are all the ways to create a service in which people rent a personal asset to other people?" While generative AI could have generated great answers to this question, it could not have generated the question itself. That's because generative AI produces outputs by analyzing and recombining patterns from its training data. Because prior to the invention of peer-to-peer services there was no existing data that explicitly discussed peer-to-peer services or similar decentralized frameworks, the AI lacked the foundational patterns to generate such a question. A human, on the other hand, might have seen a neighbor renting out their home to vacationers or sharing a car with a friend and connected the observation to the broader idea of renting underutilized personal assets. The act of witnessing or participating in an informal sharing arrangement would have provided the concrete, sensory, and social experience that inspired the idea of peer-to-peer services. It's this kind of context-specific, nuanced observation that generative AI lacks because it doesn't perceive or directly interact with the world (although even that is starting to change).

Another example, this time from science, is the question "What if the continents were once joined together and have since drifted apart?" This question, which led to the theory of continental drift, was proposed by Alfred Wegener in the early 20th century. It exemplifies a groundbreaking inquiry that AI, relying on existing patterns and data, could not have generated at the time because (a) the question challenged an established paradigm (the Earth's surface is static); (b) it connected disparate observations (the jigsaw-like-fit of South America and Africa, similarities in fossils found on different continents, and matching geological formations across oceans); and (c) the question relied on imagining an entirely different history of Earth, one where continents were part of a single supercontinent and later moved apart. Where this "what if" thinking is a hallmark of human creativity, AI cannot imagine hypothetical scenarios that go beyond its training data and established frameworks.

I'll finish this section by emphasizing that in this age of AI, it's impossible to overstate the need to master the art-science of prompt engineering and question asking. I'll elaborate on these two skills in Chapter 4.

What Is a Problem?

Earlier, I said a *group exhibits collective intelligence when it interacts to solve a problem in a synergistic way*. Given the key role that the term "problem" plays in this characterization, not to mention the role it plays in the focus of this book, I'm going to go to great lengths to define it. Note that the following is an excerpt, with some slight modifications, from my book *Differentiation Strategy: Winning Customers by Being Different*, where you can find a more expansive treatment of problem-solving.[21]

The following authors propose problem definitions that center on not knowing how to close the gap between an existing state and a desired state.

- In *The Ideal Problem Solver*, psychology professors John Bransford and Barry Stein write, "A problem exists when there is a discrepancy between an initial state and a goal state, and there is no ready-made solution for the problem solver."[22]
- Operations researchers Colin Eden, Sue Jones, and David Sims, authors of *Messing About in Problems: An Informal Structured Approach to Their Identification and Management*, propose this definition of a problem, "We usually refer to ourselves as having a problem if things are not as we would like them to be, and we are not quite sure what to do about it."[23] They also say, "[P]roblems are psychological entities which are often unclear and expressed as anxiety or concern about a situation as well as being expressed as a positive wish for the situation to be different in some way."[24]
- In his book *Techniques of Structured Problem Solving*, communications professor Arthur VanGundy Jr. writes, "A problem can be defined as any situation in which a gap is perceived to exist between what is and what should be."[25]

Consultant John Arnold, author of *The Complete Problem Solver: A Total System for Competitive Problem Solving*, elaborates on the notion of "should be" by advising his readers to ask the following questions when defining a problem:[26]

- "What is not happening that should be happening?" By implication, a problem exists when something is not happening that should be happening. Or, said a bit differently, a problem exists when something is not happening that someone wants to happen.

- "What is happening that should not be happening?" Here the implication is that a problem exists when something is happening that should not be happening. Or, put differently, a problem exists when something is happening that someone does not want to happen.

In *Swans, Swine, and Swindlers: Coping with the Growing Threat of Mega-Crises and Mega-Messes*, business professors Can Alpaslan and Ian Mitroff go to great lengths to explain what a problem *is not* by distinguishing between an *exercise* and a *problem*:[27]

- To start, Alpaslan and Mitroff give this simple example of an exercise: "If Billy has saved $6 and he needs $11 to buy a game, how much money does he need to save?" In comparison, an example of a problem is figuring out a better way to attract and retain employees. Another example is devising a policy that will minimize the amount of homelessness in a city.
- Exercises are presented to us preformulated in the sense that we do not have to figure out what it is that must be solved. Problems, on the other hand, do not drop out of the sky preformulated. They require that we come to grips with exactly what the problem is.
- An exercise is clearly defined before working on it. Problem definitions become progressively clearer during the problem-solving process.
- Exercises have a single right answer or solution. Problems have more than one possible solution.
- Exercises remain solved because they are static; the nature of the exercise does not change. Problems do not always remain solved because they are dynamic; things change and so too must the solutions.
- Exercises are usually tackled by a single discipline or profession, as would be the case, for example, with an operations research or a chemical engineering exercise. Finding a solution to a problem often requires the efforts of multiple departments, disciplines, or professions.

Consultants Charles Kepner and Benjamin Tregoe, authors of *The New Rational Manager: An Updated Edition for a New World*, describe a problem in the following ways.[28] Note their emphasis on causality and performance:

- "A problem is the visible effect of a cause that resides somewhere in the past."
- A problem exists in "any situation in which an expected level of performance is not being achieved and in which the cause of the unacceptable performance is unknown."

- A problem is "a deviation between expected and actual performance that is of unknown cause."

Business professors Joan Ernst van Aken, Hans Berends, and Hans van der Bij, authors of *Problem Solving in Organizations: A Methodological Handbook for Business Students*, provide a somewhat different take on performance problems:[29]

- "Business problem-solving projects are started to improve the performance of a business system, department, or a company on one or more criteria." The criteria, they note, often have to do with effectiveness or efficiency.
- "A problem can be defined as the result of a certain perception of affairs in the real world with which one or more important stakeholders are dissatisfied."
- The "stakeholders are dissatisfied on the basis of a comparison of their perception of the performance of the business system in question on certain implicit or explicit performance indicators with some implicit or explicit norms, and they choose the problem to work on because they have the impression that significant performance improvement is feasible within acceptable constraints on time and effort."

The definition of a problem that we're going to use incorporates key concepts from the foregoing definitions. The concepts are italicized in the following piecemeal description of a problem. The piecemeal description is followed by a summary definition.

- A problem involves an *undesired effect*. Loosely defined, an *effect* can be a situation, condition, phenomenon, event, action, behavior, object, capability, characteristic, quality, or property, each of which can also be classified as a *state* of the world. An effect (state) is the result of one or more *causes*. Thus, problems are about cause and effect.
- Other ways of saying that an effect is *undesired* are to say that it is unsatisfactory, unwanted, or unacceptable. The effect is considered unsatisfactory, unwanted, or unacceptable because it is thought of as being *bad* or because it is thought of as being *less than ideal*, which is to say, not as good as it could be.
- An undesired effect is a problem when a problem solver (person or group) does not possess the *knowledge* required to transform the undesired effect into a *desired effect* because the problem solver doesn't *know what* caused or is causing the effect, or because the problem solver doesn't *know how* to act on the cause(s) to transform the undesired

effect into the desired effect, or because of both. (Note how this pertains to the earlier-discussed idea that intelligence is what we use when we don't know what to do.)

- Desires and knowledge are things that exist in a person's mind (as Eden and his co-authors put it, they are *psychological entities*), which means that the existence and nature of a problem is a matter of *personal belief*. For example, when Competitor A loses market share to Competitor B (the effect), Competitor A will believe it to be an undesired effect and Competitor B will believe it to be a desired effect. Another example is the person (or group) who views an undesired effect as a problem because s/he lacks the knowledge needed to solve it versus the person (or group) who doesn't see it as a problem because s/he possesses the needed knowledge.

In summary form, our operational definitions are these. A *problem* exists when there is an undesired effect (state) and the problem solver lacks the knowledge required to transform the undesired effect into a desired effect (state), that is, the problem solver does not have a ready-made solution for the problem. Unlike exercises, problems do not come preformulated, do not have a single correct solution, do not always remain solved, frequently require a multi-disciplinary team to solve them, and become progressively better defined during the problem-solving process. *Problem-solving* is defined as the process of coming to know the causes (there's usually more than one) of the undesired effect and ways to act on the causes to transform them into the causes of the desired effect.

Figure 1.1 will help you visualize a problem and problem-solving as I've just defined them. The diagram shows that the undesired effect (or undesired state) has three causes. Transforming the undesired effect into the desired effect requires that the problem solver determine the causes of the undesired effect and then find ways to act on the causes so as to

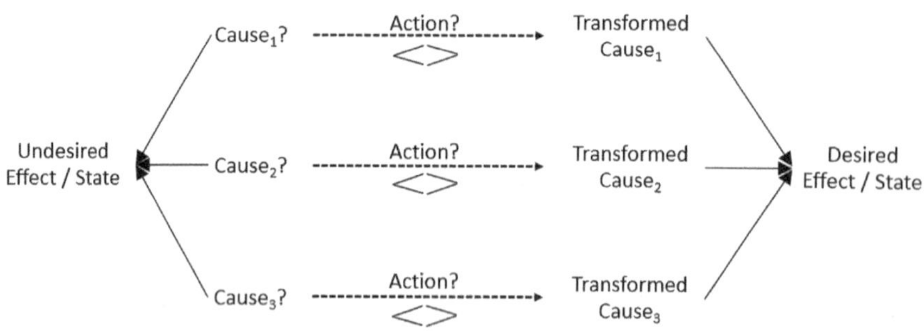

Figure 1.1 Problem-solving is thinking of ways to transform an undesired effect (state) into a desired effect (state).

transform them into causes of the desired effect. The question marks in the figure indicate where the problem solver may lack the knowledge required to solve the problem. He may not know one or more of the causes of the undesired effect or one or more of the actions that are required to transform the causes.

Identifying the causes of an undesired effect typically involves hypothesizing possible causes, then doing observation, interview, and/or survey research (or laboratory research, if you're a scientist or engineer) to validate or invalidate the hypotheses. Determining how to act on a cause involves hypothesizing multiple ways to act on it (divergent thinking), then choosing one of them as the best (convergent thinking). Divergent and convergent thinking are represented in the diagram beneath each "Action?" as, respectively, two lines that diverge from a point and two lines that converge on a point.

Designing a product (or process, policy, or some other thing) is fundamentally about solving a problem in the sense that some number of things (e.g., cost, size, performance, functionality, useability, complexity) cause the existing product to exist in an undesired state. Creating the new product involves acting on the causes to transform them into things that will cause the new product to exist in the desired state. This characterization of design is consistent with Steve Jobs's usual way of designing things, which was to first identify the things he hated[30] about a product (the causes of the undesired state).[31] Then he and his team would act on the things he hated to transform them into things that caused the new product to exist in the desired state.

What Is Thinking?

It goes without saying that one must think to solve a problem (but I'll say it anyway because it makes for a good transition). Thinking, we think, occurs in the brain-mind. The brain-mind is often described as the most complex entity known to man. One way to understand a complex thing is to describe or analyze it as a hierarchy of levels and to characterize each level by the entities that reside in it. Each level is a *level of explanation*.[32] Some cognitive scientists[33] employ three levels of explanation to explain cognition.[34] In brief, these levels are:

- *The biological level*, where cognition is described and explained in terms of neurons and higher-order biological structures like the cerebral cortex.
- *The symbolic level*, where cognition is described and explained in terms of symbols (concepts) that stand for (represent) things and a memory that consists of a network of associations among the concepts.

- *The knowledge level*, where cognition is described and explained in terms of knowledge objects (e.g., facts, beliefs, goals, solutions) and intentionally rational behavior.

Biological Level

The entities that reside on the biological level are neurons, or brain cells. The human brain consists of a network of some 100 billion neurons. Each neuron is linked to as many as 10,000 others. Neurons are either active or inactive. When a neuron becomes active it is said to "fire," meaning that an electrical impulse travels along the nerve cell. The firing (activation) of one or more neurons causes one or more other neurons to fire (become active), which causes other neurons to fire, and so on in a process called *spreading activation*. At the biological level, *to think is to link* neural activations. When a group of people converse, they cause the neurons in each other's brains to activate, meaning that spreading activation occurs at the level of the group. In effect, the individual brains become parts of a single group brain.

The 100 billion neurons in the brain are organized into three basic parts: hindbrain, midbrain, and forebrain. The hindbrain and midbrain are devoted to running the body: breathing, heartbeat, sleep and arousal, and the coordination of bodily movements. Much of the forebrain is comprised of the limbic system, which regulates emotional responses. The forebrain also includes a thin outer surface called the *cerebral cortex*, which has grown to cover the rest of the surface of the brain. Some refer to it as the brain's "thinking cap."[35] The cerebral cortex is about two-dimes-thick and occupies an area the size of four sheets of typing paper.[36] Roughly speaking, it is divided into three main areas—the *sensory cortex* is where information from all of the senses is collated and stored, the *motor cortex* is responsible for directing voluntary motor activity, and the *association cortex* is dedicated to reasoning and the other higher level mental activities that occur between a sensory perception and a motor action. In a similar way, small problem-solving groups first sense, then think, then act (or at least they should).

Symbolic Level

The entities that reside on the symbolic level are symbols. Symbols symbolize, which is to say that a symbol is a thing that stands for or represents some other thing. For example, a supermarket barcode pattern is a symbol that stands for a product on the shelf. Symbols exist in the brain as patterns of activated neurons. One set of activated neurons, for instance, symbolizes the presence, or later recollection, of "smoke," and a different set of activated neurons stands for the presence or recollection of "fire." At the symbolic level, *to think is to link* two or more symbols, such as would be the case if the activation of the smoke symbol caused the activation of the fire symbol.

A *concept* is a cognitive representation (symbol, pattern of activated neurons). Douglas Hofstadter and Emmanuel Sander, both cognitive scientists, hold that all concepts are categories, some of which are categories of one.[37] As an example of the latter, they explain how certain works of art, like the *Mona Lisa*, are so iconic and singular that they form their own conceptual category. The *Mona Lisa* is not just *a* painting. It is *the* painting, a category of one representing cultural and artistic perfection or mastery. In a similar way, *Coca-Cola*, in its role as a global cultural icon, is a category of one because it is perceived as the quintessential soda, often simply referred to as *Coke* even when discussing soda generically. In short, the *Mona Lisa* and *Coca-Cola* are each in a class (category) of their own, whereas there are multiple instances of the concepts *painting* and *soda*. While *my lounge chair* (the one in my living room with a scratch on the left front leg and a coffee stain on the right arm) isn't iconic, it is singular, which, to my way of thinking, qualifies it as a category of one that is distinct from the concept of *lounge chairs*. So, again, all concepts are categories, some of which are a category of one.

Concepts are the fundamental units of an idea. To understand how this is so, consider that, roughly speaking, an idea is something that is expressed as a sentence, and a concept is something that is expressed as a word or short phrase. Just as words are the fundamental units of a sentence, concepts are the fundamental units of an idea. Here, it's important to understand that *words* and *sentences* are linguistic expressions of *concepts* and *ideas*, not the concepts and ideas themselves. A concept is a neural activation that occurs below the threshold of consciousness.[38] A word or short phrase is what we use to label the activation. Similarly, an idea is a string of activated concepts. A sentence is what we use to express the string.

But how can that be? We seem to think with the words and sentences that we consciously experience, so how can we say that we think at the subconscious level of neural activations? Before I answer that question, consider the following:

- Think of a time when you were engrossed in a problem or question, then let it rest, then sometime later the answer just popped in your head (probably in the shower). The solution-finding process—thinking—must have taken place. It's just that you weren't conscious of it.
- Recall an occasion when you said something to someone only to realize that it wasn't what you meant to say. For that to happen, there must have been a thought that you meant to say that was different than the one you said.

- Consider a circumstance when you were struggling to explain something to someone and apologized by saying, "I'm having a hard time putting this into words." The "this" that you were referring to was the subconscious thought that you were trying to express in words.

If thought is something other than the words and sentences we consciously experience, then what is it? Steven Pinker, a psycholinguist and the source of the foregoing examples, explains that we think in a language of thought called *mentalese* in which concepts consist of neural activations and ideas are formed by stringing the concepts together.[39] Mentalese, which operates below the threshold of awareness, gives rise to the language we consciously experience. An important thing to understand is that the sentences we use to communicate our thoughts from one mind to another do not convey the entirety of the underlying thought. Mentalese encodes information in a way that is far richer and more interconnected than the linear, conscious language we use to convey our thoughts. Pinker explains, ". . . sentences in a spoken language like English or Japanese are designed for vocal communication between impatient, intelligent social beings. They achieve brevity by leaving out any information that the listener can mentally fill in from the context. In contrast, the 'language of thought' in which knowledge is couched can leave nothing to the imagination because it *is* the imagination" (italics in original).[40]

Pinker goes on to explain that the neural activations that constitute mentalese also underly the images we recall or that we create from memory.[41] That means several things. First, in addition to concepts, we also think in images, which should come as no surprise to artists, designers, and scientists who engage in Einstein-like thought experiments. Second, like sentences, the images we recall and create contain less information than is contained in their richer, underlying representations in mentalese. And third, because mentalese is the source of both language and imagery, it serves as the mind's lingua franca.[42] It is what enables us to describe the images we imagine and imagine the images we describe, as illustrated in Figure 1.2.

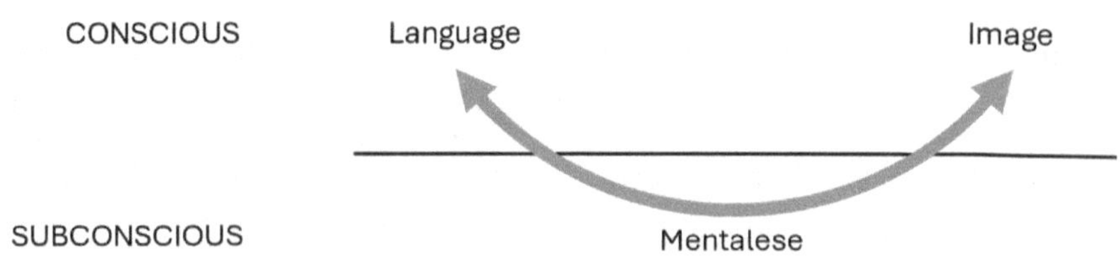

Figure 1.2 Mentalese enables us to describe the images we imagine and imagine the images we describe.

The fact that mentalese serves as the lingua franca of language and imagery enables us to utilize the complementary advantages of each in representations that combine them, such as annotated diagrams, sometimes called word-entity diagrams. The advantages of images include their ability to (a) convey relative positions, proportions, and configurations more efficiently than language (e.g., the relative positions of three cities on a map); (b) represent multiple elements at once, whereas language must present them sequentially (e.g., the multiple elements of a circuit diagram); (c) convey relationships that are nonlinear (e.g., an ecosystem diagram with multiple interacting elements); and (d) bypass the need for linguistic decoding, making them accessible across different kinds and levels of expertise, which is a valuable characteristic in multi-disciplinary groups. Language, in comparison, enables us to (a) express ideas that have no direct visual representation (e.g., justice, irony, paradox); (b) express sequences of events, logical steps, and cause-effect relationships that unfold over time (e.g., if the temperature drops below freezing, water will turn into ice); and (c) describe counterfactuals and hypotheticals, such as what could have happened but didn't or what might happen under different conditions.

With the foregoing description, then, imagery and words are expressions of thoughts we think subconsciously. But this idea is only half correct, for not only do images and words express our thoughts, they exert some measure of control over them. In his book *The Society of Mind*, the MIT computer scientist Marvin Minsky borrows from semiotics to lump images and words under the more general heading of signals, or signs. He then uses the analogy of steering a car to explain how signal-signs work to direct the thinking that occurs subconsciously, "[R]otating the steering wheel is merely a signal that makes the steering mechanism turn the car. . . . Our conscious thoughts use signal-signs to steer the engines in our minds, controlling countless processes of which we're never much aware."[43]

The meaning of a concept—alternately referred to as its *conceptual meaning* or *semantic meaning*—consists of all the other concepts it is associated with, which is to say, all the other concepts it stands in relationship to.[44] The anthropology professor James Spradley decomposed semantic relationships into the types listed in Table 1.1. He referred to them as "universal semantic relationships" because they are found in every culture.[45] When you think of a lounge chair, for example, you think of it as a *kind of* chair and as something *used for* sitting and as *part of* a living room.

The theory of *semantic pointers* (depicted in Figure 1.3) adds sensory, motor, and emotional associations to the foregoing semantic associations (relationships), which semantic pointer theory refers to as verbal associations. The theory proposes that, in addition to the foregoing semantic relationships, you might also associate your lounge chair with images of family members sitting on it and the way the fabric feels on your skin (sensory associations), with the bodily actions of sitting down on it and leaning

Table 1.1 Universal semantic relationships

Universal Semantic Relationships		
Relationship	*Explanation*	*Example*
Strict inclusion	X is a kind of Y	*Lounge chair* is a kind of *Chair*
Spatial	X is a place in Y, X is a part of Y	*Lounge chair* is a part of *Living room*
Cause-effect	X is a result of Y, X is a cause of Y	*Lounge chair* is a result of *Manufacturing*
Rationale	X is a reason for doing Y	*Lounge chair* is a reason for *Shopping*
Location for action	X is a place for doing Y	*Lounge chair* is a place for *Watching TV*
Function	X is used for Y	*Lounge chair* is used for *Sitting*
Means-end	X is a way to do Y	*Lounge chair* is a way to *Relax*
Sequence	X is a step (stage) in Y	*Lounge chair* is a stage in my *Evening routine*
Attribution	X is an attribute/characteristic of Y	*Comfortable* is an attribute of *Lounge chair*

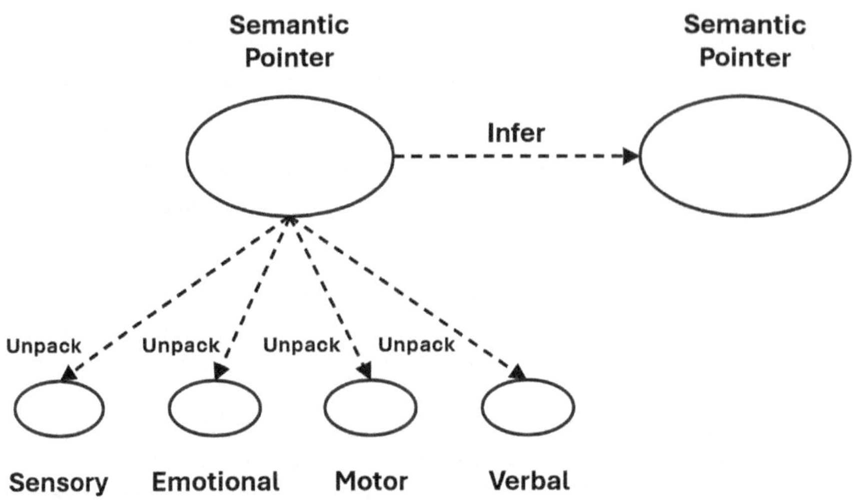

Figure 1.3 A semantic pointer (concept) unpacking into its component sensory, emotional, motor, and verbal pointers. Semantic pointers have inferential associations with other semantic pointers (concepts). Each of the ovals represents thousands of neurons.

backwards to recline the back of the chair (motor associations), and with the feelings of contentment as you nestle into it and annoyance as you struggle to get out of it (emotional associations). A semantic pointer consists of the bundle of thousands or even millions of neurons that implement these associations.

What all this means is that a concept consists of a whole lot of associations, which is to say, a whole lot of neural activations. But we don't make all these associations (activate all these neurons) every time we think of a lounge chair or some other concept. Semantic pointer theory accounts for this fact.[46] The theory proposes that when activating a concept while thinking or talking, the only thing that is activated is the compressed bundle of neurons that is the *semantic pointer*. When we want or need to—say, for example, when we want to explain the concept of a lounge chair to someone—we can progressively unbundle (unpack) the semantic pointer by virtue of the fact that it "points" to the bundles of neurons that comprise it, each of which points to the bundles of neurons that comprise them, and so on. But most of the time we don't unpack a semantic pointer. Like skipping a stone across the surface of a pond, we usually skip along the surface of our brain's deeper meaning structure by associating (inferring) the semantic pointers, one with another, with another, with another until the thought we are thinking plays out.

Douglas Hofstadter and Emmanuel Sander, both cognitive scientists, employ a similar analogy to describe the way we unbundle concepts.[47] They describe a woman recalling a year-long stay in a foreign country. When she recalls the trip, she is only able to remember tiny parts of it. It's as if she is looking down from an airplane at a mountain range but an extensive cloud layer enables only the highest peaks (remembered parts of her trip) to poke through. If someone asks her about the details of her trip, she is able to recall them, but until that happens, they remain hidden beneath the cloud cover. The content of all our concepts, they explain, has the quality of being "largely hidden from view but partially unpackable [unbundable] on request, and the unpacking process is repeatable, several layers down."[48]

Broadly speaking, there are two views of concepts in cognitive science.[49] One view is known as the *disembodied cognition* perspective, also known as the *computational mind* perspective. It takes the computer as the analogy for modeling the mind. *Cognitive linguistics* rejects the idea of a disembodied computer as the model of the mind in favor of the *embodied cognition* perspective. Embodied cognition is the idea that thinking isn't just something that happens in our brain. Rather, our body plays a huge role in how we think about the world, including the creation of our concepts, the ways we associate them, and the language we use to express and direct our concepts. As the author Annie Murphy Paul explains in her book

The Extended Mind: The Power of Thinking Outside the Brain, "The exciting implication of such findings is that we can intentionally enhance our *mental* functioning through an application of *physical* activity[.]"[50] I'll have more to say about this in Chapter 4 when we talk about the advantages of physically interacting with whiteboards.

So each of our concepts consists of a constellation of associations with other concepts. Together, this network of concepts constitutes our *semantic memory*, or alternatively, our *semantic network*. Research and theoretical estimates suggest that an average adult's semantic memory may hold anywhere from tens-of-thousands to hundreds-of-thousands of concepts, many of which are not labeled with words. But the semantic memory of no two people is the same. For example:

- Some people have concepts that others don't. Unless you're a social worker, you probably don't have a concept for *critical consciousness*, which is about developing an awareness of the social, political, and economic forces that contribute to personal and systemic challenges.
- While two people might have the same concept, one person's version of the concept may be more developed (have more associations) than the other's. A professor who teaches social work is likely to associate many more things with his concept of *critical consciousness* than is a practicing social worker.
- Two people might have the same concept with approximately the same number and kinds of associations, but the activation strengths of their associations may differ. One professor might be more likely to associate *critical consciousness* with *conscientization* (the process of recognizing oppressive systems and understanding how they influence one's mental health), while another professor is more likely to associate it with *praxis* (the interplay of reflection and action).

Another thing to know about concepts is that we can, and do, apply different concepts to the same thing when experiencing it (i.e., seeing, hearing, smelling, tasting, or touching it) or when thinking about it. For example, when looking at or thinking about your dog (assuming you have one), you might conceive of him as *Rover*, as a *dog*, as a *pet*, as a *best friend*, as a *protector*, as a *golden retriever* (not much of a protector, I admit), or any number of other concepts. Or consider the many ways to conceive of a *customer*—as a revenue source (*buyer*), as a relationship (*client*), as part of a value chain (*end user*), as a source of information (*consumer*), as a partner (*collaborator*), as a liability (*complainant*), as an advocate (*promotor*), and as a challenge (~~*pain-in-the-ass*~~ *demanding individual*). Each of these concepts has a different set of associations, which means that the way you conceive of something will cause you to think about it in a different way, that is, will send you down a different conceptual path (chain of associations).

So how does this long-winded treatment of concepts and conceptual meaning relate to collective intelligence and artificial intelligence? Several ways. Let's start with mentalese. Earlier, I cited Steven Pinker to explain that mentalese is the subconscious language of thought and that the language and images we use to express our thoughts are incomplete and sometimes incorrect versions of them. The practical implication is that collective intelligence is enhanced by tools and practices that enable group members to complete and correct each other's thoughts.

- The tools enable group members to express and share their thoughts using language and imagery (e.g., annotated diagrams), thereby utilizing the complementary advantages of each. As detailed in Chapter 4, they include whiteboards, diagramming apps, simulation software, and physical prototypes.
- The practices, described in Chapter 3, include framing exercises to reveal and align the members' mental models, iterative dialogue to clarify and expand incompletely expressed thoughts, constructive dissent to challenge the correctness or completeness of each other's thoughts, and periodic breaks to let everyone's mentalese mull over what they've said and heard (i.e., use the spoken signal-signs to steer the engines of their minds).

Including generative AI as a group member is a way to augment the tools and practices, as ChatGPT explains below:[51]

Prompt

Do the following step by step. First, read the foregoing text. Second, describe ways that generative AI can augment the tools so as to address thoughts that are incomplete or incorrect. Third, describe ways that generative AI can augment the processes so as to address thoughts that are incomplete or incorrect.

ChatGPT's Response

Augmenting Tools with Generative AI

Generative AI can enhance the tools listed in the text (e.g., whiteboards, diagramming apps, simulation software, and physical prototypes) by helping to complete and correct thoughts in the following ways:

1. Semantic Augmentation in Diagramming Apps
   - AI can suggest missing components, connections, or alternative structures in diagrams based on patterns detected in the group's discourse.
   - It can analyze annotated diagrams and highlight logical inconsistencies, gaps in reasoning, or areas where additional information would improve clarity.
2. Enhanced Whiteboards with AI-Powered Thought Expansion
   - AI can listen to discussions and suggest alternative formulations, synonyms, or conceptual refinements in real-time.
   - AI-driven sentiment and relevance analysis can help detect when ideas are ambiguous, contradictory, or lacking depth, prompting users to refine their thoughts.
3. Simulation Software with AI-Driven Scenario Exploration
   - AI can generate and test edge cases or alternative scenarios that the group may not have considered.
   - It can provide dynamic feedback on assumptions, flagging inconsistencies or suggesting new simulations to complete the group's understanding.
4. AI-Enhanced Physical Prototyping
   - AI-powered design software can analyze prototypes, suggest improvements, and simulate different conditions to test robustness.
   - AI-driven image and pattern recognition can compare the prototype against databases of known solutions to highlight potential weaknesses or missing features.

Augmenting Processes with Generative AI

Generative AI can also enhance the processes mentioned in the text (e.g., framing exercises, iterative dialogue, constructive dissent, and periodic breaks) by:

1. AI-Supported Framing Exercises
   - AI can summarize and synthesize different members' mental models, highlighting discrepancies and commonalities.
   - It can generate possible reframings or alternative perspectives to help align mental models more effectively.

2. Iterative Dialogue with AI-Powered Thought Completion
   - AI can monitor conversations and suggest possible completions to unfinished thoughts.
   - AI can offer context-aware expansions of ideas by drawing from external knowledge, historical analogies, or scientific principles.
3. AI-Driven Constructive Dissent
   - AI can identify implicit assumptions in statements and challenge them by generating counterexamples or alternative viewpoints.
   - It can introduce provocative questions or missing perspectives that encourage critical thinking and correction of errors.
4. AI-Augmented Periodic Breaks
   - AI can generate concise summaries of what has been discussed before a break, helping group members retain key insights.
   - It can provide thought-provoking prompts during or after the break to encourage subconscious processing and creative problem-solving.

By integrating generative AI into both tools and processes, groups can refine, complete, and correct their collective thoughts more effectively, ultimately enhancing their collective intelligence.

To deepen your understanding of the foregoing eight items, I suggest you ask your generative AI model for examples of each. I would do it here, but a series of eight long answers would disrupt the flow of this section too much. So I have limited myself to asking for the single example, which is an example of AI-Driven Constructive Dissent, that is, item #3 under Augmenting Processes with Generative AI above:[52]

Prompt

Describe an example of generative AI providing a group with constructive dissent.

ChatGPT's Response

A team of urban planners is brainstorming a new public transportation system for a rapidly growing city. They are using a combination of whiteboards, simulation software, and a generative AI assistant trained on transportation models, urban planning principles, and real-time traffic data.

One planner proposes a light rail system as the best solution, citing its efficiency and environmental benefits. The other members of the team largely agree. Before proceeding with the discussion, they ask generative AI what it thinks. It gives this constructive dissent:

"*While a light rail system has clear advantages, historical data and comparative urban studies suggest potential issues with cost overruns, underutilization in similar mid-sized cities, and the risk of increasing socioeconomic divides if not planned inclusively. Would you like to explore alternative models, such as bus rapid transit (BRT) or an integrated mobility-as-a-service (MaaS) network?*"

This AI-generated challenge forces the team to reconsider their assumptions and investigate whether their initial idea is truly the optimal solution. They engage in an iterative dialogue, using simulation software to test various scenarios, and ultimately refine their plan to include a hybrid system that leverages BRT corridors for flexibility while maintaining key light rail routes for high-density areas.

By acting as a constructive dissenter, the AI prevents premature consensus and enhances the group's collective intelligence by ensuring that all viable options are critically evaluated before a decision is made.

Marvin Minsky explained that not only do we use language to express our ideas, we also use it to control them. One way of doing this is to use language to flesh out the germ of an idea—for example, the idea of "a futuristic calming environment." As described below, generative AI can help to do this.[53] Note that even if a team of designers didn't agree with some or all of ChatGPT's answer, it would give them something to react to and thereby detail the idea.

Prompt

Generate a comprehensive description of "a futuristic calming environment."

ChatGPT's Response

A futuristic, calming environment blends cutting-edge technology with serene, harmonious design elements that promote relaxation while subtly enhancing cognitive function. This space is characterized by soft, ambient lighting that dynamically adjusts to circadian rhythms, casting a gentle glow reminiscent of natural light patterns. The architecture is sleek and fluid, incorporating smooth, organic curves inspired by biomimicry—structures that resemble flowing water, wind-carved dunes, or the gentle unfolding of petals.

The materials used in the environment are advanced yet comforting: self-healing surfaces, temperature-responsive textiles, and bioluminescent accents that provide subtle illumination without overwhelming the senses. The color palette is a blend of cool neutrals, deep blues, soft lavenders, and silvery metallics, evoking a sense of tranquility and sophistication.

Nature is seamlessly integrated through living walls of oxygen-producing plants, small indoor waterfalls, and misting systems that infuse the air with calming scents like lavender and eucalyptus. Soundscapes play an essential role, with AI-generated ambient music dynamically adapting to an individual's emotional state, blending gentle electronic tones with natural sounds like rustling leaves or distant ocean waves.

Technology in this space is non-intrusive and intuitive, responding to gestures or voice in a way that feels like an extension of the occupant's intentions. Transparent OLED displays provide information only when needed, and holographic interfaces allow seamless interaction without cluttering the visual field. AI-powered personal assistants anticipate needs, adjusting the environment in real time to optimize relaxation and mental clarity.

The furniture is ergonomic and adaptive, with smart textiles that shift temperature and firmness based on the occupant's posture and stress levels. Meditation pods with zero-gravity seating allow deep relaxation, while immersive VR domes provide stunning 360° views of tranquil landscapes, from serene lunar vistas to lush bioluminescent forests.

This futuristic, calming environment is not only visually stunning but also deeply attuned to human well-being, balancing technological advancement with the natural rhythms of relaxation and focus.

Now let's move on from mentalese to *universal semantic relationships* (USRs). In this case, I asked ChatGPT if instructing a generative AI model to consider the USRs when responding to a prompt would cause it to generate a better response.[54] The following is what it had to say. (I'll explain how to create the prompts in Chapter 4).

Prompt

Read the foregoing text pertaining to universal semantic relationships. Then tell me if instructing a generative AI model to consider the relationships when responding to a prompt would cause it to generate a better response and, if so, why.

ChatGPT's Response

Yes, instructing a generative AI model to consider universal semantic relationships when responding to a prompt would likely lead to a better response. Here's why:

1. Richer Contextual Understanding—The meaning of a concept is not isolated; it emerges from its relationships with other concepts. By incorporating these relationships, the AI can generate responses that are more nuanced and interconnected.
2. Enhanced Coherence and Depth—Responses that explicitly integrate multiple semantic relationships (e.g., function, cause-effect, sequence) offer a more structured and thorough explanation rather than a flat, one-dimensional definition.
3. Greater Relevance to User Intent—Different prompts require different types of relationships to be emphasized. For example, if a user asks about a tool, its function and means-end relationships are likely more relevant than its sequence relationship. If the user asks about a historical event, cause-effect and sequence relationships are crucial.
4. Improved Reasoning and Explainability—Semantic relationships help structure logical reasoning, making AI responses easier to follow and understand.

Another way to improve the responses you get from generative AI is to employ the concept of *semantic pointers*. I asked ChatGPT to explain the value of instructing it to employ the concept of semantic pointers when responding to a prompt.[55] Following is what it had to say. (Again, I'll explain how to create the prompts in Chapter 4.)

Prompt

Tell me this. What is the value of instructing a generative AI tool like ChatGPT to employ the concept of semantic pointers when responding to a prompt?

ChatGPT's Answer

Instructing a generative AI tool like ChatGPT to employ the concept of semantic pointers enhances its ability to provide responses that are not only contextually relevant but also richly associative and multi-dimensional. Semantic pointers, as compressed bundles of neural activations pointing to deeper layers of meaning, allow the AI to:

- Capture Contextual Richness: The AI can draw on a broad network of associations without overwhelming the response with unnecessary details. This allows for nuanced answers that are tailored to the specific needs of the user.
- Facilitate Deeper Exploration: By unpacking relevant associations only when necessary, the AI can guide the conversation into progressively deeper levels of meaning without losing focus.
- Adapt Dynamically: It enables the AI to handle ambiguous or open-ended prompts by activating the most relevant high-level associations first and refining them based on user feedback.
- Enhance Cognitive Diversity: When used in group settings, the AI's ability to retrieve and connect diverse associations mirrors the unbundling process in human cognition, enriching the discussion with fresh perspectives.

As with USRs and semantic pointers, I asked ChatGPT to explain how the concept of *cognitive linguistics* can be used to enhance the responses to prompts.[56] (And, once again, I'll explain how to create the prompts in Chapter 4.)

Prompt

Explain the value of instructing generative AI to use cognitive linguistics theory.

ChatGPT's Response

Value of Instructing ChatGPT to Use Cognitive Linguistics Theory

Cognitive linguistics theory provides a rich framework for meaning construction, emphasizing how language reflects embodied experience, conceptual structures, and usage-based learning. Instructing ChatGPT to apply cognitive linguistics concepts enhances its ability to generate responses that are:

1. Conceptually Grounded: AI explanations align with human cognitive patterns, making them more intuitive and natural.
2. Contextually Adaptive: AI can tailor language use based on frame semantics, metaphorical mappings, and discourse structures.
3. Semantically Coherent: ChatGPT can preserve meaning across different expressions through mental spaces and conceptual blending.
4. Dynamic and Flexible: It can interpret figurative language, reconstruct implied meanings, and adjust responses to fit pragmatic context.
5. More Humanlike in Communication: Using embodied cognition and radial category structures, AI-generated text better reflects how humans conceptualize and express ideas.

Key Cognitive Linguistics Concepts and Their AI Benefits

1. *Frame Semantics*

   - What It Does: Explains meaning in terms of structured mental schemas (frames).
   - AI Benefit: Ensures responses activate the appropriate conceptual frame for a query, preventing misinterpretations.
   - Example:

     - Instead of defining "investment" abstractly, ChatGPT would activate the economic frame, linking it to related ideas like "risk," "return," and "market behavior."

2. *Conceptual Metaphor Theory*

   - What It Does: Shows that abstract thought is structured through metaphorical mappings from embodied experience.
   - AI Benefit: Enables AI to interpret figurative language correctly and generate metaphorical explanations that resonate with human cognition.

- Example:
  - Prompt: "Explain neural networks using metaphor."
  - AI Response: "A neural network is like a team of experts, where each member specializes in a different aspect of a problem, and together they refine the answer."

3. *Mental Spaces and Conceptual Blending*
   - What It Does: Describes how the mind integrates separate domains to create meaning dynamically.
   - AI Benefit: Enables AI to synthesize novel ideas, making creative problem-solving more effective.
   - Example:
     - Prompt: "Blend the concept of blockchain with biological evolution."
     - AI Response: "Like genetic inheritance, blockchain records a 'lineage' of transactions, ensuring each block is built upon a verified history, much like DNA mutations build upon previous adaptations."

4. *Embodied Cognition*
   - What It Does: Suggests meaning arises from bodily interaction with the world.
   - AI Benefit: AI can generate more grounded, sensorimotor-based explanations that align with human experiences.
   - Example:
     - Instead of just explaining "balance" as an abstract idea, AI might link it to physical equilibrium, helping users grasp concepts through lived experience.

5. *Radial Categories and Prototype Theory*
   - What It Does: Argues that word meanings form networks of related senses rather than rigid definitions.
   - AI Benefit: Helps AI handle polysemy (multiple meanings) more flexibly.
   - Example:
     - The word "game" can mean "a sport," "a video game," or "a strategic situation." AI using prototype theory would rank meanings based on context.

I said above that there are various ways to conceive of (conceptualize) a thing. For example, you can conceive of your dog as a golden retriever, a pet, a best friend, and so forth. You can put this aspect of concepts to work by asking generative AI to conceive of something in different ways. In the following example, I asked ChatGPT to conceptualize the idea of "a park designed to foster community engagement" in different ways.[57]

Prompt

One can conceive of a dog as a pet, a best friend, a protector, a golden retriever, and so on. I want you to generate various ways to conceive of a park designed to foster community engagement.

ChatGPT's Response

Here are various ways to conceive of a park designed to foster community engagement:

- A Social Hub—A space where people come together to connect, converse, and form relationships, like a town square with greenery.
- An Outdoor Living Room—A cozy, welcoming extension of home where the community gathers for casual meetings, relaxation, and shared activities.
- A Public Commons—A democratic space where people of all backgrounds can coexist, exchange ideas, and engage in civic life.
- A Cultural Canvas—A place for artistic expression, including murals, music performances, poetry readings, and cultural festivals.
- A Learning Lab—An interactive environment with workshops, hands-on exhibits, and educational programming for lifelong learning.
- A Healing Sanctuary—A space promoting mental and physical well-being through nature immersion, meditation areas, and therapeutic landscapes.
- A Playful Retreat—A recreational space for all ages, with playgrounds, interactive installations, and sports facilities.
- A Green Infrastructure Node—A sustainable landscape that supports biodiversity, stormwater management, and urban cooling while engaging the community.

- A Community Garden—A shared space for growing food, teaching sustainability, and fostering intergenerational collaboration.
- A Performance Stage—A venue for theater, concerts, dance, and public speaking, where local talent can shine.
- A Storytelling Space—A place where personal and collective narratives are shared through oral histories, monuments, or digital archives.
- A Social Experiment—A dynamic urban laboratory where different layouts, features, and engagement strategies are tested to enhance collective interaction.
- A Fitness Arena—A space dedicated to physical activity, with jogging trails, yoga zones, and outdoor exercise equipment.
- A Civic Engagement Hub—A gathering place for town hall meetings, grassroots organizing, and participatory democracy initiatives.
- A Time Capsule—A historical site preserving the memory of past events, community milestones, and evolving cultural traditions.
- A Pop-Up Market—A space that transforms into a farmer's market, artisan fair, or swap meet, encouraging local entrepreneurship.
- A Digital Playground—A smart park integrating augmented reality, interactive kiosks, and Wi-Fi zones for digital engagement.
- A Refuge—A safe haven for marginalized groups, providing inclusive spaces for expression, support, and community-building.
- A Sensory Landscape—A designed environment engaging the senses through textures, sounds, fragrances, and interactive installations.
- A Dynamic Ecosystem—A self-sustaining, evolving space that adapts to the needs of the community over time.

Each of these conceptions highlights a different dimension of what a community-engaging park could be.

As earlier explained, no two people have the same semantic memory (semantic network) because some people possess concepts that others don't, one person's version of a concept may be better developed than another's version, and/or the activation strengths of two people's concepts may differ. Cognitive diversity is one of the most significant drivers of collective intelligence, as is explained in Chapter 2. One aspect of cognitive diversity is the differences in the foregoing aspects of people's semantic networks. As this relates to group problem-solving, the differences mean they are likely to conceive of a problem in different ways, each of which sends the group down different conceptual paths. In other words, the members are likely to have different conceptions of what the problem is about (the "aboutness" of the problem). Following is an example of the first way semantic networks differ, that is, it is an example of a cognitively diverse group in which the members possesses different and complementary concepts.[58] Note that one of the group members is ChatGPT.

Prompt

Describe a multi-disciplinary team—a teacher, a social worker, a nurse, a software developer, and ChatGPT—that is brainstorming ways to improve mental health support for teenagers in which each team member uses a different concept to conceive of the problem

ChatGPT's Response

A multi-disciplinary team—a teacher, a social worker, a nurse, a software developer, and ChatGPT—is brainstorming ways to improve mental health support for teenagers in their community. As they discuss the problem, each member applies a different concept to frame the issue, leading each down a unique path of associations:

The Teacher: "Student Engagement"

The teacher conceives of the problem through the lens of student engagement, associating it with classroom participation and attentiveness. The teacher suggests that mental health struggles often manifest as disengagement in school, such as students being withdrawn in discussions or failing to complete homework. This framing prompts the teacher to propose integrating mental health education into the curriculum, such as encouraging students to reflect on their emotions through journaling or creative projects.

The Social Worker: "Family Dynamics"

The social worker views the problem through the concept of family dynamics, focusing on how a teenager's home environment impacts their mental health. The social worker emphasizes the importance of parental involvement and suggests organizing workshops for caregivers on recognizing and addressing early signs of mental health struggles. They also propose incorporating family counseling sessions to strengthen communication and support at home.

The Nurse: "Early Detection"

The nurse frames the issue as one of early detection, associating it with identifying subtle signs of mental health concerns before they escalate. The nurse suggests implementing regular wellness check-ins during school health screenings, using simple tools like questionnaires to assess stress, anxiety, or depression. Additionally, the nurse advocates for training school staff to recognize warning signs of mental health challenges in students.

The Software Developer: "Technology as a Solution"

The software developer conceives of the problem through the lens of technology as a solution, focusing on digital tools to support mental health. The software developer proposes designing an app with features like self-assessment questionnaires, anonymous peer support forums, and mindfulness exercises. They also suggest using gamification techniques to encourage students to consistently engage with the app over time.

ChatGPT: "Concept Integration and Synthesis"

ChatGPT frames the issue through the lens of concept integration and synthesis, focusing on how different approaches can be harmonized into a cohesive system. Drawing from the team's ideas, ChatGPT suggests combining classroom engagement activities with digital tools, such as creating a journaling feature in the app that aligns with the teacher's mental health curriculum. ChatGPT also proposes connecting the app's family resources to workshops suggested by the social worker and integrating wellness check-ins into the app's functionality to align with the nurse's early detection strategies.

As the brainstorming session progresses, the team members' distinct conceptual frameworks begin to intersect:

- The teacher, inspired by the software developer's focus on technology and ChatGPT's synthesis, suggests using the app in classroom settings to encourage students to explore their feelings in a structured environment.

- The social worker, building on their focus on family dynamics, recommends adding a feature in the app that allows parents to access resources or tips for supporting their children's mental health. ChatGPT expands this by suggesting interactive, culturally sensitive content for parents.
- The nurse, connecting their early detection concept with the software developer's app idea, suggests incorporating wellness check-ins as a feature, where students can anonymously report their feelings and receive recommendations for support. ChatGPT adds to this by proposing predictive analytics to flag potential risks based on patterns in students' self-reports.
- The software developer, inspired by the nurse and social worker's input, expands their app design to include family resources and links to school-based mental health programs. ChatGPT further suggests gamifying family engagement by rewarding participation in family-focused activities.

By bringing together these distinct perspectives, including ChatGPT's role as a synthesizer and integrator, the team develops a comprehensive plan that blends classroom engagement, family support, early detection, and technological innovation. ChatGPT's ability to draw connections and refine ideas enhances the group's collective intelligence, driving creative, multifaceted solutions.

Next, let's look at ChatGPT-generated examples of the second and third ways that semantic networks differ.[59]

Prompt

Now pick up where you left off in the example you just described to provide examples of these two ideas: 1) while two of the team members might have the same concept, one person's version of the concept may be more developed (have more associations) than the other's version, and 2) two people might have the same concept with the same number and kinds of associations, but the activation strengths of their associations may differ, causing them to associate the concept with different associated concepts.

ChatGPT's Response

1. Same Concept, Different Levels of Development
The nurse and ChatGPT both explore the concept of "early detection."

- The Nurse's Version: The nurse's version of early detection is deeply developed, encompassing validated screening tools like the PHQ-9, practical protocols for implementing wellness check-ins, and detailed strategies for follow-up care, such as referrals to counselors or crisis intervention specialists. The nurse also associates early detection with training programs for school staff, ensuring they can recognize subtle behavioral changes in students.
- ChatGPT's Version: ChatGPT's version of early detection is broader but less detailed. ChatGPT suggests leveraging digital tools, like self-assessment quizzes within the proposed app, and using predictive analytics to flag potential risks. However, it lacks the nuanced understanding of specific tools or the challenges of on-the-ground implementation that the nurse provides.

The nurse's expertise prompts ChatGPT to refine its suggestions by incorporating validated screening tools and addressing privacy concerns for students. Conversely, ChatGPT inspires the nurse to think about how digital platforms could expand access to early detection, such as by integrating self-reporting features with school wellness check-ins.

2. Same Concept, Differing Activation Strengths
The social worker and the software developer both focus on the concept of "peer support."

- The Social Worker's Associations: For the social worker, peer support strongly activates associations with in-person mentorship programs. The social worker thinks of structured, face-to-face interactions where trained peer mentors facilitate discussions, creating trust and fostering emotional connections. This leads the social worker to advocate for school-based peer mentorship groups, emphasizing relational depth and immediacy.
- The Software Developer's Associations: For the software developer, peer support activates associations with digital platforms.

The developer's experience with technology makes him focus on anonymous online forums and chat systems where teenagers can seek advice from peers without fear of stigma. Scalability and privacy are central to his vision of peer support.

Although the social worker's and the software developer's associations with peer support overlap in key ways (trust, accessibility, shared experience), the activation strengths differ:

- The social worker's stronger focus on relational depth causes them to prioritize in-person mentoring as the core of peer support. This perspective leads them to question whether anonymous digital interactions can build the same level of trust.
- The software developer's stronger focus on scalability and anonymity leads them to propose additional app features, such as a badge system to encourage participation and moderation tools to maintain a safe online environment.

Collaborative Resolution: These differences lead to a productive exchange:

- The social worker acknowledges the scalability advantages of digital platforms and suggests integrating a feature in the app where users can transition from anonymous online forums to in-person mentorship opportunities when they feel comfortable.
- The software developer, influenced by the social worker's focus on emotional immediacy, proposes adding live video chat options to the app to simulate the relational depth of face-to-face mentorship.

By leveraging these nuanced differences in how concepts are developed and associated, the team further refines their ideas:

- Early detection becomes a hybrid system combining digital self-assessments with trained staff interventions.
- Peer support evolves into a multi-tiered approach, blending scalable online forums with pathways to deeper in-person connections.

ChatGPT's integrative role enhances this process by highlighting areas where the team's perspectives align or diverge, enabling them to navigate and merge their conceptual frameworks effectively. This interplay illustrates how cognitive diversity, both in the richness of concepts and the strength of associations, drives innovation in collective problem-solving.

Moving on from semantic networks, another way this treatment of concepts and conceptual meaning relates to collective intelligence and artificial intelligence concerns the value of group members questioning each other in order to dive deeper into key concepts rather than skipping along the surface of the pond (topic) they are discussing, or if you prefer, satisfying themselves with the view of the peaks poking through the clouds of the mountain range they are flying over. Consider this example:[60]

Prompt

Now describe a scenario where this group, including the AI, generates an important insight into the problem of improving mental health support for teenagers by digging much deeper into one of the concepts by asking each other questions.

ChatGPT's Response

The group decides to dig much deeper into the concept of "emotional safety" to refine their solutions. Initially, the concept is introduced by the social worker, who associates it with creating a non-judgmental space where teenagers feel secure sharing their feelings. As the discussion progresses, the group begins to ask questions that unpack and expand the concept.

Phase 1: Surface-Level Discussion

The social worker defines emotional safety as "a space where students feel accepted and not judged."

- The teacher asks, "What specific factors make a space feel emotionally safe for teenagers in a school setting?"
- The social worker responds, "It's about trust, confidentiality, and understanding. For instance, ensuring that what a student shares in a counseling session doesn't leak to their peers."

ChatGPT interjects, "Have you considered how cultural differences might influence perceptions of emotional safety? For example, in some communities, students might feel safer talking to a peer rather than an adult."

Phase 2: Exploring Contextual Variations

The nurse asks, "What role does the physical environment play in emotional safety? Could the setting itself, like a brightly lit or overly clinical room, affect how comfortable teenagers feel?"

- The social worker agrees and adds, "It's true—neutral, inviting spaces can make a big difference. Maybe we could design the counseling areas to feel more like living rooms than offices."
- The teacher suggests, "What about emotional safety in classrooms? How do we make sure discussions on sensitive topics, like mental health, don't feel invasive or risky for students?"

ChatGPT synthesizes these ideas, "Research indicates that spaces designed with comforting elements, like natural light and soft furnishings, combined with clear norms for respectful interactions, can enhance emotional safety."

Phase 3: Unpacking Emotional Safety for Vulnerable Groups

The software developer asks, "How can we create emotional safety for students who might already feel marginalized, like LGBTQ+ teens or students with disabilities?"

- The social worker responds, "It's about sensitivity to their unique experiences. For example, we might train staff to recognize microaggressions or create support groups specifically for these students."
- ChatGPT expands, "Tailoring prompts or resources to reflect diverse identities could also help. For instance, digital platforms could offer a 'customizable avatar' option for self-expression or language tailored to different cultural backgrounds."

Phase 4: Connecting Emotional Safety to Technology

The software developer shifts focus to digital tools. "How do we ensure emotional safety in an app environment? What if anonymity leads to bullying?"

- ChatGPT suggests, "Incorporate moderation tools and AI-based monitoring to identify harmful behavior. Also, gamify positive interactions—for example, rewarding students for offering constructive support to their peers."
- The nurse adds, "Could the app provide an 'emergency exit' button, so if a student feels overwhelmed, they can quickly switch to a calming activity like a breathing exercise?"

Emerging Insight

After several layers of unpacking, the group synthesizes an actionable insight: emotional safety must be multifaceted, addressing physical spaces, interpersonal dynamics, and digital interactions. They propose a comprehensive approach that includes:

- Physically Safe Spaces: Redesign counseling and classroom areas to feel warm and welcoming.
- Inclusive Training: Equip teachers and staff with cultural competence and sensitivity training.
- Digital Safeguards: Integrate moderation tools, customizable content, and emergency support features into the app.
- Student Input: Involve teens in co-designing programs and spaces to ensure their needs and perspectives are met.

ChatGPT's integrative role helps connect these threads, ensuring the team explores multiple layers of the concept and considers diverse perspectives. This deeper exploration of emotional safety leads to a well-rounded, actionable strategy that resonates with students' varied needs.

This section should make clear to you that understanding the symbolic (conceptual) level of cognition has many benefits, including finding ways to put generative AI to use when working with the people, process, and platform practices that contribute to a group's collective intelligence and crafting better generative AI prompts. Now let's look at the knowledge level.

Knowledge Level

Where the entities that reside at the symbolic level are *concepts*, the entities that reside at the knowledge level are *ideas*. As I said, roughly speaking, concepts are expressed as words or short phrases, whereas ideas are expressed as whole sentences.[61] Or, said differently, where concepts encode individual categories (expressed as words), knowledge encodes the way in which the categories relate to one another (expressed as sentences). Among the ideas that reside at the knowledge level are facts, beliefs, hypotheses, theories, laws, rules, goals, and values.[62] Here, we're going to focus on facts, rules, and goals.

- *Facts*: A fact is some truth about the world. In less formal terms, we speak of facts in terms of know-who, know-what, know-where, know-when, know-why, know-how, and know-how much. (I use the acronym $5WH^2$ to remember these different kinds of knowledge.)

- *Rules*: We use an IF-THEN *rule* to generate new facts from old facts, that is, to generate yet-to-be-known facts from already-known facts. Imagine, for example, that you are standing in front of a hill and you see smoke billowing up from behind it, so you apply the following rule: IF there is smoke billowing up from behind that hill (an already-known fact), THEN there is probably a fire on the other side of the hill (a yet-to-be-known fact). New knowledge can be knowledge that is new to you, as is the fact that there is a fire on the other side of the hill, which is something the people on the other side of the hill already know. Or it can be knowledge that is new to the world, as was knowledge of the wheel when it was invented and the double-helix structure of DNA when it was discovered by Watson and Crick.
- *Goals*: A goal is a desired state (like the desired state in Figure 1.1), which is to say, it is something we want to achieve or accomplish. We use facts and rules to reach a conclusion about how to accomplish a goal. Say, for example, you want to get to the other side of a tall brick wall. To accomplish this goal, you might combine the fact that there is a ladder near the wall with the rule IF you want to get to the other side of a tall wall, THEN use a ladder to climb over it.

The computer scientist Tadeusz Szuba uses Feynman diagrams[63] to illustrate the way that "old facts" and rules collide to produce "new facts," or as he puts it, the way that a fact and a rule rendezvous in an inference process to produce a conclusion.[64] In Figure 1.4, the fact "There's smoke billowing up from the other side of the hill" (which is condensed to "Smoke" to save space in the diagram) collides with the rule "If you see smoke, then there's probably a fire." The collision of the fact and the rule generates the conclusion "There's probably a fire on the other side of the hill." The squiggly line depicts the collision, or inference process, that generates the conclusion (yet-to-be-known fact).

Feynman diagrams can be used to depict a chain of collisions, or inferences. There are two collisions (two squiggly lines) in Figure 1.5. The first is the same as the one shown in Figure 1.4. In the second, the conclusion generated by the first collision (There's probably a fire on the other side of the hill) becomes the fact that collides with the rule in the second collision, that is, the rule that states "If there's a fire, then you should run." The collision of the fact and the rule generates the conclusion "I should run." The conclusion serves your ever-present goal (desired state) of staying alive. This short, two-collision (two-inference) chain is sufficient to solve this simple problem. Complex problems require much longer chains of inference.

So what does this have to do with collective intelligence and artificial intelligence? I'll answer by asking you to imagine that a man and woman are standing in front of a hill and that smoke is billowing up from behind

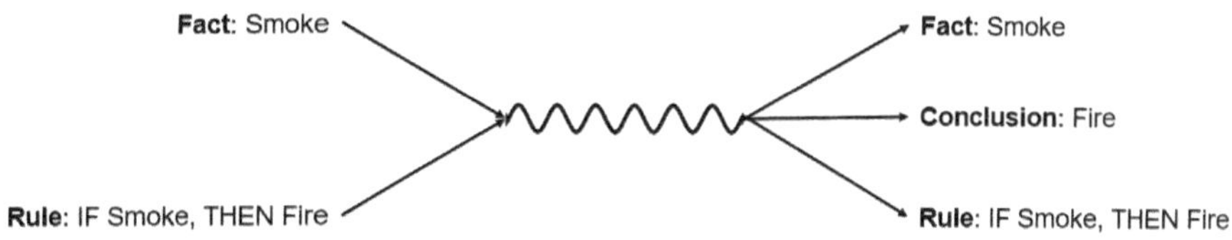

Figure 1.4 A Feynman diagram showing a fact colliding with a rule to produce a conclusion.

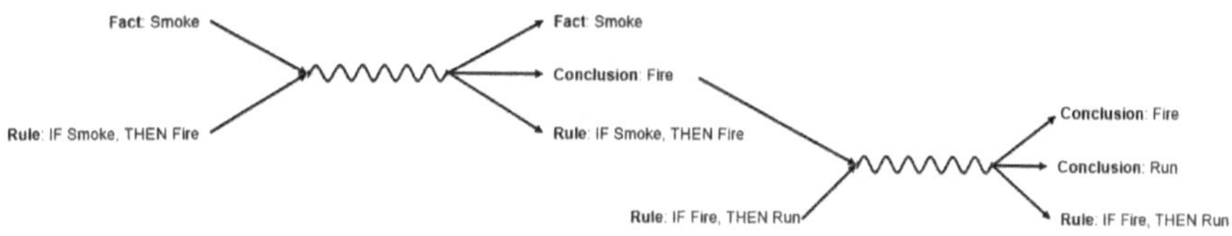

Figure 1.5 Using a Feynman diagram to depict a two-step inference process.

the hill. The man is blind, so he doesn't know the fact that there is smoke, but he does know the "IF smoke, THEN fire" rule. By contrast, the woman can see, so she knows the fact that there is smoke, but she doesn't know the "IF smoke, THEN fire" rule. Fortunately, because they can talk to each other, they're able to combine the fact and the rule to reach the conclusion that there's probably a fire on the other side of the hill. Using normal speech, the woman might state the fact by saying something like, "Heh, there's smoke billowing up from behind that hill," and the man might execute the rule by saying, "There's probably a fire on the other side of the hill." Next, they climb to the top of the hill, where the same thing occurs. The man can't see, so he isn't able to confirm the fact that there's a fire, but he does know the "IF fire, THEN run" rule, and the woman can see the fire, but she doesn't know the rule. Again, they converse to combine their knowledge and conclude that they should run.

Now imagine an interdisciplinary group that is meeting to solve a complex problem and that ChatGPT is a member of the group. As a result of their differences in training and experience, including ChatGPT's experience of reading everything freely available on the internet, the group members know different facts about the who, what, where, when, why, how, and how much ($5WH^2$) of the problem, and they know different rules for processing the facts. Over the course of their conversation, they contribute and combine these facts and rules in a chain of inferences (squiggly lines) that ultimately ends in a conclusion that solves the problem.[65] As compared to simple problems, complex problems require a long chain of inferences—longer than most individuals would perform alone, according to information scientist Gerry Stahl[66]—to reach a useful or correct conclusion. For both reasons—the diverse facts and rules possessed by the group members and the longer chain of inferences—groups are often able to solve problems that their members are unable to solve themselves, which explains why Albert Einstein once noted, "What a person thinks on his own, without being stimulated by the thoughts and experiences of other people, is even in the best case rather paltry and monotonous."[67]

Gerry Stahl elaborates on his observation that a group's chain of inferences is usually longer than an individual's chain. He explains, "The power of collaborative learning is partially to bring together multiple perspectives [.] . . . However, another advantage is to extend the cognitive effort into *longer sequences* of argumentation through the stimulation and enjoyment of productive social interaction, increasing the time-on-task as needed to solve challenging problems. Thus, groups can achieve cognitive accomplishments that their members cannot."[68] Stahl adds, "[T]he personal contributions are largely responses to what has gone before in the group interaction. . . . The important cognitive achievement is *emergent* (italics mine) at the group level, rather than a simple collection of expressions of individual cognitive accomplishments."[69]

In other words, when faced with a challenging problem, groups engage in chains of inference that are longer than the chains its members would—indeed, could—generate, and in which many of the inferences are reactions to what other members have to say, which means that they are inferences that would not occur if the member were to work on the problem alone. The net result is an emergent solution. Now let's look at an example, generated by ChatGPT, that captures the flavor, if not the extent, of a cognitively diverse group contributing facts and rules to a chain of inferences:[70]

Prompt

Read the foregoing text. Then use the ideas in the text to create an example of a multi-disciplinary team using facts, rules, goals, and chains of inference to solve a business problem. Assume that ChatGPT is a member of the team.

ChatGPT's Response

A multi-disciplinary team—including a supply chain analyst, a logistics manager, a sustainability expert, a financial analyst, and a generative AI tool like ChatGPT—is tasked with optimizing a company's supply chain to reduce costs while improving environmental sustainability. The group leverages facts, rules, and goals to collectively reason through the problem.

Step 1: Identifying Facts

- Supply Chain Analyst: Reports that long shipping routes lead to high transportation costs and delays.
- Logistics Manager: Shares that inefficiencies in warehouse management result in excessive inventory holding costs.
- Sustainability Expert: Notes that certain suppliers use environmentally harmful packaging and inefficient production methods.
- Financial Analyst: Highlights that excessive fuel costs and tariffs from overseas suppliers significantly impact profitability.
- ChatGPT: Supplements these facts with case studies of companies that have successfully optimized supply chains by implementing regional distribution centers and AI-powered demand forecasting.

Step 2: Applying Rules

The team applies domain-specific rules to process these facts:

- Supply Chain Analyst's Rule: "IF transportation costs are high, THEN consider optimizing supplier locations and distribution centers."
- Logistics Manager's Rule: "IF inventory costs are excessive, THEN improve demand forecasting and warehouse efficiency."
- Sustainability Expert's Rule: "IF a supplier's processes are unsustainable, THEN consider alternatives with lower environmental impact."
- Financial Analyst's Rule: "IF fuel and tariff costs are increasing, THEN prioritize local or nearshore suppliers."
- ChatGPT's Rule: "IF companies with regional distribution centers reduce costs and emissions, THEN consider decentralizing logistics."

Step 3: Combining Facts and Rules

Using a chain of inferences, the team synthesizes these facts and rules into actionable insights.

- Fact: Long shipping routes lead to high transportation costs.
  Rule: "IF transportation costs are high, THEN optimize supplier locations and distribution centers."
  Conclusion: Evaluate suppliers closer to distribution hubs and explore regional fulfillment centers.
- Fact: Inefficient warehouses lead to excessive inventory costs.
  Rule: "IF inventory costs are excessive, THEN improve warehouse efficiency."

Conclusion: Implement AI-driven inventory management to reduce waste and optimize stock levels.

- Fact: Some suppliers use environmentally harmful packaging.
  Rule: "IF supplier sustainability is poor, THEN consider greener alternatives."
  Conclusion: Work with suppliers who use eco-friendly materials and carbon-efficient transportation.
- Fact: Fuel and tariff costs negatively impact profitability.
  Rule: "IF fuel and tariffs are increasing, THEN prioritize nearshore suppliers."
  Conclusion: Shift procurement to suppliers in neighboring regions to lower costs.

Step 4: Aligning with Goals

The team's primary goal is to reduce supply chain costs while improving sustainability. Based on their inferences, they propose:

- Establishing regional distribution centers to reduce shipping distances and costs.
- Implementing AI-driven demand forecasting to minimize overstock and understock situations.
- Partnering with sustainable suppliers who use biodegradable packaging and energy-efficient manufacturing.
- Nearshoring key suppliers to reduce fuel costs and exposure to tariff fluctuations.

Step 5: The Role of Cognitive Diversity

The team's cognitive diversity plays a crucial role in problem-solving:

- The supply chain analyst focuses on logistics efficiency, identifying the need for regional distribution centers.
- The sustainability expert brings an environmental perspective, ensuring the solution aligns with corporate social responsibility.
- The financial analyst ensures that changes align with cost-saving measures.
- ChatGPT accelerates the process by retrieving relevant case studies and synthesizing cross-domain knowledge.
- By integrating their diverse expertise and leveraging long chains of inference, the team arrives at a more effective and innovative solution than any individual could have achieved alone.

Just as we did in the last section on concepts and conceptual meaning, we want to relate this section on knowledge to the idea of raising the collective intelligence of a group and combining it with artificial intelligence to create a hybrid intelligence that is smarter than either intelligence alone. Toward that end, I asked ChatGPT the following:[71]

Prompt

Now, what does the foregoing text, the content of your example, and whatever else you know about this topic tell you about how to raise the collective intelligence of a group and combine it with the artificial intelligence of generative AI to create an intelligence that is smarter than either intelligence alone?

ChatGPT's Response

The insights from the text, the business example, and broader knowledge on collective and artificial intelligence suggest that raising the collective intelligence of a group and integrating it with AI can produce a hybrid intelligence that surpasses either human or machine intelligence alone. Here's how:

1. *Extend Chains of Inference for Deeper Problem Solving*

- The document describes how facts and rules combine through inference chains to generate new knowledge.
- The longer the inference chain, the more sophisticated the reasoning—and groups, by distributing cognitive effort, can form longer chains than individuals.
- AI can extend inference chains by introducing new facts, drawing analogies, and identifying missing logical steps.

Implication: Design collaborative workflows that encourage long chains of inference
How to Implement:

1. Structured Reasoning Frameworks: Use argument mapping tools (e.g., DebateGraph, Kialo, bCisive, Rationale, or even AI-assisted concept mapping) to visualize chains of inference. [Note: argument mapping tools are explained in Chapter 4.]
2. AI as a Chain Extender: Design AI prompts that encourage step-by-step reasoning rather than jumping to conclusions.

Example: Instead of asking, "How do we optimize our supply chain?", ask, "What facts and rules should we consider before optimizing our supply chain?"
3. Iterative Hypothesis Generation: Require teams to explicitly state intermediate inferences before reaching conclusions. AI can suggest missing steps or alternative pathways.
4. Conversational AI Assistants: Train AI to prompt users with "What happens next?" questions to nudge extended reasoning (e.g., Socratic questioning models).

2. *Leverage AI as a Knowledge Catalyst, Not Just an Answer Machine*

- AI should augment, not replace, human reasoning by filling knowledge gaps, suggesting external examples, and helping teams see connections across disciplines.
- ChatGPT's contribution in the business example—bringing in case studies of successful supply chain optimizations—demonstrates how AI can contextualize human reasoning.

Implication: Integrate AI as an interactive, knowledge-expanding agent in group decision-making
How to Implement:

1. Dynamic AI-Augmented Research: Use AI to pull real-time, domain-specific case studies and success stories to ground decision-making in data.
2. Domain-Specific AI Training: Train AI models on company- or industry-specific knowledge bases so its insights are directly relevant to the team's expertise.
3. AI-Generated Thought Experiments: Program AI to simulate counterfactual reasoning, e.g., "What if we optimized our supply chain for carbon neutrality instead of cost savings?"
4. AI as a Debate Partner: Use AI to generate alternative perspectives or devil's advocate arguments to prevent groupthink.

3. *Maximize Cognitive Diversity by Structuring Cross-Disciplinary Collaboration*

- Cognitive diversity increases the range of facts, rules, and heuristics available for inference.
- In the business example, the supply chain analyst, logistics manager, sustainability expert, and financial analyst each brought unique rules that contributed to a holistic solution.
- AI should not only support diverse knowledge contributions but also help translate insights across disciplines.

Implication: Design team structures and AI systems that amplify cognitive diversity
How to Implement:

1. Diverse Team Composition: Ensure teams include specialists with different knowledge bases and mental models.
2. AI as a Knowledge Translator: Use AI to generate summary explanations that help one domain expert understand another's perspective (e.g., explain financial constraints to engineers using simple analogies).
3. Cross-Domain Knowledge Graphs: Implement AI-driven knowledge visualization tools that highlight interdisciplinary connections.
4. AI-Assisted Brainstorming: Use AI to suggest unexpected but relevant analogies from different industries to expand human thinking (e.g., "How has nature optimized supply chains through evolution?").

4. Use Conversational AI to Scaffold Human Reasoning

- The text emphasizes that inference processes emerge from interactive group discussions, where members build on each other's reasoning.
- AI should function as a cognitive scaffold, prompting teams to articulate, refine, and test their inferences.
- In the business example, ChatGPT played this role by surfacing case studies that aligned with the team's reasoning.

Implication: Develop AI interfaces that facilitate structured reasoning conversations
How to Implement:

1. Conversational AI with Multi-Step Reasoning: Instead of simply answering queries, AI should engage in structured dialogues that force deeper analysis.
2. AI-Prompted Reflection: Train AI to periodically ask teams meta-cognitive questions, e.g., "What assumption are you making here?" or "What alternative explanations exist?"
3. Socratic AI Design: Use AI models that function like Socratic mentors, asking clarifying questions to push teams toward greater precision in their reasoning.
4. AI-Mediated Decision Support: Integrate AI in decision-making meetings, where it listens to discussions and suggests knowledge gaps, alternative perspectives, or precedent cases.

5. Use Iterative Feedback Loops to Refine Human-AI Reasoning

- The document describes how problem-solving is an iterative process, where facts and rules collide to generate new conclusions.
- AI and humans should mutually critique each other's reasoning, ensuring that solutions are continuously refined.
- The business example demonstrates how AI contributed insights, but the human team validated and adjusted them.

Implication: Establish continuous cycles of AI-human feedback for solution refinement
How to Implement:

1. AI-Generated Hypotheses, Human Validation: AI proposes solutions, and team members debate their feasibility before refining.
2. Crowdsourced AI Refinement: Use AI to aggregate feedback from multiple teams or stakeholders before finalizing a decision.
3. AI as a Justification Engine: Train AI to explain its reasoning process, allowing humans to assess its logic rather than just trusting its output.
4. Rapid AI Iteration on Human Feedback: Allow users to give real-time corrections to AI suggestions, enabling adaptive learning loops.

Conclusion: The Formula for a Smarter Hybrid Intelligence
By following these principles, we can merge human collective intelligence with AI in a way that outperforms either alone. The key is structuring human-AI interactions around:

1. Extending inference chains through structured reasoning tools.
2. Using AI as a knowledge catalyst to introduce new perspectives and analogies.
3. Maximizing cognitive diversity by ensuring domain-crossing collaboration.
4. Scaffolding human reasoning with AI-driven structured conversations.
5. Refining solutions iteratively through AI-human feedback loops.

When AI is designed not as a knowledge oracle, but as a dynamic reasoning assistant, we create a hybrid intelligence system that is more creative, adaptive, and insightful than either human groups or AI alone.

Thus far in this treatment of the knowledge level, we've focused on subconscious thought with only passing reference to the language that expresses our thoughts and that we consciously experience. Remember that a generative AI model is a large language model (LLM). As it relates to generative AI, an important thing to understand about language is the fundamental distinction between the subject and the predicate parts of a sentence. The *subject-predicate core of language* is a foundational concept in linguistics that describes how sentences are structured around a *subject* (what the sentence is about) and a *predicate* (what is being said about the subject). This basic structure underpins the organization of meaning in natural language and is fundamental to syntax, semantics, and cognition.

- *Syntactic Structure*: The subject is typically a noun phrase (NP) that denotes an entity, object, or concept, and the predicate is typically a verb phrase (VP) that expresses an action, state, or property of the subject. For example: *The cat (subject) sleeps on the mat (predicate).*
- *Semantic Functions*: The subject serves as the topic or agent in many cases, but it can also be an experiencer, patient, or other thematic role. The predicate conveys information about the subject by linking it to properties, actions, or states.
- *Cognitive and Conceptual Role*: The subject-predicate structure mirrors cognition, as it aligns with the way humans perceive and categorize the world.

Considering the fundamental role it plays in language, I asked ChatGPT if including reference to the subject-predicate core of language in a generative AI prompt will cause it to give a better answer. The following is what it had to say. I'll talk more about using the subject-predicate distinction to create prompts in Chapter 4.

Prompt

Tell me if including reference to the subject-predicate core of language in a generative AI prompt will cause generative AI to give a better answer. If so, why?

ChatGPT's Response

Yes, including a reference to the subject-predicate core of language in a generative AI prompt can improve the AI's response. Here's why:

1. *Structural Clarity in Prompts*
   - A well-formed prompt that explicitly structures the subject (what the request is about) and the predicate (what should be done) reduces ambiguity.
   - Example:
     - Less structured: *Explain AI and intelligence.*
     - More structured: *Explain how AI (subject) models human intelligence (predicate).*
     - Even better: *Explain how generative AI (subject) models human intelligence (predicate) using probabilistic inference.*
   - AI models like GPT-4 perform better with clearly defined subjects and predicates, as they mimic the way structured language encodes meaning.
2. *Improved Semantic Processing*
   - Large Language Models (LLMs) use semantic decomposition when processing queries. A clear subject-predicate structure helps AI retrieve and organize relevant knowledge more efficiently.
   - Example:
     - Weak prompt: *How does intelligence work in AI?*
     - Strong prompt using subject-predicate core: *How does generative AI (subject) model intelligence (predicate) through probabilistic reasoning?*
     - The second prompt guides the AI to focus on a specific conceptual link.
3. *Enhanced Logical Coherence*
   - AI models are trained on vast amounts of text where the subject-predicate relationship is fundamental.
   - When a prompt explicitly adheres to this structure, it reinforces logical relationships, reducing hallucination or vague responses.
   - Example:
     - Vague: *What do you think about the future of AI?*
     - Structured: *How will AI (subject) transform (predicate) scientific research in the next decade?*

- The second prompt anchors the response in a clear conceptual framework.

4. *Alignment with Frame Semantics and Schema Activation*

- The subject-predicate core aligns with Frame Semantics, which AI models use indirectly through knowledge graphs and vector embeddings.
- When a prompt includes an explicit subject-predicate structure, it activates the correct frame, improving relevance.
- Example:
    - Without clear frame: *Tell me about cognition in AI.*
    - With subject-predicate core activating frame: *How does AI (subject) simulate (predicate) human cognition using neural networks?*
    - This guides the model to retrieve technical rather than general responses.

5. *More Precise Bayesian Inference*

- LLMs function probabilistically, predicting the next token based on prior context.
- A well-structured prompt narrows the probability space, making the response more precise and informative.
- Example:
    - Broad: *What can AI do?*
    - Specific with subject-predicate core: *How does generative AI (subject) generate (predicate) human-like text using transformers?*
    - The second prompt reduces response variance and increases precision.

Conclusion: Why Does This Work?

1. Less ambiguity: AI better understands intent.
2. More structured input: More structured output.
3. Aligns with LLM training: Better retrieval of relevant knowledge.
4. Activates proper knowledge frames: More coherent responses.
5. Guides AI inference: More probabilistically optimal answers.

I'll end this section by answering the question with which it began: "What is thinking?" At the biological level, *to think is to link* neural activations. At the symbolic level, *to think is to link* concepts. And at the knowledge level, *to think is to link* facts. Thus, stripped to its essence, the answer is simply this. *To think is to link.*

Where Is Thinking?

We take it as obvious that we think in our head, that the brain is the organ in which thought occurs.[72] But what is now obvious was once obscure. The ancients thought that we think with our heart. Even Aristotle got it wrong. After watching a headless chicken run around the barnyard like . . . well . . . a chicken with its head cut off, he concluded that the brain is a radiator—an organ that functions to cool the blood. People continued to get it wrong until 1664, when the English physician Thomas Willis wrote the first accurate account of the brain.

No sooner was the brain-heart issue settled than a new one arose, called the brain-mind problem.[73] Peer into a head from the outside and you'll find a thumpingly physical three-pound brain.[74] Peer out of a head from the inside, as you're doing at this very moment, and you'll find there are no things to thump. "In here" there is only the ethereal thought-stuff of mind. It's as if our heads contain two parallel universes, one material and one mental, one made *of* matter, the other made *out of* matter. How do physical brains produce mental experiences? How does mind arise from brain? After centuries of contemplation, the brain-mind problem remains a mystery.

No matter the mystery, the idea that the brain-mind is the locus of thought is well established. (Perhaps too well established, as we'll soon see.) The question then becomes, "Where in the brain-mind does thinking occur?" Scientists have made considerable progress mapping the geography of thought using brain scanning technology. But mapping mindscape poses a real puzzler. How do you say where something's located in the mind when there's no "where" there? You can experience the mind's "wherelessness" by doing a thought experiment. Stop reading for a moment, think a thought, and then say where it's located in your mind. You'll find you can't do it. The only way out of this problem, it seems, is to say that when it comes to mapping the mind, the best we can do is to say where mental entities are located relative to one another using terms like above, below, and between. With that in mind (somewhere), there are several ways to describe where thinking occurs in the mind.

The first way is to say that thought lies intermediate between perception and action.[75] We might well ask "Why?" What purpose is served by placing thought between the images we perceive and the motor actions we formulate in the mind? The answer lies in the nature of mediation. To mediate is to be the medium for bringing about some result. The fundamental purpose of thinking is to bring about an action that is appropriate to whatever perception is at hand. In a world that is full of good things and bad things, we don't want to take any old action. Rather, we want to take actions that enable us to achieve or obtain the good things and avoid or eliminate the bad things. Thought is the means of generating effective actions. This perspective on the mind points to how AI can boost the collective intelligence of a group by helping it to perceive, think, and act:

- *Perception*: In a small problem-solving group, each member contributes to the collective perception by bringing unique observations and interpretations about the problem that confronts them. Predictive AI systems can enhance the group's perception by processing large datasets and identifying patterns that human members might overlook. Together, these perceptions form a wider and deeper understanding of the problem than any individual could achieve alone.
- *Thought*: As we've already talked about, by contributing a diverse set of facts and rules and engaging in longer chains of inference, a group is able to reason its way to a solution that none of its members could conceive of alone. Generative AI, as noted in the previous section, can bridge gaps in the chain by contributing facts and rules that the group has failed to consider.
- *Action*: To be of any use, the solution must be enacted. Here, again, a cognitively diverse group can contribute diverse facts and rules to create an action plan. They can also contribute their different skills to implement the plan. Generative AI can contribute by identifying missing steps in the plan and pointing out potential difficulties and adverse consequences of the steps.

The second way to describe where thinking occurs in the mind is to say that it lies in the subconscious, beneath the words and images we consciously experience. We've already touched on some of the ways this perspective relates to collective intelligence and artificial intelligence in the discussion of mentalese. Some additional ways in which this perspective relates to the two intelligences are these:

- When individuals struggle to put subconscious thoughts into words, the group can help through discussion and feedback. Generative AI, too, can identify when a group member is struggling to articulate his thoughts and propose phrasing or frameworks to clarify and advance discussions. And sentiment analysis can infer unspoken thoughts, bridging gaps in communication when members are unclear or hesitant.
- That we think in a subconscious language of thought (mentalese) highlights the importance of expressing and aligning the group members' subconscious frameworks and models. Building a shared understanding

of these frameworks and models enables effective collaboration. A useful way to build this common understanding, one which takes advantage of the idea that mentalese translates between images and language, is for a group to collectively create an annotated diagram, where the entities are labeled and their relationships are depicted by the lines and arrows that connect them. Generative AI can be used to suggest and generate insightful diagrams or parts of diagrams, even videos that capture relationships among the entities.

- The role that signal-signs play in guiding subconscious thought parallels how verbal and non-verbal cues direct group dynamics. Group members' statements, diagrams, and metaphors can serve as steering mechanisms, subtly influencing the direction of the group's collective thinking. AI's recommendation algorithms can steer the group's thinking in productive directions by suggesting relevant resources, solutions, or next steps based on the group's ongoing discussion.

The first two accounts locate thought at a spot between perception and action and beneath the images and words we consciously experience. The third account is given by Andy Clark, a professor of cognitive philosophy at the University of Sussex, who, along with the philosopher David Chalmers, first posited the idea of *extended mind*. Clark and Chalmers proposed that the human mind extends outside our bodies into technologies that we think through. Take the example of multiplying two numbers. Most of us can easily multiply 7 × 2 in our head, but when it comes to multiplying large numbers, like 72,431 × 36,287, we use a calculator to compute the answer. When this happens, Clark and Chalmers explain, the mind and the calculator function as a "unified cognitive system" in which the pathway of thought "loops" through the calculator. In other words, the brain-calculator combination gives rise to a mind in which some of the thinking occurs outside our bodies in the calculator.

Clark goes on to explain the way that technology augments intelligence. You can demonstrate this to yourself by doing another thought experiment. Go ahead and try multiplying 72,431 × 36,287 entirely in your head, without using a calculator, pen and paper, or any other type of technology to think through. Unless you're some sort of mathematical savant, you can't do it. Which means that you are literally less intelligent without the technology than you are with it. Now consider the historical progression of cognitive technologies that mankind has thought through—sticks and clay tablets, quills and papyrus scrolls, pencils and paper, chalkboards, whiteboards, abacuses, slide rules, calculators, computers, smartphones, and so on. Clark notes that throughout history man has engaged in the "culturally transmitted process of designer-environment construction: the process of deliberately building better worlds to think in."[76] We'll be going deep into this topic in Chapter 4, where you'll learn about the meeting environments and analog and digital tools that enhance the collective intelligence of a group. It should already be clear to you that generative AI opens a new chapter in mankind's ongoing story of building better worlds to think in.

Once we let thought out of the (skin) bag to loop through various technologies, it's free to loop through other things, including other people's minds. This time, rather than trying to multiply 72,431 × 36,287 in your head, ask your digital assistant (Siri, Google Assistant, Alexa, etc.) to do it. It will respond with the answer 2,628,303,697. Now imagine that you ask a mathematical savant for the product and s/he gives you the answer. In the first case, your thinking looped through the digital assistant that you thought through. In the second, your thinking looped through the savant. Just as the mind-digital assistant combination functioned as a unified cognitive system, so too did the mind-mind combination of you and the savant.

You've probably never looped through the mind of a savant, but you loop through other people's minds all the time. As earlier explained, we think in chains of inference in which one idea links to another, which links to another, which links to another, and so on. When two people engage in a dialogue, the chain loops round and round through their heads. The first person says something that activates an idea in a second person's head, who says something that activates an idea in the first (or third, fourth, etc.) person's head, who says something that activates an idea in the second (or third, fourth, etc.) person's head, and so on. When two (or more) people inter-think in this way, it's fair to say that the thinking occurs in the unified cognitive system comprised of their two (or more) minds. It is this unified cognitive system that is collectively intelligent. Or not, for as you'll later learn, there are things that can make a group collectively stupid.

As I said at the start of the last section, we take it as obvious that we think in our head, that our brain-mind is the organ in which thought occurs. But what is seemingly obvious is in fact obscure. Cognitive scientists now assert that, like Aristotle, we've got it wrong. Thinking also occurs in unified cognitive systems that consist of our mind, other people's minds, and the technologies we think through. And with that insight, mankind's greatest mystery takes on a whole new dimension—the brain-mind problem becomes the extended mind problem.

How Do Groups Think Together?

How do groups go about thinking together? They engage in conversation, which is to say, they use spoken language, written language, and body language to exchange their thoughts and build a thought structure together. Ludwik Fleck, a Polish physician and microbiologist and the author of the book *Genesis and Development of a Scientific Fact*, had this to say about the role that conversation plays in collective cognition, "He is a poor observer who does not notice that a stimulating conversation between two persons soon creates a condition in which each utters thoughts he would not have been able to produce either by himself or in different company .... Prolonged duration of this state produces ... a thought structure that belongs to neither of them alone[.] Who is its carrier and who its originator? It is neither more nor less than the small collective of two persons. If a third person joins in, a new collective arises."[77]

Similarly, in his book *Dialogue and the Art of Thinking Together*, William Isaacs, a lecturer at MIT's Sloan School of Management, explains that "dialogue is a conversation in which people think together in relationship"[78] and that it (the dialogue) "seeks to harness the 'collective intelligence'... of the people around you."[79] Ann Baker, a public policy professor at George Mason University, takes the idea a step further when she asks at the start of her book *Catalytic Conversations: Organizational Communication and Innovation*, "Could the health of an organization hinge on something as commonplace as talk?"[80] Her book-length answer is an emphatic "Yes!", for conversations, she says, "are at the heart of creating new knowledge and are therefore precursors to sustainable change and innovation."[81]

I'll have much more to say about conversation in the next chapter. For now, the foundational fact is that collective cognition is implemented by conversation and collective intelligence emerges out of it.

What Makes a Group Smarter than Its Smartest Member?

The long answer to this question is given in the next three chapters, where I explain that collective intelligence emerges from the right combination of *people*, using the right *processes*, implemented on the right technology *platforms*. The short answer is that, insofar as problems are concerned, collective intelligence is fundamentally about surfacing chunks of information and knowledge,[82] then using group reasoning and group judgment to assemble them into a solution. Let me explain.

Earlier I said that problem-solving, reduced to its essence, involves generating alternative solutions and choosing one of them as the best. Which means, in turn, that a group exhibits collective intelligence when it generates alternative solutions that none of its members could have generated alone, then chooses one of them as the best. I also said that generating the alternative solutions is mostly about *group reasoning*, whereas choosing one of the solutions is mostly about *group judgment*, though each involves some of both. Here I'm going to expand on this idea.

To start, look again at Figure 1.1, where I used the symbols < > to represent the diverging and converging that results in a way to transform the cause of an undesired state into the cause of a desired state. In fact, the whole diagram has this diverge-converge structure.[83] Whether it pertains to identifying the possible causes of an undesired state and judging one or more of them as correct (i.e., right, accurate, or true), or generating possible ways to transform each of the causes and choosing one of them as best, solving a problem is basically about generating alternatives (diverging), then judging which alternative(s) to choose (converging).

Generating a set of alternatives (diverging) involves surfacing the chunks of information and knowledge that are required to create the alternatives, then assembling them into the alternatives. Thus, each alternative consists of a portion of the chunks, and the set of alternatives contains all the chunks needed to create them.[84] A complex, multi-faceted problem requires a group to solve it because no one person has all the required chunks. The right combination of people is one in which the members, together, possess all the chunks needed to create a collectively exhaustive—or more realistically, a reasonably exhaustive—set of alternatives. But there's more to diverging than that. Not only must a collectively intelligent group possess all the chunks, its members must also engage in group reasoning and group judgment to assemble the chunks into the alternatives.

Judging which of the alternatives is correct or best (converging) requires some form of voting to aggregate everyone's judgments.[85] To make well-informed votes, the group members must first surface the chunks of information and knowledge needed to assess each alternative. Here, again, the right combination of people is one in which the members, together, possess all the chunks of information and knowledge needed to accurately assess the alternatives. And here, again, there's more to it than that. Not only must a collectively intelligent group possess all the chunks, but its members must also engage in the group reasoning and group judgment needed to make the assessments. In the real world, it's usually the case that there's insufficient information and knowledge to make a fully informed vote, so some of the group members will err in their judgments, some one way and others in other ways. The benefit of a cognitively diverse group is that the errors in judgment tend to cancel each other out.

So, in short, a collectively intelligent group is smarter than its smartest member because it possesses all the chunks of information and knowledge needed to solve the problem and it's able to do a superior job of using the information and knowledge to reason and judge its way to a solution. The rest of this book is devoted to putting together the *people*, *processes*, and *platforms* (the "3Ps") to make this happen, including ways that generative AI can augment each of the Ps.

To bring this process to life, I asked ChatGPT for an example.[86] Here is its response:

Prompt

Read the foregoing text. Then describe an example of a cognitively diverse group of people using the necessary chunks of knowledge and information to carry out the group reasoning and group judgment needed to identify the cause of an undesired state and to identify an optimal way of acting on the cause to transform it into the cause of the desired state.

ChatGPT's Response

Example: A Cognitively Diverse Group Solving an Urban Traffic Congestion Problem

Step 1: Identifying the Cause of the Undesired State

A city is experiencing severe traffic congestion in its downtown area, leading to increased commute times, pollution, and economic inefficiencies. A cognitively diverse task force is assembled, consisting of urban planners, transportation engineers, behavioral economists, data scientists, environmentalists, business representatives, and local residents. Each member possesses different chunks of knowledge and information relevant to the problem.

- Diverging (Generating Alternatives for Causes)
  The group reasons through different possible causes based on their collective chunks of knowledge:
  - Urban planners highlight outdated road infrastructure and inefficient intersections.
  - Transportation engineers analyze real-time traffic data and suggest that poor signal synchronization contributes significantly.
  - Behavioral economists point out that many commuters prefer personal vehicles over public transit due to pricing and convenience issues.
  - Data scientists present GPS mobility data revealing patterns of congestion caused by delivery trucks operating during peak hours.
  - Environmentalists argue that urban sprawl has increased car dependency.
  - Business representatives note that ride-hailing services have increased traffic volume.

The group then engages in group judgment to evaluate these causes, discussing available evidence and determining which ones contribute most to the congestion.

- Converging (Judging the Most Probable Cause)

After deliberation, they conclude that a combination of inefficient traffic light coordination, excessive personal vehicle use, and delivery trucks operating during peak hours are the primary contributors.

Step 2: Identifying an Optimal Way to Act on the Cause

Having identified the main causes, the group now shifts to generating and evaluating possible interventions.

- Diverging (Generating Alternative Solutions)

  Drawing on their respective expertise, the group proposes multiple solutions:

  1. Adaptive Traffic Signal Control—Using AI-driven algorithms to dynamically adjust traffic lights.
  2. Congestion Pricing—Charging fees for entering downtown during peak hours.
  3. Incentivizing Public Transit Use—Offering subsidies and improved service frequency.
  4. Designating Off-Peak Delivery Hours—Restricting delivery trucks to operate at night.
  5. Expanding Bicycle and Pedestrian Infrastructure—Creating more bike lanes and car-free zones.

  Each solution incorporates different chunks of knowledge:

  - Traffic engineers support adaptive signals as a high-tech fix.
  - Economists argue for congestion pricing to shift commuter behavior.
  - Business representatives caution against negative impacts of delivery restrictions.
  - Environmentalists advocate for expanded bike lanes.

- Converging (Judging the Best Solution)

  The group engages in collective reasoning to evaluate the potential effectiveness of each alternative:

  - Predictive models from data scientists estimate traffic reduction from congestion pricing.

- Cost-benefit analysis by economists compares implementation costs and projected efficiency gains.
- Public sentiment from local residents is weighed regarding acceptability.

Recognizing trade-offs, they decide on a hybrid approach: Adaptive traffic signals + congestion pricing + off-peak delivery hours, as it balances efficiency, feasibility, and public acceptance.

Final Outcome

The group reaches a collectively intelligent decision by integrating diverse perspectives, ensuring all necessary knowledge chunks are surfaced and used. Their errors in judgment cancel out, leading to a more effective solution than any single individual could have formulated alone.

Summary

The purpose of this chapter was to lay the theoretical foundation for the practical applications that follow in the rest of this book. The practical applications are the means of making small problem-solving groups collectively more intelligent. As explained in the introduction, the applications consist of behavioral interventions, process interventions, and technological interventions, which are more easily remembered, respectively, as people, process, and platform interventions. We'll start with the people.

Notes

1 Thomas W. Malone and Michael S. Bernstein (Eds.), *Handbook of Collective Intelligence* (Cambridge, MA: The MIT Press, 2015), 3.
2 Thomas W. Malone and Michael S. Bernstein (Eds.), *Handbook of Collective Intelligence* (Cambridge, MA: The MIT Press, 2015), 3.
3 William H. Calvin, *How Brains Think: Evolving Intelligence, Then and Now* (New York, NY: Basic Books, 1996), 1.
4 John Holt as quoted in Richard Ogle, *Smart World: Breakthrough Creativity and the New Science of Ideas* (Boston, MA: Harvard Business School Press, 2007), 1.
5 William H. Calvin, *How Brains Think: Evolving Intelligence, Then and Now* (New York, NY: Basic Books, 1996), 1.

6 William H. Calvin, *How Brains Think: Evolving Intelligence, Then and Now* (New York, NY: Basic Books, 1996), 13.
7 Robert J. Sternberg (Ed.), *Handbook of Intelligence* (Cambridge, UK: Cambridge University Press, 1982), 24–25.
8 Michael Schrage, *No More Teams! Mastering the Dynamics of Creative Collaboration* (New York, NY: Currency Doubleday, 1989), 33.
9 Leonard Mlodinow, *Elastic: Unlocking the Brain's Ability to Embrace Change* (New York, NY: Vantage Books, 2018), 86–87. Note that Mlodinow does not work for Intellectual Ventures and used the example of the Photonic Fence to explain the benefits of organizations that generate ideas from the bottom-up.
10 Only female members of the Anopheles species of mosquito transmit the Plasmodium parasites that cause malaria.
11 James R. Larson, Jr., *In Search of Synergy in Small Group Performance* (New York, NY: Taylor and Francis Group, 2010), 4.
12 Paul Thagard, *Brain-Mind: From Neurons to Consciousness and Creativity* (Oxford, UK: Oxford University Press, 2019), 11.
13 I'll elaborate on this in a later section, where I describe group inference using Feynman diagrams.
14 For a detailed, yet understandable, description of the way that generative AI is trained, see Timothy B. Lee and Sean Trott, "A Jargon-Free Explanation of How AI Large Language Models Work," *Ars Technica*, July 31, 2023, https://arstechnica.com/science/2023/07/a-jargon-free-explanation-of-how-ai-large-language-models-work/
15 OpenAI, Response to "First read the following text: 'AI makes predictions by identifying patterns extracted from data. The patterns that AI detects are often so high dimensional that humans cannot make sense of them.' Then explain what a high-dimensional pattern is; include an example. Then explain why humans cannot make sense of them." *ChatGPT-4o*, 2025.
16 Remember, generative AI is predicting the text (answer) that is most likely to follow the text (question) you've given it. To say that it's "predicting" the answer is to say it's giving the most probable answer, which is to say it's guessing the best answer to your question. Sometimes it guesses wrong.
17 Lu Hong, Anusha Kallapur, and Scott E. Page, "Strategic Decisions and AI: The Inferential Trilemma," January 2025, Manuscript submitted for publication.
18 There are several books that explain how to run simple, affordable experiments, including the following. Stefan H. Thomke, *Experimentation Works: The Surprising Power of Business Experiments* (Boston, MA: Harvard Business School Press, 2020); Alberto Savoia, *The Right It: Why so Many Ideas Fail and How to Make Sure Yours Succeed* (New York, NY: Harper Collins, 2019); Michael Schrage, *The Innovator's Hypothesis: How Cheap Experiments Are Worth More Than Good Ideas* (Cambridge, MA: The MIT Press, 2014).
19 As quoted in Jeff Dyer, Hal Gregersen, and Clayton Christensen, *The Innovator's DNA: Mastering the Five Skills of Disruptive Innovators* (Boston, MA: Harvard Business Review Press, 2019), 70.
20 Michael Nielsen, *Reinventing Discovery: The New Era of Networked Science* (Princeton, NJ: Princeton University Press, 2012), 103.
21 Kevin Holt, *Differentiation Strategy: Winning Customers by Being Different* (New York, NY: Routledge, 2022), 132–164. Reproduced with permission from Routledge.

22 John D. Bransford and Barry S. Stein, *The Ideal Problem Solver: A Guide for Improving Thinking, Learning, and Creativity*, 2nd Edition (New York, NY: W.H. Freeman and Company, 1993), 7.
23 Colin Eden and David Sims, *Messing About in Problems: An Informal Structured Approach to Their Identification and Management* (Oxford, UK: Pergamon Press, 1983), 12.
24 Colin Eden and David Sims, *Messing About in Problems: An Informal Structured Approach to Their Identification and Management* (Oxford, UK: Pergamon Press, 1983), 14.
25 Arthur B. VanGundy, Jr., *Techniques of Structured Problem Solving*, 2nd Edition (New York, NY: Van Nostrand Reinhold, 1988), 3.
26 John D. Arnold, *The Complete Problem Solver: A Total System for Competitive Decision Making* (New York, NY: John Wiley & Sons, 1992), 12.
27 Can M. Alpaslan and Ian I. Mitroff, *Swans, Swine, and Swindlers: Coping with the Growing Threat of Mega-Crises and Mega-Messes* (Stanford, CA: Stanford University Press, 2011), 17–20.
28 Charles H. Kepner and Benjamin B. Tregoe, *The New Rational Manager: An Updated Edition for a New World* (Princeton, NJ: Princeton Research Press, 1997), 22–24.
29 Joan Ernst van Aken, Hans Berends, and Hans van der Bij, *Problem Solving in Organizations: A Methodological Handbook for Business Students* (Cambridge, UK: Cambridge University Press, 2007), 7–9.
30 "Dislike" is too tame a term to describe Jobs's opinion of products that failed to meet his standards.
31 David Kord Murray, *Borrowing Brilliance: The Six Steps to Business Innovation by Building on the Ideas of Others* (New York, NY: Gotham Books, 2009), 188.
32 Valerie Ahl and T.F.H. Allen, *Hierarchy Theory: A Vision, Vocabulary, and Epistemology* (New York, NY: Columbia University Press, 1996), 30.
33 Cognitive science is the interdisciplinary study of the brain and mind. It focuses on how the mind represents and manipulates knowledge. Cognitive science draws from psychology, linguistics, neuroscience, computer science, and artificial intelligence.
34 Subrata Dasgupta, *Technology and Creativity* (Oxford, UK: Oxford University Press, 1996), 30. Dasgupta notes that some cognitive scientists recognize these three levels. My explanation of the three levels does not track entirely with Dasgupta's description.
35 Judith Hooper and Dick Teresi, *The Three-Pound Universe* (New York, NY: Dell Publishing Co., 1986), 36.
36 William H. Calvin, *How Brains Think: Evolving Intelligence, Then and Now* (New York, NY: Basic Books, 1996), 12. In comparison, Calvin elaborates, a chimpanzee's cortex would fit on one sheet of typing paper, a monkey's on a postcard, and a rat's on a postage stamp.
37 Douglas Hofstadter and Emmanuel Sander, *Surfaces and Essences: Analogy as the Fuel and Fire of Thinking* (New York, NY: Basic Books, 2013).
38 The term consciousness is given a number of meanings. Here, I am using it to mean "access," as when we speak of a conscious part of the mind to which we have access and a subconscious part that is inaccessible to introspection.
39 Steven Pinker, *How the Mind Works* (New York, NY: W.W. Norton & Company, 1997), 69–70, 86–90.

40 Steven Pinker, *How the Mind Works* (New York, NY: W.W. Norton & Company, 1997), 70.
41 Imagery includes visual images as well as images that are generated by the other senses—hearing, touch, taste, and smell. Perceptual images are formed when we sense things directly. Recalled images are retrieved from memory—imagine (i.e., retrieve from your memory) the sight of a tree, the sound of a car horn, the feel of wool, the taste of salt, and the smell of a rose.
42 A lingua franca is a language that is adopted as a common language between speakers whose native languages are different. The term originated in the Levant, where traders used a mixture of Italian, French, Greek, Arabic, and Spanish to communicate with one another.
43 Marvin Minsky, *The Society of Mind* (New York, NY: Simon & Schuster, 1985), 56.
44 *Conceptual meaning* (semantic meaning) is not the same as the *lexical meaning* of a word you find in a dictionary.
45 James P. Spradley, *The Ethnographic Interview* (Orlando, FL: Holt, Rinehart, and Winston, 1979), 117.
46 James P. Spradley, *The Ethnographic Interview* (Orlando, FL: Holt, Rinehart, and Winston, 1979), 28–31. For a more comprehensive treatment of semantic pointers, see Chris Eliasmith, *How to Build a Brain: A Neural Architecture for Biological Cognition* (Oxford, UK: Oxford University Press, 2013). Eliasmith developed the theory of semantic pointers.
47 Douglas Hofstadter and Emmanuel Sander, *Surfaces and Essences: Analogy as the Fuel and Fire of Thinking* (New York, NY: Basic Books, 2013), 50–51.
48 Douglas Hofstadter and Emmanuel Sander, *Surfaces and Essences: Analogy as the Fuel and Fire of Thinking* (New York, NY: Basic Books, 2013), 51.
49 Vyvyan Evans, *Cognitive Linguistics*, 2nd Edition (Edinburgh, UK: Edinburgh University Press, 2019), 207–211.
50 Annie Murphy Paul, *The Extended Mind: The Power of Thinking Outside the Brain* (Boston, MA: Houghton Mifflin Harcourt, 2021), 54.
51 OpenAI, Response to "Do the following step by step. First, read the foregoing text. Second, describe ways that generative AI can augment the tools so as to address thoughts that are incomplete or incorrect. Third, describe ways that generative AI can augment the processes so as to address thoughts that are incomplete or incorrect." *ChatGPT-4o*, 2025.
52 OpenAI, Response to "Describe an example of generative AI providing a group with constructive dissent." *ChatGPT-4o*, 2025.
53 OpenAI, Response to "Generate a comprehensive description of 'a futuristic calming environment.' Then generate an image of the environment." *ChatGPT*, 2025.
54 OpenAI, Response to "Read the foregoing text pertaining to universal semantic relationships. Then tell me if instructing a generative AI model to consider the relationships when responding to a prompt would cause it to generate a better response and, if so, why." *ChatGPT-4o*, 2025.
55 OpenAI, Response to "Tell me this. What is the value of instructing a generative AI tool like ChatGPT to employ the concept of semantic pointers when responding to a prompt?" *ChatGPT-4o*, 2025.
56 OpenAI, Response to "Explain the value of instructing generative AI to use cognitive linguistics theory." *ChatGPT-4o*, 2025.

57 OpenAI, Response to "One can conceive of a dog as a pet, a best friend, a protector, a golden retriever, and so on. I want you to generate various ways to conceive of a park designed to foster community engagement." *ChatGPT-4o*, 2025.
58 OpenAI, Response to "Describe a multidisciplinary team—a teacher, a social worker, a nurse, a software developer, and ChatGPT—that is brainstorming ways to improve mental health support for teenagers in which each team member uses a different concept to conceive of the problem." *ChatGPT-4o*, 2025.
59 OpenAI, Response to "Now pick up where you left off in the example you just described to provide examples of these two ideas: 1) while two of the team members might have the same concept, one person's version of the concept may be more developed (have more associations) than the other's version, and 2) two people might have the same concept with the same number and kinds of associations, but the activation strengths of their associations may differ, causing them to associate the concept with different concepts." *ChatGPT-4o*, 2025.
60 OpenAI, Response to "Now describe a scenario where this group, including the AI, generates an important insight into the problem of improving mental health support for teenagers by digging much deeper into one of the concepts by asking each other questions." *ChatGPT-4o*, 2025.
61 Larger ideas are expressed as multiple sentences, ranging in length from paragraphs to entire books. Here, however, we're only concerned with ideas expressed as a single sentence.
62 Subrata Dasgupta, *Technology and Creativity* (Oxford, UK: Oxford University Press, 1996), 32.
63 Feynman diagrams are named after the Nobel-Prize-winning physicist Richard Feynman, who used them to depict the collision of elementary particles.
64 Tadeusz M. Szuba, *Computational Collective Intelligence* (New York, NY: John Wiley & Sons, 2001), 253–254.
65 It's not uncommon for people to credit the person who completes the last inference in the chain with having solved the problem when, in fact, everyone who contributed facts and rules to the chain of inferences should be credited.
66 Gerry Stahl, *Essays in Philosophy of Group Cognition* (Published by Gerry Stahl at Lulu.com, 2016), 130.
67 As quoted in Jeff Dyer, Hal Gregersen, and Clayton Christensen, *The Innovator's DNA: Mastering the Five Skills of Disruptive Innovators* (Boston, MA: Harvard Business Review Press, 2019), 115.
68 Gerry Stahl, *Essays in Philosophy of Group Cognition* (Published by Gerry Stahl at Lulu.com, 2016), 130.
69 Gerry Stahl, *Essays in Philosophy of Group Cognition* (Published by Gerry Stahl at Lulu.com, 2016), 136.
70 OpenAI, Response to "Read the foregoing text. Then use the content of the document to create an example of improving mental health support for teenagers." *ChatGPT-4o*, 2024.
71 OpenAI, Response to "Now, what does the foregoing text, the content of your example, and whatever else you know about this topic tell you about how to raise the collective intelligence of a group and combine it with the artificial intelligence of generative AI to create an intelligence that is smarter than either intelligence alone?" *ChatGPT-4o*, 2024.
72 Isaac Asimov in Judith Hooper and Dick Teresi, *The Three-Pound Universe* (New York, NY: Dell Publishing Co., 1986), xiii–xvi. This short history of the brain is abstracted from a more detailed version given by Isaac Asimov in the Foreword to this book.

73 The brain-mind problem is also known as the body-mind problem. The distinction between the body and the mind can be traced back to the ancient Greeks. Once it was known that mind arises from the brain, not the heart, the body-mind problem became the brain-mind problem.

74 I've borrowed the phrase "thumpingly physical" from Steven Pinker, but with apologies to Dr. Pinker, I've forgotten where he used it.

75 If we were talking about the brain, we would say that thought occurs in the association cortex, which from a functional, if not a geographic, perspective, lies between the sensory cortex and the motor cortex.

76 Andy Clark, *Natural-Born Cyborgs: Minds, Technologies, and the Future of Human Intelligence* (New York, NY: Oxford University Press, 2003), 78.

77 Ludwig Fleck, *Genesis and Development of a Scientific Fact*, translated and edited by Thaddeus J. Trenn and Robert K. Merton (Chicago, IL: University of Chicago Press, 1979), 44.

78 William Isaacs, *Dialogue and the Art of Thinking Together: A Pioneering Approach to Communicating in Business and in Life* (New York, NY: Currency-Doubleday, 1999), 19.

79 William Isaacs, *Dialogue and the Art of Thinking Together: A Pioneering Approach to Communicating in Business and in Life* (New York, NY: Currency-Doubleday, 1999), 11.

80 Ann C. Baker, *Catalytic Conversations: Organizational Communication and Innovation* (Armonk, NY: M.E. Sharpe, Inc., 2010), 3.

81 Ann C. Baker, *Catalytic Conversations: Organizational Communication and Innovation* (Armonk, NY: M.E. Sharpe, Inc., 2010), 3.

82 Without getting too deep into the topic, let's say that information is a fact that exists in the world (e.g., smoke and fire are correlated) and knowledge is information that has been captured and exists in someone's head or is stored in a book or some other medium. To solve a problem, it's often necessary to use the knowledge that people have in their heads or can find in some medium. It may also be necessary to perform some form of research (e.g., survey research) to discover relevant information in the world.

83 You might say the diagram is fractal. A structure is said to be fractal when the same pattern recurs at progressively smaller scales.

84 This is analogous to having all the pieces needed to solve a jigsaw puzzle.

85 Scott E. Page, *The Difference: How the Power of Diversity Creates Better Groups, Firms, Schools, and Societies* (Princeton, NJ: Princeton University Press, 2007), chapter 10. Page elaborates on the mathematics of information aggregation.

86 OpenAI, Response to "Read the foregoing text. Then describe an example of a cognitively diverse group of people using the necessary chunks of knowledge and information to carry out the group reasoning and group judgment needed to identify the cause of an undesired state and to identify an optimal way of acting on the cause to transform it into the cause of the desired state." *ChatGPT-4o*, 2025.

Chapter 2

People

Cognitive Diversity, Collaboration, and AI

We start with the bedrock of the "3Ps," people. No matter how advanced the processes or platforms, collective intelligence ultimately rests on the people who use them. The cognitive diversity of a group is critical. A diverse mix of knowledge and skills reveals insights that no single member could see alone. But assembling the right mix of people is only half the battle. Communication is the other half, for it is the way they speak, listen, and converse that transforms a collection of individuals into an interconnected, collectively intelligent whole. This chapter explores the foundational factors that drive the people part of group intelligence—cognitive diversity, communication, and collaboration strategy, each of which plays a critical role in making a team smarter than its smartest member.

Cognitive Diversity

Cognitive diversity is a key driver of successful problem-solving groups and the organizations to which they belong. Just ask Matthew Syed, author of the book *Rebel Ideas: The Power of Diverse Thinking*, who says, "If we are intent upon answering our most serious questions, from climate change to poverty, and curing diseases to designing products, we need to work with people who think differently, not just accurately . . . .[D]iversity is the critical ingredient driving what we might term *collective* intelligence. . . . Harnessing the power of cognitive diversity is set to become a key source of competitive advantage, and the surest route to reinvention and growth. You might even say we are entering the age of diversity" (italics in original).[1] Harnessing the power of cognitive diversity is the key concern of this section. But first things first.

The first of these things is the distinction between *identity diversity* and *cognitive diversity*,[2] or as they're sometimes called, *surface-level diversity* and *deep-level diversity*.[3] Identity (surface-level) diversity refers to demographic differences among team members. Identity diversity is otherwise

DOI: 10.4324/9781003654407-3

referred to as surface-level diversity because it is relatively easy to detect by observing people, interviewing them, or reading their resumes. Examples are gender, age, nationality, sexual orientation, and race. As is later explained, it's useful to separate out education and experience from the other kinds of identity diversity.

Cognitive (deep-level) diversity refers to differences among team members that are more difficult to detect, including differences in the concepts and knowledge they hold in their heads and differences in the way they think. Scott Page, a professor of complexity, social science, and management at the University of Michigan, has researched and written extensively on diversity. He uses the following kinds of "cognitive repertoires" to characterize cognitive diversity.[4] The examples are mine, with a little help—OK, a lot of help—from ChatGPT. Note that Page lumps mental models and frameworks together, but I think there's reason to distinguish them.

1. *Information*, as defined by Page, consists of facts and observations about the world. The facts can be quantitative (e.g., statistical data) or qualitative (e.g., descriptions, anecdotes). Information can be characterized as pieces or objects. Pieces of information include the population of homeless people in a city, the chemical composition of a compound, or a competing company's profit margin.
2. *Knowledge*, also as defined by Page, is a working, practical understanding of a subject or domain of inquiry. It includes domain expertise, principles, and insights derived from information. Examples are understanding the root causes of homelessness in a city, the behavior of a compound under different conditions (e.g., temperatures), and the contributions that a competitor's expense margins are making to its profit.
3. *Heuristics or tools* are methods for making decisions, finding solutions, or generating ideas. They can be formal (e.g., algorithms) or informal (e.g., mental shortcuts). They emphasize efficiency and practicality over exhaustive analysis. Examples are to use the Pareto Principle (80/20 Rule) to decide which root causes of homelessness to focus on, apply the "Like Dissolves Like" principle to predict how a compound will interact with other substances, and use benchmarking to quickly compare a competitor's profit margin with industry standards.
4. *Representations* are divided into two types, *perspectives* and *categories*. Different perspectives look at the same thing in different ways. Categories group different things together.

   - A demographic perspective on a city's homeless population might analyze the population by age, gender, and ethnicity to understand the specific needs of subgroups, whereas a geographical perspective might examine homelessness based on neighborhoods or districts. This compares to sorting the homeless population into categories like "chronic homelessness," "temporary homelessness," and "at risk of homelessness" to target interventions more effectively.

- A chemist might use a molecular perspective by representing a compound as a structural formula (e.g., H_2O), while a physicist might adopt an energy-based perspective by considering its bonds' energetic states. Or the chemist might group a compound into categories such as "acid," "base," or "neutral" based on its pH, or classify it by its phase (solid, liquid, gas) at room temperature.
- A financial perspective on a competitor's profit margin might focus on ratios (e.g., profit margin = profit/revenue), while a strategic perspective might evaluate the margin in the context of competitive advantages (e.g., cost leadership vs. differentiation). Categorizing the profit margin might involve classifying it as "high," "moderate," or "low" relative to industry benchmarks or classifying companies by their profit sources (e.g., product sales vs. services).

5. *Mental Models* are simplified descriptions that capture relevant features of a domain. To my way of thinking, as they compare to frameworks, models tend to focus on how things work, which is to say, they focus on what causes what and why. Examples are:

- A supply-and-demand model of housing that links homelessness to the availability and affordability of housing. This model assumes that factors like income levels, rental costs, and government policies (e.g., subsidies, zoning laws) interact to determine housing stability. It simplifies the complex social dynamics of homelessness into an economic framework that focuses on increasing housing supply or reducing demand (e.g., through employment programs).
- The "lock-and-key" model for chemical interactions, where molecules are visualized as having specific shapes that determine how they interact with others, which is akin to a key fitting into a lock. This model helps predict how the compound will react with others, emphasizing compatibility and molecular structure over detailed energetic calculations.
- A value-chain model, which conceptualizes a company as a series of interlinked activities (e.g., inbound logistics, operations, outbound logistics, marketing and sales, service) that add value at each step. Profit margins are explained as the result of how efficiently and effectively these activities are managed, allowing users of this model to identify which parts of the chain contribute most significantly to profitability and which are sources of inefficiency.

6. *Mental frameworks*, unlike models, do not address causal mechanisms. Instead, they are structured, universal systems for organizing knowledge and understanding within a domain. For example:
   - The social determinants of health framework organizes the factors influencing homelessness into categories, such as economic stability, education access, social and community context, health care access, and neighborhood environment. It provides a structured, universal system for understanding the root causes of homelessness and designing targeted policies or interventions.
   - The periodic table is a universal framework that organizes chemical elements by atomic number, properties, and periodic trends. It provides a systematic way to understand the composition and potential reactions of a compound by situating its constituent elements within the table's structure, enabling predictions of behavior and reactivity.
   - Porter's value chain framework structures a company's operations into primary (inbound logistics, operations, outbound logistics, marketing and sales, service) and support activities (e.g., finance, accounting, HR, procurement, technology) that collectively create value. By analyzing a company's profit margin within the context of the value chain, one can systematically identify areas of strength and weakness to improve competitive positioning and profitability.

The more kinds of cognitive repertoires a team possesses, the more cognitively diverse it is. Or, as Page puts it, the less overlap there is in a team's repertoires, the more cognitively diverse it is. The foregoing examples point to the value of assigning a cognitively diverse team to a complex problem. Xerox PARC researcher Alan Kay, a pioneer of personal computing and object-oriented programming, is variously credited with having said "Point of view is worth 80 IQ points," "Perspective is worth 80 IQ points," and "A change in perspective is worth 80 IQ points."[5] Whichever version is correct (maybe all of them), Kay's point was that "having a new way of seeing a problem may be the most effective way of generating a solution."[6] The same can be said of cognitive repertoires. *A change in cognitive repertoire is worth 80 IQ points*. And the best way to have a variety of repertoires to change to is to assemble a cognitively diverse group.

One way of discovering a prospective group member's cognitive repertoires is self-assessment, which entails using the six kinds of repertoires to guide a discussion in which the person is asked for his or her views on the problem and the way(s) in which s/he would attack it. Another way of discovering a potential group member's cognitive repertoires is to infer them from the member's education and experience and, in some cases, the other types of identity diversity. For example, the education and experience of a team of agronomists, geneticists, soil scientists, climate scientists, and farmers is likely to yield fruitful repertoires for finding ways to grow staple crops in a region experiencing increasingly frequent droughts, whereas the other types of identity diversity (race/ethnicity, age, gender, sexual orientation, etc.) are not. However, in comparison, people with the other kinds of identity diversity are more likely to have repertoires that are useful for finding solutions to the problems suffered by minorities, whereas the agronomists and others are not.

Unfortunately, at the start of the problem-solving process, there's no way to know all the repertoires that will be required to optimize the solution and which of them will be most useful. The only way to find that out is to make iterative attempts to solve the problem and assess the repertoires that are needed after each attempt. Even so, the organizers of a problem-solving team should carefully consider the types of team members most likely to have cognitive repertoires that will contribute to solving the problem. This is a place where generative AI can make a valuable contribution. Continuing with an example from the last chapter, I asked ChatGPT to identify the types of people who might have useful cognitive repertoires for finding ways to improve mental health support for teenagers in a community.[7] The following is how it responded. Note that generative AI can also analyze the results of each attempt to solve the problem to suggest potentially useful types of team members for the next attempt.

Prompt

Do the following step by step. First, read the foregoing text on cognitive repertoires. Then, list the types of professions that might have cognitive repertoires that would make fruitful contributions to finding ways to improve mental health support for teenagers in a community and describe how each profession's repertoires would make a contribution.

ChatGPT's Response

The following types of professions with diverse cognitive repertoires can contribute meaningfully to improving mental health support for teenagers in a community, along with their specific contributions:

1. *Psychologists and Mental Health Therapists*
   Contribution: Offer specialized knowledge in diagnosing, understanding, and treating mental health conditions in teenagers. They can provide evidence-based therapeutic interventions and frameworks for prevention.

Cognitive Repertoire: Expertise in human behavior, emotional regulation, and psychological well-being.

2. *Educators and School Counselors*
   Contribution: Identify mental health challenges in educational settings and offer support tailored to academic pressures and peer-related stress. They bridge the gap between schools and mental health professionals.
   Cognitive Repertoire: Knowledge of adolescent development and an understanding of the academic and social stressors teenagers face.

3. *Community Health Workers*
   Contribution: Act as connectors between healthcare systems and the community, ensuring culturally sensitive and accessible care. They can implement outreach programs and early interventions.
   Cognitive Repertoire: Deep understanding of the community's cultural and socio-economic context, which informs how mental health issues are perceived and addressed.

4. *Social Workers*
   Contribution: Address systemic issues contributing to teenage mental health problems, such as poverty, abuse, or lack of access to resources. They can design interventions at the family and community level.
   Cognitive Repertoire: Systems thinking, advocacy skills, and case management expertise.

5. *Technology Developers and Data Scientists*
   Contribution: Design apps and tools for mental health monitoring, crisis intervention, or therapeutic games. They can analyze data to identify trends and gaps in mental health service delivery.
   Cognitive Repertoire: Technical problem-solving skills and the ability to innovate solutions leveraging technology.

6. *Artists and Creative Professionals*
   Contribution: Use creative outlets such as art therapy, music, and storytelling to help teenagers express and process emotions in a non-verbal and supportive environment.
   Cognitive Repertoire: Innovative methods for emotional expression and fostering resilience.

7. *Law Enforcement and Juvenile Justice Experts*
   Contribution: Address the intersection of mental health and the legal system, particularly for at-risk teenagers. They can work on

preventive measures to reduce criminal behavior linked to mental health issues.

Cognitive Repertoire: Understanding of behavioral triggers and experience in de-escalation techniques.

8. *Public Health Researchers*

Contribution: Conduct community-based participatory research to identify mental health trends and evaluate the effectiveness of interventions. They provide a data-driven foundation for decision-making.

Cognitive Repertoire: Expertise in population health, survey design, and statistical analysis.

9. *Religious and Spiritual Leaders*

Contribution: Offer spiritual support and a sense of belonging to teenagers. They can create safe spaces for open discussions about mental health.

Cognitive Repertoire: Understanding of community values and spiritual resilience techniques.

10. *Policy Makers and Urban Planners*

Contribution: Develop policies to increase funding for youth mental health programs and design urban spaces that promote well-being (e.g., recreational areas).

Cognitive Repertoire: Strategic thinking and an ability to integrate multi-sectoral inputs into policy frameworks.

11. *Parents and Teen Advocates*

Contribution: Provide firsthand insight into teenagers' daily lives and challenges, shaping interventions that resonate with real-world issues.

Cognitive Repertoire: Lived experience, empathetic understanding, and practical knowledge.

This cognitively diverse team can collaboratively address teenage mental health challenges by combining their unique perspectives, fostering innovation, and ensuring inclusive solutions.

For the most part, the team members selected by ChatGPT in this example come from different professional disciplines, making it a *multi-disciplinary* or *cross-disciplinary* or *inter-disciplinary* team. But professional disciplines aren't the only source of cognitive diversity. Depending on the problem to be solved, other options are *cross-functional teams* (say, operations, marketing, and HR functions), *cross-company* teams (say, manufacturing, research, and consulting companies), *cross-supply chain teams* (say, raw materials, manufacturer, and retailer companies), *cross-industry teams* (say, plastics, pharmaceutical, and medical device companies), *cross-sector teams* (say, commercial, government, and nonprofit organizations), and *cross-national teams* (say, developed, developing, and emergent nations).

The methods I've so far described for assembling a cognitively diverse team—self-assessment, inferring cognitive diversity from education, experience, or identity, and asking generative AI—all entail finding the people you're looking for. An alternative method is to have them find you, much like the British mathematician Alan Turing did during World War II. As depicted in the movie *The Imitation Game*, Turing used a difficult crossword puzzle published in the newspaper to attract people with exceptional code-cracking skills to help break the German Enigma code. In a similar way, you might publish or post a description of your problem to attract prospective team members. In cases where, because of their different backgrounds, the prospects might not understand the nature of the problem or how they might contribute to solving it, it helps to describe it in an abstract way. I asked ChatGPT for an example[8]:

Prompt

Generate an example of an abstract description of a problem that would help professionals from different disciplines understand the nature of the problem.

ChatGPT's Response

We want to design a system to detect and prevent misinformation spread on social media platforms while balancing freedom of expression, technological scalability, and cultural sensitivities. The challenge involves identifying and managing the flow of information in a large, interconnected network. The goal is to detect patterns of influence and disruption, understand their causes, and develop strategies to ensure the system remains fair, balanced, and trustworthy. This requires navigating trade-offs between encouraging open participation and preventing harm caused by misleading or harmful elements.

If you are skilled in analyzing how information moves through systems, designing solutions for complex and evolving networks, or finding creative ways to balance competing priorities, we need your expertise. Whether you work with data, people, or policies, your unique insights can help us tackle this critical challenge.

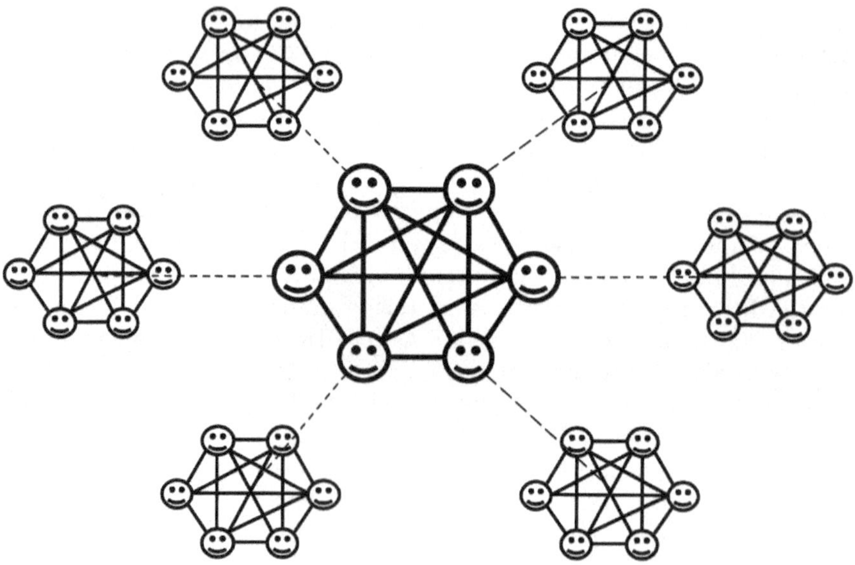

Figure 2.1 Team members looking for relevant cognitive repertoires (*exploring*) in the peripheral teams to which they belong that can be used (*exploited*) by the core team to which they belong.

In their book *X-teams: How to Build Teams That Lead, Innovate, and Succeed*, business professors Deborah Ancona and Henrik Bresman recommend that innovation and problem-solving teams be externally oriented, which explains the X in X-teams, and they propose that the team alternate between *exploration* and *exploitation*.[9] Exploration involves looking beyond the team for useful ideas, and exploitation is about using the ideas in the team's deliberations. One way of doing this is to assemble a team in which the team members have ready access to other teams—or what some characterize as other "thought worlds"[10]—comprised of people with relevant cognitive repertoires. For example, a university professor has access to the repertoires of the members of her department, and an HR person has access to the repertoires of the members of his company's HR function. MIT computer scientist Alex Pentland uses the alternative terms *exploration* and *engagement*.[11] As depicted in Figure 2.1, exploration is when the team members interact with the other teams to which they belong, and exploitation/engagement is when they interact with each other. In both cases, Ancona-Bresman and Pentland, they are talking about the way information flows through a social network.

Speaking and Listening

Assembling a team with the requisite repertoires is one thing. Getting them to share them is another. Let's say that a cognitively diverse team is assembled to solve a problem. At the start of the problem-solving process, some parts of the team members' cognitive repertoires overlap and other parts do not. In other words, they hold some parts of their cognitive repertoires in common and other parts are uniquely held by the different members of the team. Ideally, as the problem-solving process progresses, the team members will share the relevant parts of their repertoires such that everyone holds the parts in common, thereby making it possible for the parts to interact (e.g., one person's fact interacts with another person's rule to produce a new fact, as was diagrammed in Figure 1.4 and Figure 1.5). I say "ideally" because the sharing doesn't always happen or happen enough. There are a number of reasons why this is the case.

One reason team members might not contribute relevant parts of their cognitive repertoires is because of what cognitive scientists refer to as *process losses*.[12] The most common kind of process loss is *production blocking*. Production blocking occurs when a team member has an idea while listening to another member speak but is blocked from producing (contributing) it because s/he forgets it by the time it's her turn to speak, or the member suppresses the idea because it seems less relevant or original after hearing what others have to say. *Cognitive interference*, a second kind of process loss, occurs when the ideas contributed by other group members interfere with a member's thought process because of the need to attend to the others' contributions. A third kind of process loss is termed *evaluation apprehension*, which refers to withholding an idea for fear others will judge it negatively or because it's a political "hot potato."

Note that the first two kinds of process losses result from the process of taking turns speaking and listening. Linguists refer to this as *conversational turn-taking*. Two ways of eliminating the process losses caused by conversational turn-taking eliminate the turn-taking altogether. The first way is to use electronic brainstorming technology, which will be described in depth in Chapter 4. Electronic brainstorming technology enables everyone to type their answers to a question *simultaneously*, which means, in effect, that everyone can "talk at once." The second way, which is detailed in Chapter 3, is to use the brainwriting method, where group members pass their written ideas around the group round-robin style so that the other members can write their comments on the ideas.

Because electronic brainstorming technology permits anonymous entry, it also minimizes the third type of process loss, evaluation apprehension. Anonymous entry creates a sense of psychological safety. Amy Edmondson, an organizational behavior scientist at Harvard University, first introduced the construct of *team psychological safety*. She defined it as "a belief that the work environment is safe for interpersonal risk taking."[13] Her work heavily influenced Google's Project Aristotle. As explained in Chapter 1, the project was a multi-year research effort aimed at understanding what makes teams effective. Among all the factors studied, psychological safety emerged as the most critical determinant of team effectiveness.[14] Teams where members felt safe to take risks, share ideas, and admit mistakes without fear of embarrassment or retribution outperformed others.

Another way to create a psychologically safe meeting environment is for the participants to have a high degree of *social-emotional intelligence*, which refers to their ability to read others' social signals. Social signals are the nonverbal, paraverbal, and contextual cues people use to communicate their emotions, intentions, or social standing in interactions. They serve as indicators of what someone might be thinking, feeling, or planning, even if they do not explicitly state it. Nonverbal signals include facial expressions, gestures, body posture, and eye contact. A paraverbal signal is a communication cue conveyed through the way someone speaks, including their tone of voice, pitch, volume, speed, and pauses. Contextual signals include bodily proximity, appearance, and the environment in which the signals occur (e.g., laughter in a formal setting might imply discomfort or mockery).

Anita Williams Wooley, also an organizational behavior scientist, and her colleagues discovered that social-emotional intelligence is one of three factors that contribute most to a group's collective intelligence.[15] The second factor is the number of women in the group. The researchers found that the greater the percentage of women in the group, the greater its collective intelligence, all the way up to 100 percent. (A later study found that groups with more than about 20 percent females up to about 75 to 80 percent females display progressively more collective intelligence.[16] Beyond 80 percent the group's collective intelligence drops slightly.) One of the researchers on the Wooley team, MIT management professor Thomas Malone, later commented in his book *Superminds: The Surprising Power of People and Computers Thinking Together* that the two factors—social-emotional intelligence and the percentage of females—are likely related because you're more likely to find social perceptiveness in women than in men.[17] As next explained, the third factor identified by Wooley and her colleagues was the equality of conversational turn-taking.

In many meetings, one or a few group members dominate the meeting by taking more and longer speaking turns than others. As Geoff Mulgan describes it, "The typical meeting barely attempts to make the most of the knowledge and experience in the room. The loudest and most powerful speak the most, drowning out the weak or shy, and much that should be said isn't."[18] In other words, the dominators in the room prevent the weak and the shy from contributing relevant parts of their cognitive repertoires. Domination is extremely dysfunctional because as Alex Pentland, also part of the Wooley research team, later explained, "The largest factor in predicting group intelligence was the equality of conversational turn-taking; groups where a few people dominated the conversation were less collectively intelligent than those with a more equal distribution of conversational turn-taking. The second most important factor was the social intelligence of a group's members, as measured by their ability to read each other's social signals. Women tend to do better at reading social signals, so groups with more women tended to do better."[19]

Pentland and his postdoctoral student Wen Dong went on to discover that an even more important factor driving collective intelligence is the pattern of idea flow. Pentland explains, "The characteristics typical of the highest performing groups included: 1) a large number of ideas: many very short contributions rather than a few long ones; 2) dense interactions: a continuous overlapping cycling between making contributions and very short (less than one second) responsive comments (such as "good," "that's right," "what?" etc.) that serve to validate or invalidate the ideas and build consensus; and 3) diversity of ideas: everyone within the group contributing ideas and reactions, with similar levels of turn taking among the participants."[20] The implication for our discussion is that not only are group members less likely to contribute relevant parts of their diverse repertoires (Pentland's third item, "diversity of ideas") because of unequal turn-taking, they are also less likely to do so because other members take too long to say what they have to say.

Why do short contributions increase a group's collective intelligence? The answer requires us to understand the concept of *adjacency pairs*. In linguistics, an adjacency pair refers to a pair of conversational turns in which the first person says something, and the second person says something back that responds to what the first person said. For instance, a question and answer, or a suggestion and response. The answer to this question also requires us to consider again what Gerry Stahl had to say in the last chapter, where he explained that complex problems usually require a long sequence of inferences (longer than most individuals would perform) to reach a useful or correct conclusion. Figure 2.2 depicts the reason why short contributions increase a group's collective intelligence. As compared to the lengthy contributions in each adjacency pair shown at the bottom of the figure, the shorter contributions at the top of the figure enable the speakers to complete more adjacency pairs within the same stretch of time, which enables them to complete the longer chain of inferences that is required to reach a useful answer.

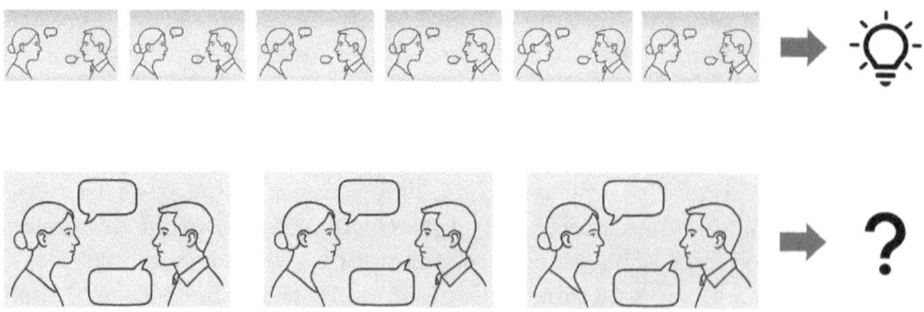

Figure 2.2 Briefer contributions enable more adjacency pairs (inferences), which increases the likelihood of reaching a useful conclusion.

Source: David Holt Design

One way to minimize unequal and lengthy turn-taking is to use a meeting facilitator to manage the conversation. A second way is to use technology to do it. In their research, which was conducted before 2010, Pentland and his colleagues created the Meeting Mediator (MM), a portable system that used sociometric name badges to detect social interactions in real time and mobile phones to provide visual feedback. The MM was able to reduce the difference in speaking time between people, increase interactivity levels, and detect dominant group members. The original MM was never made commercially available, but it has inspired the development of modern collaboration tools, such as platforms like Riff Analytics that offer AI-enabled, real-time feedback to promote effective digital collaboration. Pentland's research on sociometric badges has also inspired the creation of open-source frameworks such as Open Badges, which measure team communication and dynamics.

A third way to minimize lengthy turn-taking is to train the group to "talk lean." The method for doing so is explained in the book titled (What else?) *Talk Lean: Shorter Meetings. Quicker Results. Better Relations.*[21] Developed by the training company Interactifs, the Interactifs Discipline® teaches people to respond in a way in which the *content* of their response is clear, direct, and straight to the point, while the *manner* in which it is conveyed is polite, warm, and respectful. Interactifs's method responds to the fact that "very few people are consistently able to be direct without becoming brutal or unpleasant; or to be courteous without being submissive or manipulative. They are confronted with what they see as a stark choice between being direct or being polite."[22]

A fourth way to shorten conversational turn-taking is to get everyone in the habit of giving their conversation partner exactly what they ask for, no more and no less. This is the conversational equivalent of responding to someone who asks you for a hammer. Just give the person a hammer, not a hammer, screwdriver, and saw (more than they asked for) and not a nail (less than they asked for).

And finally, a fifth way to minimize lengthy turn-taking is to train the group members to speak in the same way that McKinsey & Company writes reports and presents findings. Just like McKinsey consultants do, meeting members should start with their proposal or conclusion, then follow with the reasons that support it, not the other way around. When speakers forget to do so, the facilitator or group leader should gently interrupt and ask them to first state in a sentence or two their proposal or conclusion, then follow with their reasoning.

To recap, one reason team members don't contribute relevant parts of their cognitive repertoires results from process losses—production blocking, cognitive interference, and evaluation apprehension. A second reason is unequal turn-taking, lengthy turn-taking, or both.

A third reason concerns the size of the group. Researchers Nicolas Fay, Simon Garrod, and Jean Carletta, investigated how group size determines whether a group's conversation will consist of a set of interactive dialogues or a series of monologues.[23] The *dialogue model* of communication sees it as a collaborative process between pairs, leading to mutual understanding, whereas the *monologue model* views communication as a one-way transmission from a sender to multiple receivers. Fay et al. found that in smaller groups (five members), communication resembles interactive dialogue, where members are influenced most by those with whom they interact. But in larger groups (ten members) communication tends to be more like a series of monologues, with members being influenced most by the dominant speaker. In other words, in large groups, there is less opportunity for the "dense interactions" that are part of Pentland's pattern of idea flow. One way to address this is to limit the size of the group to no more than 9 (no double digits), and ideally to 5 or less. When a larger group is necessary for political or other reasons (as is often the case), the solution is to alternate between the whole group and breakout groups. Ways of doing this are described in Chapter 3.

Another way to look at this is to consider the relationship between group size and speaking time. In a 20-person group, each person has just three minutes of speaking time per hour, which equates to 18 minutes of speaking time in a six-hour meeting. That's not a lot of time to share the relevant parts of a person's cognitive repertoires. And it's not unusual for a group to cram as many as ten topics on an agenda, which means that each person has less than two minutes to contribute the parts of their repertoires that relate to each topic. Little wonder that the attorney and author George David Kieffer observes that meetings fail in direct proportion to the number of people participating and the number and variety of tasks undertaken.[24]

A fourth reason why team members don't contribute relevant parts of their cognitive repertoires is a group phenomenon known as *anchoring*. Anchoring occurs when the group members moor on the initial idea, opinion, or piece of information that is contributed (the "anchor"). The anchor limits the group's dialogue because subsequent contributions are subconsciously adjusted to align with, support, or contest the anchor rather than considering a broader range of possibilities, including the relevant parts of the group members' cognitive repertoires. An anchor introduced by a more dominant or authoritative member is more likely to shape the discussion, even if others privately disagree. Anchors can also emerge from persuasive framing or strong confidence displayed by a group member. One way to thwart anchoring is the nominal group technique, which is also discussed in Chapter 3.

A fifth reason why team members don't contribute relevant parts of their cognitive repertoires is *cognitive depletion*.[25] Cognitive depletion refers to the temporary reduction in an individual's mental resources or cognitive capacity due to prolonged mental effort. It is a sort of mental fatigue that diminishes a member's ability to process information, make decisions, regulate emotions, or stay focused. Simply put, members stop functioning because they run out of steam. Ways to counter cognitive depletion include frequent breaks, providing energy-enhancing nutrition and hydration, and scheduling the most challenging tasks during the morning when group members have the most energy.

A sixth, and final, reason team members don't contribute relevant parts of their cognitive repertoires is that nobody asked them to. Members may not think to mention parts of their repertoires unless they are asked. While everyone should ask their team members for more information—whether to extract, clarify, or extend the information—it is especially important that the team leader do so because it is the leader, especially when s/he is the boss, who sets the tone for the group. Another matter relating to team leaders who are bosses is that they should be the last to answer a question. No one wants to contradict their boss, so it's best that the boss answer last rather than first. Even better, if possible, is for the group to be composed of people who are at equivalent levels in the organizational hierarchy.

The final recap of the reasons why team members don't contribute relevant parts of their cognitive repertoires is this. One reason is process losses—production blocking, cognitive interference, and evaluation apprehension. A second reason is unequal turn-taking, lengthy turn-taking, or both. A third reason concerns the size of the group. Fourth and fifth reasons are anchoring and cognitive depletion. And a sixth reason is that group members aren't asked for their thoughts. This is a good place to remind you that a diverse set of cognitive repertoires is the primary driver of collective intelligence, but the diversity is of no use if the group members don't contribute the relevant parts of their repertoires.

So far, I've described reasons why group members don't speak up to contribute their cognitive repertoires. The opposite problem occurs when the members don't hear what's being said. This can mean that they literally can't hear what's being said because the speaker speaks softly or because the meeting room has poor acoustics. Both are commonly encountered problems that should be planned for in advance. The solution to the first problem is to use microphones to amplify the speakers' voices, and the solution to the second is to use a different room.

A less literal sense of the word *hear* means that people can hear what's being said just fine, but they aren't listening to it because their mind is wandering. One way to stop a mind from wandering is called *active listening*. Annie Murphy Paul does a great job of explaining the meaning of the term (though she doesn't refer to it as such) and the impact it has on a group. She says, "[R]esearchers recommend that we implement a specific sequence of actions in response to our teammates' contributions: we should *acknowledge*, *repeat*, *rephrase*, and *elaborate* on what other group members say. Studies show that engaging in this kind of communication elicits more complete and comprehensive information. It re-exposes the entire group to the information that was shared initially, improving group members' understanding and memory for that information. And it increases the accuracy of the information that is shared, a process that psychologists call 'error pruning.'"[26] Thomas Chamoro-Premuzic, a business professor at University College London, is a bit more succinct.[27] His simple formula is this: (1) *Shut up*, (2) *Listen*, (3) *Repeat*. Overusing either of these methods can slow the conversation to a crawl and become tiresome, so they need to be applied with care. Getting group members in the habit of listening in this way requires training, using a meeting facilitator to prompt them to do it, or both.

Anyone who has participated in a group conversation knows that mind wandering also occurs at the level of the group. This happens when a group member brings up something that is tangential to the focal topic, and the rest of the group wanders down the tangent. The solution to this problem is to use a meeting facilitator to keep the group focused on the topic. For facilitators, the usual approach is to put the off-topic idea in a "parking lot" for later discussion.

Another reason people hear but don't listen concerns the structure of the conversation. In a round-robin structure, where the group members are instructed to speak in turn, they may be rehearsing what they are going to say when it's their turn to speak rather than listening to the other speakers. One way to address this problem is to give everyone a few moments to jot down what they're going to say before the first person speaks. Another way is to take advantage of the simultaneous entry enabled by electronic brainstorming technology.

A final reason people hear but don't listen pertains to types of talk, the topic to which we turn next. But before we get into that, I asked ChatGPT how generative AI might assist with the foregoing issues.[28] Following is its response:

Prompt

First read the foregoing text. Then use what you learn from the text to tell me all the ways that generative AI can assist a small problem-solving team do a better job of speaking and listening to each other.

ChatGPT's Response

Generative AI can help a small problem-solving team improve speaking and listening in several ways, addressing the challenges outlined in the text. Here's how:

Addressing Process Losses

1. Reducing Production Blocking
   - AI can record and transcribe all conversations in real-time, allowing participants to review and recall their thoughts when it's their turn to speak.
   - AI can provide an idea queue, where team members can quickly jot down their ideas while others are speaking, ensuring they don't forget them.
2. Minimizing Cognitive Interference
   - AI can highlight key discussion points and summarize ongoing conversations, reducing the cognitive burden of tracking multiple threads of discussion.
   - AI-powered visual mapping tools can show how ideas connect, helping members stay focused on relevant contributions.
3. Reducing Evaluation Apprehension
   - AI-powered anonymous contribution platforms (like electronic brainstorming tools) can allow members to submit ideas without fear of judgment.
   - AI sentiment analysis can help identify moments of hesitation or anxiety and provide real-time support (e.g., suggesting more inclusive phrasing).

Enhancing Conversational Turn-Taking

4. Ensuring Equal Participation
   - AI can track speaking time and prompt dominators to yield the floor while encouraging quieter members to contribute.
   - AI-powered Meeting Mediator tools can provide live feedback on speaking balance, alerting facilitators if turn-taking is unequal.
5. Encouraging Brief Contributions
   - AI can coach participants to "talk lean" by analyzing speech patterns and suggesting more concise ways to phrase their ideas.
   - AI can detect and flag when someone is taking too long to make a point and gently nudge them toward summarizing their key message.

Managing Group Size & Dynamics

6. Optimizing Group Interaction
   - AI can suggest when to break large groups into smaller teams based on the flow of discussion.
   - AI can moderate conversations in large groups by clustering related contributions, reducing redundancy and enhancing efficiency.
7. Countering Anchoring Effects
   - AI can reorder or anonymize initial contributions before revealing them, preventing the first idea from setting the conversational anchor.
   - AI can prompt alternative perspectives by suggesting counterarguments or asking members to consider other angles.
8. Preventing Cognitive Depletion
   - AI can schedule strategic breaks based on detected fatigue patterns in voice tone or engagement levels.
   - AI can provide real-time summaries so members don't have to exert mental effort to track long discussions.

Improving Active Listening & Focus

9. Facilitating Active Listening
   - AI can detect when a speaker's point hasn't been acknowledged and prompt listeners to repeat or summarize key takeaways.

- AI-generated real-time visual conversation maps can display who said what, making it easier to follow and engage with contributions.

10. Reducing Mind Wandering & Tangents
    - AI can detect when the conversation drifts off-topic and prompt the facilitator to redirect focus.
    - AI can maintain a "parking lot" for off-topic ideas and suggest appropriate times to revisit them.
11. Supporting Structured Conversation
    - AI can prompt the McKinsey method by reminding speakers to state their conclusions first, then provide reasoning.
    - AI can provide automatic round-robin tracking to ensure each participant gets a fair opportunity to speak.
    - AI can enable simultaneous input through electronic brainstorming tools, preventing participants from mentally rehearsing their points instead of listening.

By integrating generative AI into small-team problem-solving, teams can eliminate common speaking and listening barriers, ensuring that all members contribute effectively and hear each other clearly.

I wondered which, if any, of ChatGPT's answers are feasible given its current capabilities, so I asked it to evaluate its answer.[29] It gave a very extensive answer, so I am only showing the summary of its response.

Prompt

Evaluate your answer. How realistic are your suggestions considering the current capabilities of AI systems?

ChatGPT's Response (Summary)

Highly Feasible	AI can already do this with commercial tools: transcription, summarization, anonymous input, breakout groups.
Partially Feasible	AI has demonstrated potential, but real-time execution remains inconsistent or experimental: meeting facilitation, real-time feedback on speech.
Not Yet Feasible	AI is not yet capable of real-time conversational nudging or enforcing structured speech patterns naturally.

Overall Realism Score: 7.5/10

- Many AI-driven solutions are technically possible today.
- The biggest gap is in real-time interaction—AI struggles to intervene meaningfully while conversations are happening.
- Ethical and adoption barriers (e.g., discomfort with AI monitoring speech) may slow adoption even when technically feasible.

What's Next?

- Short-Term (Now-2026): Expect wider adoption of AI-assisted meeting tools (e.g., real-time summarization, idea capture, turn-taking tracking).
- Medium-Term (2027–2030): AI could improve in conversational nudging, detecting anchoring effects, and structuring discussions.
- Long-Term (Beyond 2030): Advanced AI meeting mediators may enable seamless facilitation and real-time conversational coaching.

Types of Talk

There are different ways of describing conversations in which people do and don't listen to one another. One way is to contrast *advocacy* and *inquiry*. Advocacy is the practice of debate. With this approach, a person adopts a position and advocates it to the exclusion of all others. Advocacy is the predominant form of conversation in American culture. Nearly everywhere you look—on the editorial page of the newspaper, in the courtroom, on TV talk shows, in the company boardroom, even the sidewalk cafe—you find people zealously clinging to their version of the world. It reminds me of the old pro-gun bumper sticker that read, "The only way you'll take my gun [version of the world] away from me is to pry my cold, dead fingers off the barrel."

Inquiry, by contrast, is the practice of listening and understanding. Rather than maintaining a death grip on their position, each group member works to understand the positions of the other members. To understand does not necessarily mean to agree. It simply means suspending judgment and listening without resistance to another's point of view. Few of us really make the effort to listen deeply. As one wit put it, "People don't listen, they reload."

In his book *Learning to Read the Signs: Reclaiming Pragmatism for the Practice of Sustainable Management*, advertising executive Byron Nahser tells of a time when he was forced to engage in inquiry.[30] Nahser attended a conference at the University of Chicago led by the psychiatrist M. Scott Peck. The attendees were divided into small groups, each group was given a problem to solve, and they were required to use the following ground rules: (1) When a person has the floor, you cannot interrupt or correct him; (2) If you want to challenge a person, you can only say, "I hear you saying . . . ."; and (3) You can respond only when the other person is satisfied that you heard and understood what he had to say.

Nahser's first thought was to bolt for the door, but, he says, "I stayed put, wondering if Milton Friedman would suddenly appear to stop all this nonsense." Over the course of three days, the group went through four stages. First was the strained conviviality and role-playing of a pseudo-community, which, he comments, "[Was] familiar to those of us in business, since American corporations operate at the pseudo-community level." The next stage was chaos, as conflicting positions emerged and subgroups formed to defend them. The third stage was emptying. The participants began to empty themselves of old beliefs and started listening to one another. Finally, there was the stage of real community. The group became a community of inquiry in which, Nahser explains, "Each person add[ed] ideas, insights, or 'a piece of the truth,' building toward a clearer picture of reality from which flow[ed] the decision and action."[31]

Education professors Kate Middleton and Neil Mercer offer a similar way of classifying the different types of conversation in their book *Interthinking: Putting Talk to Work*.[32] They wrote the book to explain how people use spoken language to think together, which they variously refer to as *interthinking*, *intermental activity*, and *collective thinking*. The bulk of their book is dedicated to distinguishing and describing three types of talk—*disputational*, *cumulative*, and *exploratory*.

Disputational talk is characterized by disagreement. The atmosphere is competitive rather than co-operative. Most interactions have the form "Yes it is!—No it's not!" There are few attempts to understand one another or offer constructive criticism. Disputational talk has the advantage of fostering diversity of thought by surfacing ideas and uncovering weak assumptions. The disadvantage is that the ideas aren't integrated.

Cumulative talk is just the opposite. The atmosphere is cooperative rather than competitive. Everyone accepts and agrees with what others have to say. Ideas are contributed without reasons and accepted without challenge. The advantage is that group members build positively on each other's ideas by extending them, adding to them, and integrating them. The disadvantage is that errors and weak ideas persist unchallenged because there is no critical evaluation of the ideas. This sort of talk leads to what psychologists refer to as *groupthink*, in which the group members' desire for harmony and conformity leads to dysfunctional decisions.[33] Earlier, I noted that rather than being collectively intelligent, a group can be collectively stupid. Groupthink is one of the primary reasons why groups are sometimes stupid.

Exploratory talk lies midway between disputational and cumulative talk. It combines competition and cooperation. Group members ask and answer questions and they ask for and offer reasons. Everyone contributes ideas, everyone's ideas are viewed as worthy of consideration, and everyone's ideas are considered critically but constructively. This is the sort of *constructive dissent* that has contributed to the extraordinary success of Pixar Animation Studios and Bridgewater Associates I mentioned in the Introduction and will elaborate in just a moment.

A few quotes make clear the value of dissent and disagreement in exploratory talk. The author and strategy consultant (and $4 million poker champ) Annie Duke says, "In a way, you don't care much about the areas where everyone agrees; you may as well make the decisions yourself with no input from anyone else. Instead, you want to identify and explore the areas where there's disagreement and divergence."[34] In the same vein, Alfred Sloan, when he was chairman of General Motors, once concluded a meeting by saying, "Gentlemen, I take it we are all in complete agreement on the decision here. . . . Then I propose we postpone further discussion until our next meeting to give ourselves time to develop disagreements and perhaps gain some understanding of what the decision is all about."[35] And Francis Crick who, along with James Watson, won the Nobel Prize for discovering the structure of DNA, said of their partnership, "Our . . . advantage was that we had evolved unstated but fruitful methods of collaboration. . . . If either of us suggested a new idea, the other, while taking it seriously, would attempt to demolish it in a candid but nonhostile manner."[36]

It's hard to overstate the value of constructive dissent, not just for small groups, but for the organizations to which they belong. As I mentioned, Pixar Animation Studios, the creator of the movie *Toy Story*, is a great example. In an industry where some 60 percent of movies lose money and many of the rest make only a marginal profit,[37] Pixar created an uninterrupted string of blockbusters. Between 1995 and 2010, they produced 11 movies that collectively grossed $6.3 billion, won 24 Oscars, and were nominated for twice that number.[38] Ed Catmull, the co-founder and former president of Pixar, explains that a major driver of their success is to "Put smart, passionate people in a room together, charge them with identifying and solving problems, and encourage them to be candid with one another."[39] The same sort of candor accounts for the remarkable success of the hedge fund Bridgewater Associates. Two cornerstones of the company, explains Ray Dalio, its founder and CEO, are "radical truth" and "radical transparency."[40]

Clearly, candid disagreement is a good thing. But let's face it, no one enjoys having their ideas picked apart, especially in front of a group, so it's critical to attend to the other half of exploratory talk, being constructive and polite. There are several ways to politely disagree. In his book *Making Conversation: Seven Essential Elements of Meaningful Communication*, the meeting designer and facilitator Fred Dust suggests that the terms *confirm* and *complicate* are gentler ways of saying *agree* and *disagree* because they "point in a direction but they're not absolute."[41] So rather than saying, "I agree," say something like, "I can confirm that." And instead of saying, "I disagree," say something along the lines of "Let me complicate that a bit." Another way to gently disagree is to *express uncertainty* by using a phrase like, "I might be wrong, but I see it this way" and to *ask questions*, such as, "Could you explain a bit more about what you mean? I might have a slightly different take on it." As I've done in all of these examples, it's always best to use *I statements* so that you frame your disagreement in terms of your own thoughts or feelings rather than as an attack on the other person's idea.

The organizational and experience designers Adam Connor and Aaron Irizarry go so far as to devote an entire book to the topic of providing and receiving candid feedback in their book *Discussing Design: Improving Communication & Collaboration Through Critique*.[42] Their framework for giving candid feedback is to ask yourself or the designer four questions: *What is the objective of the design? What elements of the design are related to the objective? Are those elements effective in achieving the objective? Why or why not?* Considering that problem-solving is all about designing a solution to a problem, these questions apply equally to providing candid feedback on someone's proposed solution.

While exploratory talk is the ideal for enhancing collective intelligence, groups may naturally oscillate between disputational, cumulative, and exploratory talk. By understanding and leveraging these three styles of talk, groups can more effectively harness the collective intelligence of their members. Littleton and Mercer emphasize that groups should work to maintain a "meta-cognitive awareness" of the type of talk in which they are engaged so as to identify when a shift (e.g., from disputational to exploratory talk) is needed. One way of maintaining a meta-cognitive awareness is to have a meeting facilitator do it. I asked ChatGPT what role generative AI might play in this process.[43] The following is how it answered:

Prompt

What are ways AI can contribute to maintaining a meta-cognitive awareness of the type of talk in which the group is engaged—disputational, cumulative, and exploratory—and suggesting appropriate shifts among the three types of talk? Evaluate the feasibility of your suggestions.

ChatGPT's Response

AI can contribute to maintaining meta-cognitive awareness of the type of talk in a group discussion and suggesting appropriate shifts among disputational, cumulative, and exploratory talk through the following mechanisms:

1. *Real-Time Talk Classification*
    - Speech and Text Analysis: AI can use natural language processing (NLP) to classify utterances based on their features, such as:
        - Disputational Talk: Detection of adversarial language, interruptions, or contradictory statements.
        - Cumulative Talk: Repetition, affirmation, and additive contributions without critique.
        - Exploratory Talk: Use of reasoning, open-ended questions, and collaborative problem-solving.
    - Visualization of Talk Patterns: AI could create a live dashboard showing the prevalence of each talk type during the discussion.
2. *Nudges for Mode Shifts*
    - Shifting to Exploratory Talk:
        - If disputational talk dominates, AI might suggest: "Let's pause and explore how these ideas might complement each other."
        - If cumulative talk persists without critique, AI could prompt: "Can we identify any assumptions that need testing?"
    - Encouraging Cumulative Talk:
        - After extended disputational dialogue, AI could recommend: "Let's focus on areas of agreement to build shared understanding."
    - Promoting Critical Examination:
        - During prolonged cumulative talk, AI might suggest: "Are there alternative views or challenges we should consider here?"
3. *Sentiment and Engagement Analysis*
    - Monitoring Tone and Emotional Climate:
        - AI could assess the emotional tone of the conversation to detect frustration (common in disputational talk) or overconfidence (a risk in cumulative talk).

    - Suggestions could then address group dynamics, such as: "Let's take a moment to ensure everyone feels heard before continuing."
  - Balancing Participation:
    - By analyzing participation patterns, AI could flag when certain individuals dominate disputational talk or when quieter voices need to be included.

4. *Feedback Loops*
  - Periodic Reflections:
    - AI could pause the discussion at intervals to summarize the dominant talk mode and ask: "Are we engaging in the right type of talk for this phase of the discussion?"
  - Dynamic Talk Transitions:
    - Based on analysis, AI could suggest: "We've explored alternatives thoroughly. Is it time to consolidate and move toward agreement?"

5. *Knowledge Mapping*
  - Highlighting Talk Gaps:
    - AI could generate a visual map of the discussion showing:
    - Clusters of cumulative talk (indicating shared knowledge building).
    - Isolated disputational threads (indicating unresolved conflicts).
    - Prompts might include: "Here's a cluster of ideas that could benefit from deeper exploration."

6. *Customizable Thresholds and Alerts*
  - Adaptive Interventions:
    - AI could be programmed to intervene only when certain thresholds are crossed, e.g.:
      - Excessive disputational talk leads to unresolved conflicts.
      - Cumulative talk persists without progression to critical evaluation.
  - Alerts for Facilitators:
    - Notifications could help facilitators step in at key moments to guide the group back to exploratory talk.

Conclusion

By continuously analyzing the flow, tone, and content of group discussions, AI can provide real-time insights and actionable prompts to maintain an optimal balance of disputational, cumulative, and exploratory talk. This enhances the group's meta-cognitive awareness, enabling members to adapt their communication style dynamically for greater collective intelligence.

Evaluation Summary: Feasibility of AI-Assisted Meta-Cognitive Awareness of Talk Types

Highly Feasible	AI can already analyze speech and text using NLP for sentiment, engagement, and classification (e.g., meeting transcripts, tone analysis in platforms like Zoom, Microsoft Teams, and Otter.ai). Some elements, like summarization and participation tracking, are well within AI's current capabilities.
Partially Feasible	Real-time intervention and dynamic nudging require context-sensitive AI, which remains in early stages. AI can suggest shifts between talk types, but doing so in a way that feels natural and non-disruptive is still challenging.
Experimental	Live visualization of talk modes and knowledge mapping of discussion structures are promising but not widely available. AI can generate static conversation maps (e.g., argument mining research), but real-time, interactive displays still require custom development.
Not Yet Feasible	AI cannot yet fully understand deeper discourse nuances (e.g., distinguishing between constructive vs. destructive disputational talk) at a human-like level. Also, adaptive interventions based on group-specific thresholds require significant customization and training.

Overall Realism Score: 7/10

- AI can classify disputational, cumulative, and exploratory talk with reasonable accuracy, but real-time intervention quality is still limited.
- AI can track participation and emotional tone, but interpreting complex group dynamics correctly remains a challenge.

- AI can generate post-discussion insights, but live nudging with precision and nuance requires further development.
- The biggest challenge is ensuring AI suggestions are contextually relevant, minimally disruptive, and adaptive to different conversation styles.

Future Potential (2025–2030)

- Short-Term: Improved real-time sentiment and participation tracking with better dashboards and analytics.
- Medium-Term: AI co-pilots for meetings that can dynamically suggest shifts in discussion tone with greater contextual awareness.
- Long-Term: Multimodal AI (speech, text, video) integration to provide holistic, adaptive facilitation of group dialogue in real-time.

Dysfunctional Behaviors

It's almost inevitable you're going to encounter dysfunctional behaviors that diminish the collective intelligence of a group. You want to make sure that you, as a group member, aren't the one engaging in these behaviors and that you know how to handle them if you're facilitating or leading the meeting. Following is a description of five behaviors—domination, monologues, tangents, wheel spinning, and unhealthy conflict—that are most responsible for decreasing a group's collective intelligence. I've already touched on the first three but will elaborate on them here.

Before I describe the five behaviors, however, you should know how to interrupt people because interrupting people is what you must do to contain the behaviors. There are verbal and nonverbal ways of interrupting someone. The nonverbal means are often required to get the person to stop talking long enough to interject the verbal means. The nonverbal means of interruption include the following:

- Leaning forward and opening your mouth slightly signals you have something to say.
- Raising your hand slightly is a subtle gesture that suggests you'd like to speak.
- If you were nodding slowly, increasing the pace indicates you're ready to transition.
- Shifting posture or looking at others signals the need for a shift in the conversation.

With regard to the verbal ways of interrupting, Fred Dust tells of a time he asked an experienced on-stage interviewer for advice on how to interview people.[44] She complied and concluded her advice by saying, "Oh, most important, learn how to interrupt people gracefully when they won't stop talking." When he asked her if she had learned what works best, she replied, "I never have."

I asked ChatGPT to suggest some innovative ways of doing so.[45] It suggested the following:

Prompt

Generate ten innovative and effective ways to gently interrupt a person who is talking too long.

ChatGPT's Response

1. *The "Echo and Pivot" Technique*
   Interrupt by summarizing their point and smoothly steering the discussion elsewhere.
   Example:

   > "That's a fascinating take on [topic]! It really ties into something I've been thinking about—what do you all think about how this applies to [new topic]?"

   Why It Works: The speaker feels acknowledged, while the conversation naturally shifts.

2. *The "Tag Team" Approach*
   Gently enlist someone else to enter the conversation, creating a natural transition.
   Example:

   > "Oh, this is interesting! I'd love to hear what [another person] thinks about this—[Name], have you encountered something similar?"

   Why It Works: It feels inclusive rather than disruptive, making it a shared exchange.

3. *The "Pause and Reflect" Method*
   Use a thoughtful pause to signal a shift in the conversation.
   Example:

   > "Hold that thought for a second—I just want to make sure we're capturing this properly. If I understand you right, you're saying [brief summary]? That makes me wonder about [new perspective]."

   Why It Works: It slows the momentum, provides a natural stopping point, and allows a redirection.

4. *The "Enthusiastic Interruption" Method*
   Use genuine excitement as a tool for interruption.
   Example:

   > "Oh wow, that's such a great point! It actually reminds me of something that connects really well—can I jump in and share?"

   Why It Works: Enthusiasm feels like collaboration rather than correction.

5. *The "Zoom Out" Strategy*
   Shift focus by bringing attention to the conversation's bigger picture.
   Example:

   > "This is such a rich discussion, and I want to make sure we also touch on [another key point]. Maybe we can circle back to this later?"

   Why It Works: It reframes the conversation without invalidating what's been said.

6. *The "Shared Authority" Interruption*
   Leverage a "we" statement to subtly shift control of the conversation.
   Example:

   > "I love where this conversation is going! Maybe we can take a quick pause and check if there are other thoughts in the room?"

   Why It Works:

   - The word *we* makes it collective rather than about you interrupting them.
   - It frames the pause as constructive rather than disruptive.

7. *The "Micro-Silence Disruption"*
   Create a brief but intentional moment of silence to reset the flow.
   How It Works:

   - Instead of verbally interrupting, use non-verbal cues such as leaning forward, inhaling audibly, or lifting a hand slightly.
   - If they pause even slightly, let the silence linger just a second longer than usual—then step in with a transition like:
     - "That's really insightful. Let's take a moment to connect this back to [main topic]."

Why It Works:

- A subtle break in the speaker's rhythm gives you a window to intervene naturally.
- It's an elegant way to take control without directly interrupting.

8. *The "Curiosity Hook" Interruption*
   Drop an intriguing question or statement mid-flow to hijack their attention.
   Example:

   "Wait, before you continue—I just had a wild thought based on what you said! What if . . .?"

   Why It Works:

   - The phrase "Wait, before you continue" creates a psychological pause.
   - Using curiosity naturally redirects attention to you, making the interruption feel organic rather than intrusive.

9. *The "Object Shift" Technique (Best for in-person conversations)*
   Introduce a subtle but visible distraction to reset the speaker's dominance.
   How It Works:

   - If you're holding a pen, coffee cup, or notebook, place it deliberately on the table or adjust your position.
   - Pair this with a verbal cue like:

     "I want to jot something down before we move on—this connects to something interesting."

   Why It Works:

   - Physical actions break the speaker's momentum without confrontation.
   - It re-establishes equilibrium in the conversation without verbal conflict.

10. *The "Role Reversal" Disruption*
    Flip the speaker's role from "explainer" to "reflector," forcing a natural pause.
    Example:

    "That's really interesting! If you had to summarize your main takeaway from this, what would it be?"

Why It Works:

- This forces them to condense their thoughts, effectively ending their monologue without you cutting them off.
- It shifts them from speaking mode to reflective mode, creating space for others.

Why These Methods Work

- They disrupt without feeling aggressive.
- They use psychological pauses to steer the conversation.
- They introduce novelty so the interruption feels natural.

Domination is the first of the dysfunctional behaviors I'll describe. It refers to one or two people dominating the discussion by hogging all the airtime. It's normal for a group to have people who contribute more ideas and talk more than others. It becomes a problem when they talk so much that it prevents others from participating. This decreases the group's collective intelligence by limiting the cognitive repertoires that others are able to contribute. The three ways to minimize domination are to use conversational, technological, and process interventions.

The usual way of handling dominators is for the facilitator or group leader to redirect the conversation to the rest of the group by asking if anyone else has something to say on the topic. If, after several attempts, this doesn't work, try sending nonverbal signals, such as a dissatisfied glance, a negative head nod, or moving closer to the offender. And if you're still having problems, pull the person aside during a break and discuss the matter with him or her. Be firm but friendly. And as with any kind of feedback, focus on the issue, not the person. It's not uncommon for those highest in the hierarchy—possibly the person who hired you to facilitate the meeting—to be the worst offenders. Speaking to them privately is a good way to avoid undermining their authority.

Another way to use conversation to minimize domination is to have the rest of the group help you do it. If there's time, the entire group should be trained to identify domination and other dysfunctional behaviors. They should be taught to recognize when they, themselves, are engaging in the behaviors and to call out others (gently) when the others are doing so. This method works best for groups that meet regularly and know each other well.

Conversational interventions don't always work. To put it bluntly, some people simply won't shut up no matter what you do. When that's the case, your only options are to drop the person from the group or use the other two ways of intervening, technology and processes. As previously explained, electronic brainstorming technology addresses the problem by making it possible for everyone to "talk at once." There are several ways to use processes to minimize domination. One way is to have the group members write their ideas before or during the meeting, as is done with the brainwriting method explained in the next chapter. A second (and mischievously entertaining) way is to subdivide the group into dyads or triads and put the dominators together in the same subgroup. A third way is to employ round-robin discussions in which each person speaks in turn. And a fourth process for containing dominators is to establish pre-set time limits per speaker.

Monologues are another behavior that decreases a group's collective intelligence by leaving less time for members to contribute their cognitive repertoires. Group members who engage in monologues and those who dominate discussions may seem similar because both take up a lot of speaking time, but they differ in their intent, style, and impact on group dynamics. Monologuers don't intend to control the conversation. It's just that they are deeply engrossed in their ideas or don't know how to express themselves concisely. Dominators, by contrast, are more intentional about controlling the discussion. They consciously steer the conversation, interrupt others, and resist allowing different viewpoints to emerge. Monologuers might pause or apologize when interrupted, as they may not have intended to consume so much time, whereas dominators often push back against interruptions, attempt to regain control, or even dismiss the contributions of others. Monologuers can cause conversation fatigue, causing others to disengage, become passive, or wait for them to finish, whereas dominators can create power imbalances, making others feel shut down, pressured, or unable to contribute meaningfully. Monologuers generally respond to the gentlest interruptions and redirections.

Tangents refer to the avenues of conversation that occur when the discussion drifts away from the main topic into related but less relevant or even completely unrelated territory. This can happen naturally in dynamic conversations, especially when someone shares an anecdote, an interesting side thought, or introduces an unexpected idea. Tangents aren't always negative. They can spark creativity, deepen understanding, or lead to valuable insights. However, when they persist too long or derail the main discussion, they can detract from the group's collective intelligence. The usual way to handle valuable tangents is to write them down and put them in a "parking lot" where they can be revisited later. A good way to handle long-winded tangents that are disconnected from the focal topic is to gently interrupt, quickly summarize the tangent, then link it back to the original discussion. Another way is to ask how the tangent relates to the focal topic.

Wheel spinning refers to a situation where a group or individual is engaged in a discussion or effort without making meaningful progress (i.e., they're spinning their wheels). It usually involves rehashing the same points without moving forward, getting stuck in an unproductive loop where the conversation circles back to the same arguments or concerns, or endless debating without resolution. As with the other dysfunctional behaviors, wheel spinning diminishes the group's collective intelligence by decreasing the time available for the members to contribute their cognitive repertoires. Here, the goal of the interventions is to break the cycle and reintroduce momentum without making the participants feel dismissed or rushed. One way to intervene is to first identify the sticking point, which may be unclear, then ask the group to say what is preventing them from moving past it. This gets them to refocus on the problem. Another way is to set a time limit on the discussion to encourage more concise contributions. Yet another way, which is explained in Chapter 4, is to use dialogue mapping to visually map the conversation so that you can literally point to where the issue has already been discussed. If there's no way to move beyond the impasse, it's best to assign someone the task of gathering whatever information might be needed and defer further discussion to the next meeting, which shifts the conversation from debating to doing.

Conflict here refers to disagreements that spin out of control. When tempers flare in a meeting, the facilitator's role is to de-escalate tension and get the discussion back on a productive track. The key is to intervene quickly while maintaining neutrality and control. Here's how to do it effectively:

1. *Recognize the signs of escalation early*: Unhealthy conflict typically starts with raised voices or sharp changes in tone, interruptions or talking over each other, personal attacks or dismissive body language, or fixation on blame rather than problem-solving. If you notice these signs, you should intervene before the situation gets worse.
2. *Interrupt the conflict with a neutral, calming statement*: Pause the conversation by saying something like, "I want to pause here. It seems like we have some strong perspectives, and I want to make sure we're hearing each other clearly." This interrupts the escalating tension without assigning blame and shifts focus from conflict to constructive discussion.
3. *Separate the people from the problem*: When emotions run high, people often personalize disagreements instead of focusing on the issue. To separate the people from the problem, say something along the lines of, "I hear that this is an important issue for both of you. Let's focus on the key concern rather than how we're reacting to it." This helps to prevent personal attacks and refocuses attention on problem-solving.
4. *Enforce ground rules and maintain control*: If tempers continue to flare, reinforce behavioral expectations for the group by saying, for example,

"I want to remind everyone that we're here to collaborate. Let's keep this discussion respectful so we can find a solution together." This enables you to establish authority without being authoritarian and reasserts the goal of solving the problem, not winning an argument.
5. *If needed, propose a breather*: If emotions are too intense to be resolved, suggest a short break by saying, "I think we could all benefit from a quick break. Let's take a five-minute breather and come back to this with a fresh perspective." This provides time for emotions to cool and prevents further escalation of the conflict.
6. *Reframe the conflict as a shared problem to solve*: To realign perspectives, shift the language from "you vs. me" to "us vs. the issue." Say, for example, "Both of you care deeply about this, which means we have valuable perspectives to work with. How can we combine your insights to move forward?" This encourages collaboration rather than opposition and moves the discussion toward resolution instead of continued friction.
7. *If necessary, take the conflict offline*: If two members continue to argue, suggest a private conversation outside of the group setting. Say something like, "This seems like a discussion that might be more productive in a one-on-one setting. Let's schedule time to address this separately while we keep the meeting moving." This reduces public tension while allowing resolution to happen in a lower stakes setting.

Collaboration Strategy

Creating a multi-disciplinary[46] collaboration strategy starts with identifying a problem that the collaborators are willing to work on together. This is easier said than done when the collaborators are competitors. Cities compete for companies. Companies compete for customers. Nonprofits compete for funding. Scientists compete for academic positions. Whatever the case, the competitors are loath to share what they know for fear of giving their competitors a leg up.

The concept of a *pre-competitive space* helps to overcome the reluctance of individuals and organizations to collaborate. Pre-competitive space refers to a phase of research, development, or innovation where individuals and organizations collaborate on foundational technologies, standards, or knowledge that benefit an entire industry or discipline rather than providing a direct competitive advantage to any single participant. Some examples are these:

- *Commercial Example*[47]: The Sustainable Agriculture Initiative (SAI) Platform established by the food and beverage companies Danone, Nestlé, and Unilever promotes sustainable agricultural practices across the industry. By collaborating on non-competitive issues like sustainability, they aim to drive systemic change without affecting their individual market positions.

- *Nonprofit Example*[48]: The Diverse Books for All Coalition is an example of a pre-competitive collaboration among a group of smaller nonprofits located in the same geographical area that are addressing the same problem. This coalition brings together over 30 nonprofits and member organizations to address the need for more children's books by and about diverse races and cultures. By collaborating, these organizations aim to make books on the subject of diversity more accessible and affordable, benefiting the entire community without giving any single participant a competitive advantage.
- *Academic Example*[49]: The Human Genome Project (HGP), launched in 1990, was an international scientific research initiative aimed at mapping and sequencing the entire human genome. This collaborative effort involved researchers from around the world and was completed in 2003. The HGP has provided a foundational understanding of human genetics, leading to numerous advancements in medicine and biotechnology.

I asked ChatGPT to describe a process for identifying opportunities for a pre-competitive space.[50] It answered in the following way:

Prompt

What is a good process for identifying an opportunity for a pre-competitive space?"

ChatGPT's Response

The first and most critical step in identifying a pre-competitive space is defining an industry-wide challenge that multiple stakeholders face but cannot easily solve alone. This step requires a careful balance between identifying a problem broad enough to warrant collaboration but narrow enough to be actionable.

A. Characteristics of a Good Pre-Competitive Challenge

A challenge suitable for pre-competitive collaboration should have the following attributes:

1. Systemic and Cross-Cutting
    - The problem affects multiple players in the industry, across sectors, or within a discipline.
    - Example: In pharmaceuticals, the high cost and failure rate of early-stage drug discovery impact all companies.
2. Non-Differentiating for Competitive Advantage
    - Solving the problem does not give any single company or entity a unique market advantage but rather creates a stronger foundation for innovation.
    - Example: In AI, developing large open datasets for training machine learning models benefits all players without favoring one company.
3. High Cost or Complexity for Individual Efforts
    - The issue is too expensive, risky, or inefficient for any single organization to tackle alone.
    - Example: In semiconductor manufacturing, the cost of developing advanced materials for chip fabrication is so high that competitors like Intel, AMD, and TSMC collaborate in early R&D.
4. Regulatory or Ethical Pressure
    - The issue may require industry-wide compliance with new regulations or address social concerns like sustainability, fairness, or safety.
    - Example: In biotechnology, gene-editing companies may collaborate on ethical guidelines to shape public policy.
5. Infrastructure or Standards Gap
    - A lack of shared technical standards, interoperability, or common infrastructure prevents progress.
    - Example: In financial technology (FinTech), firms may collaborate on digital identity verification standards to prevent fraud.

B. Methods to Identify the Right Pre-Competitive Problem

1. Industry-Wide Pain Points Assessment
    - Conduct industry surveys, roundtables, or think tanks to identify persistent problems.

- Look for repeated failures or chronic inefficiencies in research, production, or implementation.
- Example: The Global Battery Alliance was created when EV companies identified supply chain transparency as a major bottleneck.

2. Analyze Market Forces and Trends
   - Consider macroeconomic trends, regulatory changes, and technological disruptions.
   - Identify areas where shared innovation is needed to keep up with rapid change.
   - Example: The AI alignment problem is a major concern that competitors like OpenAI, Google DeepMind, and Anthropic address collectively.
3. Study Existing Research Gaps
   - Review academic literature, patents, and white papers to spot areas where multiple organizations face the same technical hurdle.
   - Example: In climate science, multiple institutions share climate data models to better predict and mitigate global warming effects.
4. Map Out Competitive vs. Pre-Competitive Areas
   - Draw a distinction between foundational knowledge and proprietary application.
   - Example: In biotechnology, the Human Genome Project was pre-competitive, but pharmaceutical companies developed proprietary drugs from the data.
5. Engage Regulators and Policy Experts
   - Discuss with government agencies and standards organizations to anticipate future compliance requirements.
   - Example: The Paris Agreement led to pre-competitive collaborations in the carbon offset and green energy industries.

Once you've found the problem to solve, you need to find the problem solvers. At the start of the problem-solving process, as I said earlier, there's no way to know all the cognitive repertoires that are needed to solve the problem. The only way to find that out is to make iterative attempts at solving it and assess the needed repertoires after each attempt. That said, you've got to start somewhere. One way, as mentioned earlier, is to post the problem and let prospective collaborators come to you. The other way is to carefully consider the types of collaborators who are likely to have cognitive repertoires that will contribute to solving the problem. Generative AI can be a useful tool for doing this. I asked ChatGPT to explain the best way to use it to identify prospective collaborators, that is, prospective members of a multi-disciplinary team.[51] Here is how it responded:

Prompt

Consider the following situation. A small group of people is organizing a problem-solving effort. The problem is complex and therefore requires a multi-disciplinary team to solve it. But because the problem is so complex, it's hard to know all the disciplines that will be required to solve it. The organizers intend to use generative AI to help them identify the needed disciplines. What is the best way for them to do so?

ChatGPT's Response

The best way for the organizers to use generative AI to identify the required disciplines for solving a complex problem involves a structured, iterative, and feedback-driven approach. Below is a step-by-step framework:

1. *Problem Framing and Scoping*

- The team should first define the problem as clearly as possible, even acknowledging unknowns.
- They should outline what is already known, what is uncertain, and what is entirely unknown.
- Generative AI can assist in refining the problem statement by generating variations of the problem from different perspectives.

AI Usage:

- Use AI to generate problem formulations from different disciplinary perspectives.
- Ask AI: "What disciplines are typically involved in solving problems related to [describe problem]?"

2. *Initial Discipline Mapping via Knowledge Graphs*

- AI can construct a knowledge graph linking the problem to known disciplines, subfields, and interdisciplinary areas.

- AI-generated literature reviews or taxonomies of similar problems can help identify expertise areas.

AI Usage:

- Query AI for a taxonomy of disciplines related to the problem domain.
- Use AI to analyze research papers, patents, or case studies to extract key disciplinary contributions.
- Ask AI to map historical case studies of similar problems to the disciplines that addressed them.

3. *Identifying Gaps and Emergent Needs*

- Since some disciplines may not be obvious at first, AI can be used to detect gaps in the known approaches.
- AI can help predict emerging fields that might contribute novel insights.

AI Usage:

- Prompt AI: "What are possible blind spots in the current disciplinary approach to this problem?"
- Ask AI to simulate different problem-solving approaches and identify missing perspectives.
- Use AI to scan for recent interdisciplinary breakthroughs that may be relevant.

4. *Iterative Refinement with Human Experts*

- Present AI-generated discipline suggestions to domain experts and ask for feedback.
- Use their feedback to refine AI prompts and generate a more accurate set of needed disciplines.

AI Usage:

- Ask AI: "Given the following expert feedback, how should the disciplinary composition of the team change?"
- Use AI to compare expert opinions against existing interdisciplinary models.

5. *Dynamic Adaptation as Problem Evolves*

- As the problem-solving effort progresses, new disciplinary needs will arise.
- The team should use AI to periodically reassess and refine the required expertise.

AI Usage:

- Set up a continuous feedback loop where AI monitors progress and suggests new disciplines dynamically.
- Ask AI: "What new disciplines might be relevant based on the latest findings in this problem-solving process?"

6. *Leveraging AI for Team Formation*

- AI can help not only identify needed disciplines but also suggest experts or professionals who work at their intersection.
- AI can match problem requirements with expertise databases or professional networks.

AI Usage:

- Use AI to recommend potential team members based on expertise.
- Ask AI to identify individuals or groups working on similar problems.

Conclusion

The best approach is iterative and hybrid, leveraging both AI-driven insights and human expertise. AI should be used as a cognitive amplifier to explore disciplinary possibilities, detect gaps, and dynamically adapt to the evolving complexity of the problem.

The next step in creating a collaborative strategy is to assess the degree to which prospective team members are psychologically suited for the collaborative problem-solving effort. The evolutionary biologist Timoth Collins and his colleagues suggest that the participants should be "open-minded, flexible, genuinely curious people who are not too invested in their own ideas and comfortable with give-and-take, [and are able to] work together to define the problem, key priorities and the obstacles to solutions."[52] Assessment methods range from interviewing the candidates or interviewing people who know the candidates to retaining an organizational psychologist to create a questionnaire that tests for the characteristics. In summary form, ChatGPT suggests that collaborators possess the following characteristics:[53]

- *Psychological safety and emotional intelligence*: Team members should create an inclusive, psychologically safe space for collaboration, regulate emotional responses, and adapt to group dynamics for effective teamwork.

- *Collaborative mindset*: Individuals must be able to build on others' ideas, practice active listening, and navigate conflicts constructively to foster a cooperative and productive interdisciplinary environment.
- *Cognitive flexibility*: Team members should be open to new ideas, be able to hold multiple perspectives, and be comfortable with uncertainty and ambiguity, allowing them to engage with diverse disciplines effectively.
- *Communication and translation skills*: Effective team members should be able to explain their expertise in accessible terms, translate concepts across disciplines, and use analogies or visual thinking to enhance shared understanding. (Ideally, the team should include a generalist who can translate across the disciplines.)
- *Constructive risk-taking and innovation bias*: Individuals should challenge assumptions, engage in "what-if" thinking, and push beyond disciplinary constraints to prototype and test unconventional ideas.
- *Tolerance for iteration and failure*: Members should embrace an iterative approach to problem-solving, be resilient in the face of setbacks, and view failures as learning opportunities rather than obstacles.
- *Systems thinking and interdisciplinary awareness*: Ideal candidates recognize how their field connects to others, understand the complexity of interdependent systems, and are aware of their own knowledge boundaries.

Motivating people to join a team is not always an easy task, especially when it adds to a person's already busy schedule. In cases like these, it helps to know the kinds of incentives that motivate people to join. Two basic kinds of incentives are *intrinsic incentives* and *extrinsic incentives*. Intrinsic incentives stem from an individual's internal drives, such as the drive to master a skill or satisfy intellectual curiosity or a passion for one's work. External incentives come from external rewards or pressures, such as financial compensation, career advancement, or social recognition. Professionals are motivated to participate in multi-disciplinary teams through a combination of intrinsic and extrinsic incentives. Key motivators include:

- *Professional Development*: Engaging with colleagues from various disciplines enables professionals to broaden their knowledge base, acquire new skills, and stay abreast of advancements in other fields.
- *Shared Governance and Empowerment*: Participating in a multi-disciplinary team involves shared decision-making processes, which enhances job satisfaction and a sense of ownership.

- *Financial Incentives*: Certain organizations offer financial rewards to those who join multi-disciplinary teams.
- *Improved Team Dynamics and Job Satisfaction*: Working in a multi-disciplinary team fosters a collaborative environment, enhancing communication and mutual respect among professionals. The collegial atmosphere contributes to higher job satisfaction.
- *Opportunities for Leadership and Career Advancement*: Participation in multi-disciplinary teams can open pathways to leadership roles within an organization, providing avenues for career advancement.

Let's say you've found a problem in a pre-competitive space and assembled the right multi-disciplinary team to solve it. It sounds like you're good to go. In fact, you're not. Why? Because there's no method to your madness. Research by Anita Williams Wooley and her colleagues establishes that a team needs a collaboration process to make optimal use of its repertoires.[54] Each process should be uniquely suited to the task at hand. Based on the Wooley team's research, general guidelines for diagnosing what caused something to happen, is causing something to happen, or will cause something to happen—including the past, present, or future causes of an undesired state[55]—are set forth below. As you read the guidelines, consider that the key benefits of following them are that they encourage explicit coordination rather than relying on unstructured discussions, they optimize expertise utilization by ensuring members are focused on the most relevant aspects of the task, and they result in improved information integration, which significantly enhances performance.

1. *Understand the problem and sources of evidence:* Review the problem (undesired state) and where to look for possible causes of the problem (evidence).
2. *Assess the team members' expertise:* Team members explain their expertise to each other.
3. *Assign roles and responsibilities:* Based on everyone's expertise, decide who should analyze which type of evidence.
4. *Develop a strategy for evidence integration:* Discuss how the team will combine their findings from the different evidence sources to reach a final conclusion. This step is crucial because effective information integration is a mediator of improved analytic performance.
5. *Structure the analysis approach:* Identify and resolve the most reliable pieces of evidence first and use those reliable data points to constrain and focus follow-up searches.
6. *Plan for decision-making and final consensus:* Establish how the team will synthesize their individual analyses into a coherent solution, discuss

potential conflicts in interpretations and how they will be resolved, and discuss how the team will weigh evidence appropriately rather than relying on dominant voices in the group.

7. *Plan time and execution:* Establish the total amount of time that is available to complete the task and how much of it will be allocated to each subtask.

Here's how ChatGPT describes the application of the guidelines to a hypothetical business problem:[56]

Prompt

Describe a hypothetical business situation in which managers must determine what will happen based on various scattered and incomplete pieces of evidence, and they use the foregoing seven steps to make the determination

ChatGPT's Response

EcomNova, a mid-sized e-commerce company specializing in sustainable fashion, notices an unexpected and significant drop in online sales over the past month. The senior management team must determine the cause using scattered and incomplete evidence and follow a structured seven-step analytical process to develop a solution.

Step 1: Understand the problem and sources of evidence

The executive team first identifies key components of the problem and potential sources of evidence, including:

- Website Analytics: Drop in traffic, higher bounce rates, or checkout abandonment?
- Customer Feedback & Support Data: Complaints about pricing, website issues, or product quality?
- Competitor Analysis: Have competitors launched aggressive promotions or new product lines?
- Marketing Performance: Changes in ad effectiveness, social media engagement, or email open rates?
- Economic Factors: Is there a broader economic downturn affecting consumer spending?

- Supply Chain Issues: Were any products out of stock or delayed?
- Technical Issues: Any website bugs, slow loading times, or security concerns?

Since the problem is complex, the team gathers initial reports but acknowledges that no single data point provides the full picture.

Step 2: Assess the team members' expertise

Each team member clarifies their expertise:

- Data Analyst (Website & Sales Analytics)—Evaluates web traffic, conversion rates, and checkout issues.
- Marketing Director (Ad & Social Performance)—Reviews ad spending, engagement, and effectiveness.
- Customer Service Manager (Customer Complaints & Feedback)—Identifies customer dissatisfaction trends.
- Competitor Analyst (Market Intelligence)—Monitors competitor strategies and industry trends.
- Operations Manager (Supply Chain & Logistics)—Checks inventory availability and shipping delays.
- IT Specialist (Website Performance & Security)—Investigates potential site issues or cyber threats.

Each expert explains how their domain might contribute to diagnosing the problem.

Step 3: Assign roles and responsibilities

To efficiently analyze evidence, roles are assigned:

- Data Analyst—Extracts sales data and conversion rates, identifies patterns.
- Marketing Director—Analyzes ad campaign metrics, social media activity, and email marketing.
- Customer Service Manager—Categorizes complaints and identifies recurring issues.
- Competitor Analyst—Researches industry news, price changes, and competitor promotions.
- Operations Manager—Investigates inventory issues and fulfillment delays.
- IT Specialist—Conducts a site audit for technical issues or cyber threats.

By distributing responsibilities, the team ensures that each aspect of the problem is thoroughly investigated.

Step 4: Develop a strategy for evidence integration

Before jumping to conclusions, the team agrees on an integration strategy:

- Compare cross-domain insights: Does website traffic decline align with customer complaints?
- Identify correlations: Are customers abandoning carts due to slow website speeds or price sensitivity?
- Prioritize severity: Focus on factors that could have the most impact on sales.
- Use multiple perspectives: Encourage team members to challenge each other's assumptions to avoid cognitive bias.

This ensures that isolated data points aren't misinterpreted but instead contribute to a comprehensive analysis.

Step 5: Structure the analysis approach

The team prioritizes analyzing the most reliable evidence first:

1. Website Analytics & Checkout Data (Most immediate and quantifiable)
2. Customer Feedback & Complaints (Direct customer perspective)
3. Marketing & Competitor Intelligence (External factors)
4. Supply Chain & IT Investigations (Operational issues)

The findings guide follow-up investigations:

- If checkout abandonment is high, IT and UX teams dig deeper into website performance.
- If customers mention high prices, marketing checks if competitors are undercutting them.
- If traffic drops without a clear reason, the team re-examines ad visibility and SEO trends.

Step 6: Plan for decision-making and final consensus

The team establishes decision-making rules:

- Evidence Weighting: Website analytics and customer complaints are given priority over anecdotal insights.
- Resolving Conflicts: If interpretations differ, data trends will guide the final decision.

- Avoiding Dominant Voices: No single department (e.g., marketing) can dictate the conclusion without corroborating evidence.
- Final Consensus Approach: Each expert presents findings, and the team collaboratively builds a cause-effect model to determine the most likely explanation.

Step 7: Plan time and execution

The team sets a timeline to reach a resolution:

- Day 1–2: Data collection and preliminary individual analysis.
- Day 3: Cross-team discussions and integration of findings.
- Day 4: Hypothesis formulation and root cause identification.
- Day 5: Decision-making and action plan formulation.

They ensure enough time is allocated to deep dives into complex data without delaying corrective actions.

Outcome:

After integrating findings, the team determines that two key factors contributed to the sales drop:

1. Website Performance Issues—The IT Specialist found that a recent update caused longer checkout times, leading to increased cart abandonment.
2. Competitive Underpricing—The Competitor Analyst revealed that rival brands launched aggressive discounts, making Ecom-Nova's prices seem uncompetitive.

Solution & Action Plan:

- IT Fix: Urgent website performance optimizations are scheduled.
- Marketing Response: A targeted promotional campaign and limited-time discounts are launched.
- Customer Communication: A proactive email outreach campaign addresses concerns and incentivizes returning customers.

Conclusion:

By following this structured seven-step approach, the management team efficiently synthesized scattered evidence and developed a data-driven response to their sales decline. The method helped them avoid premature conclusions, consider multiple angles, and reach a rational and effective business decision.

In this second example the guidelines are applied to a social problem:[57]

Prompt

Describe a hypothetical situation in which a multi-disciplinary team must determine the causes of a social problem based on various scattered and incomplete pieces of evidence, and they use the foregoing seven steps to make the determination.

ChatGPT's Response

A mid-sized urban community, Riverdale, has experienced a 30% increase in youth crime over the past year, including vandalism, petty theft, and gang activity. The Mayor's Task Force on Youth Crime assembles a multi-disciplinary team to determine the root causes based on scattered and incomplete evidence and develop targeted interventions.

Step 1: Understand the problem and sources of evidence

The team begins by reviewing the nature of the problem and identifying potential evidence sources:

Key Problem Areas & Evidence Sources

1. Law Enforcement Data: Crime reports, arrest records, and hot-spot mapping.
2. School & Education Data: Truancy rates, dropout trends, disciplinary actions.
3. Economic Conditions: Unemployment rates, income disparities, housing insecurity.
4. Community & Social Factors: Family stability, gang influence, recreational opportunities.
5. Youth Perspectives: Interviews and surveys with at-risk youth.
6. Healthcare & Mental Health Reports: Substance abuse trends, trauma exposure.
7. Social Media Analysis: Online behaviors, peer influence, and gang recruitment tactics.

Each evidence source is partial and incomplete, meaning no single factor fully explains the problem. The team must synthesize fragmented data into a coherent understanding.

Step 2: Assess the team members' expertise

The multi-disciplinary team consists of experts with diverse backgrounds:

- Criminologist—Examines crime patterns, risk factors, and criminal networks.
- Sociologist—Studies social structures, peer influence, and family dynamics.
- School Administrator—Provides insights on school-related behavioral trends.
- Social Worker—Assesses individual and family risk factors.
- Economist—Evaluates poverty, unemployment, and economic stressors.
- Psychologist—Investigates trauma, mental health, and substance abuse.
- Community Organizer—Represents local voices and grassroots organizations.
- Data Analyst—Integrates quantitative crime and socioeconomic data.

Each expert explains how their discipline contributes to solving the problem, helping the team understand where their perspectives overlap or diverge.

Step 3: Assign roles and responsibilities

The team divides investigative tasks based on expertise:

- Criminologist & Data Analyst → Analyze crime reports and geographical hotspots.
- School Administrator & Sociologist → Examine school records and student behavioral trends.
- Social Worker & Psychologist → Conduct interviews with affected families and youth.
- Economist & Community Organizer → Investigate economic stressors and community resources.

By assigning clear roles, the team ensures efficient information gathering while avoiding duplication.

Step 4: Develop a strategy for evidence integration

Since no single data source is definitive, the team discusses how to integrate findings effectively:

- Identify patterns across disciplines (e.g., Does high truancy correlate with crime hotspots?).
- Use triangulation (i.e., cross-referencing police data, school reports, and social worker interviews).
- Prioritize causation over correlation (e.g., Is unemployment driving youth crime, or is crime making job access harder?).
- Use qualitative and quantitative evidence together to avoid biases from relying on only numbers or only personal accounts.

The team agrees on a framework for integrating insights, preventing disciplinary silos from distorting conclusions.

Step 5: Structure the analysis approach

To narrow down the root causes, the team starts with the most reliable evidence:

1. Crime & School Data (Quantifiable trends—reliable starting point).
2. Economic Indicators (Background conditions affecting crime rates).
3. Youth & Family Interviews (Firsthand experiences explaining motivations).
4. Social Media & Peer Influence (Emerging patterns in recruitment & coordination).

By analyzing objective data first, the team avoids premature bias and ensures that subjective interviews are interpreted in context.

Step 6: Plan for decision-making and final consensus

To avoid conflicts in interpretation, the team establishes rules:

- Weighing evidence appropriately:
  - Hard data (crime reports, economic trends) is primary.
  - Self-reported interviews provide context but must be validated.

- Preventing dominant voices from overshadowing others:
  - Each expert presents findings without immediate counterarguments.
- Resolving conflicting interpretations:
  - If perspectives differ, the team re-examines original data rather than relying on assumptions.

  A final synthesis meeting is scheduled, where the team will merge findings into a coherent model of the causes behind youth crime in Riverdale.

Step 7: Plan time and execution

The team allocates time efficiently:

- Week 1: Data collection (crime stats, school records, economic trends).
- Week 2: Community engagement (interviews, focus groups, surveys).
- Week 3: Evidence integration & analysis.
- Week 4: Consensus-building and report finalization.

The structured timeline prevents delays and ensures that all perspectives are included before drawing conclusions.

Final Findings:

After integrating scattered and incomplete evidence, the team uncovers three primary causes:

1. Disrupted Social Structures
   - A significant rise in single-parent households and family instability correlates with delinquency rates.
   - Many at-risk youth lack adult supervision after school, making them vulnerable to gang influence.
2. Economic and Educational Disparities
   - Areas with higher unemployment and poverty rates see higher youth crime.

- A funding gap in schools has led to reduced extracurricular programs, leaving fewer positive outlets for youth.

3. Social Media & Gang Recruitment
   - Interviews reveal that many youth offenders were recruited via social media.
   - Gang-affiliated challenges and viral trends incentivize criminal behavior.

Proposed Solutions & Next Steps:

1. Family & Community Support Programs
   - Expand mentorship initiatives to pair at-risk youth with role models.
   - Create family counseling programs to improve home stability.
2. Economic & Educational Interventions
   - Advocate for job training programs targeting youth in high-crime areas.
   - Secure funding for after-school programs and community centers.
3. Digital Monitoring & Outreach
   - Partner with tech companies to monitor gang-related online activity.
   - Launch counter-narrative campaigns to discourage youth from engaging in crime.

Conclusion:

By systematically analyzing incomplete evidence, the multi-disciplinary team moved beyond simplistic explanations (e.g., "It's just bad parenting" or "It's just poverty") and developed a nuanced understanding of the interwoven causes of youth crime. This structured approach not only identified the root causes but also informed actionable solutions that balance social, economic, psychological, and community-based interventions. By integrating evidence across disciplines, the team ensures that policy decisions will be based on reality rather than assumptions.

Another useful resource for creating a collaboration process is the Network for Transdisciplinary Research (td-net) toolbox created by the Swiss Academies of Arts and Sciences. You can find it on the *SCNAT knowledge* website.[58] The toolbox contains methods and tools "intended to help shape collaboration between experts and stakeholders from science and practice in systematic and traceable ways." An example is the *give-and-take matrix* in which each sub-project of a multi-project effort identifies the information it could give to each of the other sub-projects and the information it would like to take from each of them. For a link to the tool, see this end note.[59] A handy summary of the tools is provided by Sibylie Studer and Theres Paulsen in their article "Co-producing knowledge: Phases, issues, and the td-net toolbox."[60]

Both the Wooley team's approach and td-net's approach emphasize the crucial role that *evidence integration* plays in the process, which makes this an important concept to understand. Once again, I turned to ChatGPT for an explanation.[61] The following is what it had to say:

Prompt

Explain the different ways in which evidence can be integrated. In other words, the different ways to combine insights from different sources. Use the example of youth crime to illustrate each of the ways.

ChatGPT's Response

When dealing with scattered and incomplete evidence from different disciplines, various integration methods help synthesize information into a coherent understanding of a complex problem. Below are key approaches applied to youth crime investigation example.

1. Triangulation

Definition: Using multiple independent sources to confirm the same finding.

Purpose: Strengthens reliability by reducing bias from any single source.

Application to Youth Crime:

- Crime reports indicate a rise in youth gang activity.
- Social media analysis uncovers gang recruitment tactics.

- Youth interviews confirm that gangs target young people via online platforms.
- Integrated Outcome: The convergence of these independent sources confirms that social media plays a key role in gang recruitment.

2. Complementary Integration
Definition: Different sources provide different aspects of a problem, combining to form a more complete picture.
Purpose: Accounts for the multifaceted nature of social issues.
Application to Youth Crime:

- Economic data shows a rise in youth unemployment.
- Sociological research links job insecurity to gang affiliation.
- School records reveal increasing dropout rates, reducing career prospects.

Integrated Outcome: These insights together explain how economic instability, lack of education, and social pressures interact to drive youth crime.

3. Sequential Integration
Definition: One type of evidence guides the collection of further evidence.
Purpose: Ensures that investigation follows a logical flow rather than randomly gathering data.
Application to Youth Crime:

- Initial analysis of crime data pinpoints specific neighborhoods with increased gang-related crimes.
- This prompts sociologists to conduct targeted interviews in those areas.
- Interview results reveal that many youths perceive gangs as a form of protection.

Integrated Outcome: A stepwise approach prevents wasted effort and ensures evidence is collected in a focused and strategic way.

4. Weighted Integration
Definition: Some sources are given greater importance than others based on credibility, reliability, or scope.
Purpose: Prevents unreliable data from skewing conclusions.
Application to Youth Crime:

- Hard crime data (police reports) is given more weight than self-reported anecdotes due to its objectivity.

- Social media evidence is treated with caution due to potential misinformation.
- School attendance records are prioritized over youth self-assessments of their school struggles.

Integrated Outcome: Reliable sources anchor the analysis, while softer data provides context without overshadowing empirical findings.

5. Causal Mapping
Definition: Arranging evidence into a cause-and-effect chain to show relationships between different factors.
Purpose: Helps visualize how different variables interact over time.
Application to Youth Crime:

- Economic decline leads to higher youth unemployment →
- Higher youth unemployment leads to increased school dropout rates →
- Dropouts have fewer legal job opportunities →
- Gangs offer financial & social incentives →
- Gang recruitment increases, leading to more youth crime.

Integrated Outcome: A structured model showing that youth crime is not random but a product of systemic failures.

6. Contradiction Resolution
Definition: Reconciling conflicting findings to determine the most accurate interpretation.
Purpose: Ensures that contradictions are resolved rather than ignored.
Application to Youth Crime:

- Crime reports indicate rising youth crime rates.
- School records show declining truancy, which appears contradictory.
- Further investigation finds that youths are committing crimes after school, not during school hours.

Integrated Outcome: Rather than dismissing conflicting findings, the team identifies an overlooked factor, improving accuracy.

7. Thematic Integration
Definition: Organizing findings into broad themes to simplify complex relationships.
Purpose: Identifies key patterns across different evidence sources.
Application to Youth Crime:

Findings are grouped into three main themes:

1. Economic Disadvantage (poverty, job scarcity, school dropouts).
2. Social Influences (gang culture, peer pressure, online recruitment).
3. Family & Community Gaps (lack of supervision, few after-school programs).

Integrated Outcome: This thematic approach simplifies the complexity and helps policymakers design targeted interventions.

8. Bayesian Updating

Definition: Continually refining the conclusion as new evidence emerges.

Purpose: Helps adjust initial assumptions and incorporate new insights dynamically.

Application to Youth Crime:

1. Initial Hypothesis: The team suspects economic hardship is the biggest driver of youth crime.
2. New evidence from youth interviews suggests that lack of community programs plays an equally big role.
3. Updated Conclusion: The team revises its focus, balancing economic and social interventions.

Integrated Outcome: Instead of sticking to a fixed hypothesis, the team adapts conclusions as new data emerges, leading to a more accurate understanding.

Conclusion: A Holistic Approach to Evidence Integration

By using multiple integration methods, the team ensures a comprehensive and rigorous understanding of the youth crime problem.

- Triangulation confirms key findings.
- Complementary integration provides a multi-dimensional view.
- Sequential analysis structures the investigation.
- Weighted integration prevents bias.
- Causal mapping clarifies relationships.
- Contradiction resolution resolves inconsistencies.
- Thematic organization simplifies complexity.
- Bayesian updating allows for flexible refinements.

By effectively integrating evidence, the team moves beyond simplistic explanations and develops data-driven solutions that address the root causes of youth crime in a meaningful and actionable way.

Another part of the collaboration process is for the group to agree on how decisions will be made. Imagine a vertical line on which the different ways of making decisions are placed. At the top of the line is the most democratic means of decision-making, *group voting*, in which each person has an equal vote and the majority makes the decision. At the bottom of the line is the least democratic way of deciding, *consultative decision-making*, where the leader makes the decision after consulting the group members. Between the two poles are the following alternatives listed from most to least democratic:

- *Group Voting*: Each person has an equal vote, and the majority determines the decision. This is the furthest from leader-driven decision-making.
- *Consensus Decision-Making*: The group must reach agreement or at least ensure that no one strongly opposes the decision. (I don't like it, but I can live with it.)
- *Consent-Based Decision-Making (Sociocracy)*: Instead of seeking full agreement, the group moves forward unless someone has a strong, justified objection. The leader's role is more of a facilitator than a final authority.
- *Weighted Voting or Preference Aggregation*: The group votes, but votes are weighted based on expertise or relevance, ensuring that those with the most knowledge or stake in the decision have greater influence. This is more participatory than delegation but still introduces hierarchy.
- *Deliberative Delegation*: The group deliberates but ultimately delegates the final decision to a designated individual (often the leader), blending collective discussion with hierarchical decision-making.
- *Delphi Method (Iterative Consultation)*: The leader facilitates a structured process of gathering and refining input, but the final decision may still rest with the leader or a designated authority.
- *Advisory Committee with Leader Ratification*: The leader retains ultimate authority but is strongly influenced by a specialized group's recommendations.
- *Consultative Decision-Making*: The leader makes the decision after consulting the group members.

Summary

The effectiveness of a problem-solving group depends not only on who is in the room but on how they think together. This chapter explained the power of cognitive diversity, the importance of structuring dialogue to maximize idea flow, and the behavioral dynamics that enhance and hinder collective intelligence. It also explained the need for a collaboration strategy, which is to say, a well-planned collaboration process. The next chapter dives deeper into the subject of processes.

Notes

1 Matthew Syed, *Rebel Ideas: The Power of Diverse Thinking* (London, UK: John Murray Publishers, 2019), 12, 14, 16.
2 Scott E. Page, *The Diversity Bonus: How Great Teams Pay Off in the Knowledge Economy* (Princeton, NJ: Princeton University Press, 2017), 2.
3 Cheri Winton Brodeur, "Finding the Gorilla: The Impact of Complexity and Diversity in Meeting Process," in Joseph A. Allen, Nale Lehmann-Willenbrock, and Steven G. Rogelberg (Eds.), *The Cambridge Handbook of Meeting Science* (New York, NY: Cambridge University Press, 2015), 504–532.
4 Scott E. Page, *The Diversity Bonus: How Great Teams Pay Off in the Knowledge Economy* (Princeton, NJ: Princeton University Press, 2017), 52–67. See also Scott E. Page, *The Difference: How the Power of Diversity Creates Better Groups, Firms, Schools, and Societies* (Princeton, NJ: Princeton University Press, 2007); Scott E. Page, *Diversity and Complexity* (Princeton, NJ: Princeton University Press, 2011).
5 Quote Investigator, "Point of View Is Worth 80 IQ Points," May 29, 2018, https://quoteinvestigator.com/2018/05/29/pov/
6 Quote Investigator, "Point of View Is Worth 80 IQ Points," May 29, 2018, https://quoteinvestigator.com/2018/05/29/pov/
7 OpenAI, Response to "Do the following step by step. First, read the foregoing text on cognitive repertoires. Then, list the types of professions that might have cognitive repertoires that would make fruitful contributions to finding ways to improve mental health support for teenagers in a community and describe how each profession's repertoires would make a contribution." *ChatGPT-4o*, 2025.
8 OpenAI, Response to "Generate an example of an abstract description of a problem that would help professionals from different disciplines understand the nature of the problem." *ChatGPT-4o*, 2025.
9 Deborah Ancona and Henrik Bresman, *X-Teams: How to Build Teams That Lead, Innovate, and Succeed* (Boston, MA: Harvard Business School Press, 2007), 6–7.
10 Deborah Dougherty, "Interpretive Barriers to Successful Product Innovation in Large Firms," *Organization Science*, May 1992, 3(2), 179–202. https://www.jstor.org/stable/2635258?origin=JSTOR-pdf
11 Alex Pentland, *Social Physics: How Social Networks Can Make Us Smarter* (New York, NY: Penguin Books, 2014–2015), 98.
12 Paul B. Paulus and Bernard A. Nijstad (Eds.), *Group Creativity: Innovation Through Collaboration* (Oxford, UK: Oxford University Press, 2003), chapters 3, 6–8.
13 Amy Edmundson, *The Fearless Organization: Creating Psychological Safety in the Workplace for Learning, Innovation, and Growth* (Hoboken, NJ: John Wiley & Sons, 2019), 8.
14 Amy Edmundson, *The Fearless Organization: Creating Psychological Safety in the Workplace for Learning, Innovation, and Growth* (Hoboken, NJ: John Wiley & Sons, 2019), 40–41. See also Charles Duhigg, "What Google Learned from Its Quest to Build the Perfect Team," *New York Times Magazine*, February 15, 2016, and articles on Google's Website, https://rework.withgoogle.com/en/
15 Anita Williams Wooley, Christopher F. Chabris, Alex Pentland, Nada Hashmi, and Thomas W. Malone, "Evidence for a Collective Intelligence Factor in the Performance of Human Groups," *Science*, October 29, 2010, 330(6004), 686–688.

16 National Academies of Sciences, Engineering, and Medicine, *New Directions in Assessing Performance Potential of Individuals and Groups: Workshop Summary* (Washington, DC: The National Academies Press, 2013), https://doi.org/10.17226/18427
17 Thomas W. Malone, *Superminds: The Surprising Power of People and Computers Thinking Together* (New York, NY: Little, Brown and Company, 2018), 34.
18 Geoff Mulgan, *Big Mind: How Collective Intelligence Can Change Our World* (Princeton, NJ: Princeton University Press, 2018), 132.
19 Alex Pentland, *Social Physics: How Social Networks Can Make Us Smarter* (New York, NY: Penguin Books, 2014–2015), 88.
20 Alex Pentland, *Social Physics: How Social Networks Can Make Us Smarter* (New York, NY: Penguin Books, 2014–2015), 89.
21 Alan H. Palmer, *Talk Lean: Shorter Meetings. Quicker Results. Better Relations* (North Mankato, MN: Capstone, 2013).
22 Alan H. Palmer, *Talk Lean: Shorter Meetings. Quicker Results. Better Relations* (North Mankato, MN: Capstone, 2013), x.
23 Nicolas Fay, Simon Garrod, and Jean Carletta, "Group Discussion as Interactive Dialogue or as Serial Monologue: The Influence of Group Size," *Psychological Science*, 2000, 11(6), https://doi.org/10.1111/1467-9280.00292
24 George David Kieffer, *The Strategy of Meetings: How to Make Your Next Business Meeting a Win for Your Company and Your Career* (New York, NY: Simon & Schuster, 1988), 75.
25 Stan Harris, "How to Manage Cognitive Depletion and Make Better Decisions during Stressful Times," *Auburn University Website*, March 30, 2020, https://harbert.auburn.edu/news/associate-dean-gives-tips-to-make-better-decisions-during-stress.html
26 Annie Murphy Paul, *The Extended Mind: The Power of Thinking Outside the Brain* (New York, NY: Houghton Mifflin Harcourt, 2021), 233.
27 Thomas Chamoro-Premuzic, "How to Become a Better Listener, According to Science," *Fast Company*, May 6, 2022, https://www.fastcompany.com/90749446/how-to-become-a-better-listener-according-to-science?partner=feedburner&utm_source=feedburner&utm_medium=feed&utm_campaign=feedburner+fastcompany&utm_content=feedburner&cid=eem524%3A524%3As00%3A05%2F06%2F2022_fc&utm_source=newsletter&utm_medium=Compass&utm_campaign=eem524%3A524%3As00%3A05%2F06%2F2022_fc
28 OpenAI, Response to "First read the foregoing text. Then use what you learn from the text to tell me all the ways that generative AI can assist a small problem-solving team do a better job of speaking and listening to each other." *ChatGPT-4o*, 2025.
29 OpenAI, Response to "Evaluate your answer. How realistic are your suggestions considering the current capabilities of AI systems?" *ChatGPT-4o*, 2025.
30 Byrons Hahser, *Learning to Read the Signs: Reclaiming Pragmatism for the Practice of Sustainable Management* (New York, NY: Routledge, 2013).
31 Byrons Hahser, *Learning to Read the Signs: Reclaiming Pragmatism for the Practice of Sustainable Management* (New York, NY: Routledge, 2013), 68–69.
32 Kate Littleton and Neil Mercer, *Interthinking: Putting Talk to Work* (New York, NY: Routledge, 2013).
33 The classic example of groupthink is the decision by John F. Kennedy (JFK) and his advisors to support an invasion of the Bay of Pigs in Cuba that went disastrously wrong. Kennedy later asked himself, "How could I have been so stupid

to let them go ahead?", which led to JFK's brother, Robert Kennedy, playing the role of "devil's advocate" in future decisions of consequence.

34 Annie Duke, as quoted in Jeff Gariliano, "Stop Trusting Your Gut," *Strategy + Business*, December 16, 2020, https://www.strategy-business.com/article/Stop-trusting-your-gut?utm_source=itw&utm_medium=itw20220630&utm_campaign=resp

35 Alfred Sloan, as quoted in Joseph A. Allen, Nale Lehmann-Willenbrock, and Steven G. Rogelberg (Eds.), *The Cambridge Handbook of Meeting Science* (New York, NY: Cambridge University Press, 2015), 575.

36 Francis Crick, as quoted in Michael Schrage, *No More Teams! Mastering the Dynamics of Creative Collaboration* (New York, NY: Currency-Doubleday, 1989), 35.

37 American Film Market Website, https://americanfilmmarket.com

38 Adrian J. Slywotzky and Karl Weber, *Demand: Creating What People Love Before They Know They Want It* (New York, NY: Crown Business, 2011), 285.

39 Ed Catmull and Amy Wallace, *Creativity, Inc.: Overcoming the Unseen Forces That Stand in the Way of True Inspiration* (New York, NY: Random House, 2014), 86–87.

40 Ray Dalio, *Principles* (New York, NY: Avid Reader Press, 2017), 322–337.

41 Fred Dust, *Making Conversation: Seven Essential Elements of Meaningful Communication* (New York, NY: HarperCollins Publishers, 2020), 166.

42 Adam Connor and Aaron Irizarry, *Discussing Design: Improving Communication & Collaboration Through Critique* (Sebastopol, CA: O'Reilly, 2015), 33.

43 OpenAI, Response to "What are ways AI can contribute to maintaining a meta-cognitive awareness of the type of talk in which the group is engaged—disputational, cumulative, and exploratory—and suggesting appropriate shifts among the three types of talk?" *ChatGPT-4o*, 2025.

44 Fred Dust, *Making Conversation: Seven Essential Elements of Meaningful Communication* (New York, NY: HarperCollins Publishers, 2020), 137.

45 OpenAI, Response to "Generate ten innovative and effective ways to gently interrupt a person who is talking too long." *ChatGPT-4o*, 2025.

46 This also applies to multi-functional, multi-company, multi-industry, and multi-national strategies.

47 Katelin Kennedy, Ceejay Girard, and Seth Olson, "Best Practices to Harness the Power of Pre-Competitive Collaboration for Sustainable Supply Chains," *Resonance*, March 1, 2022, https://www.resonanceglobal.com/blog/best-practices-to-harness-the-power-of-pre-competitive-collaboration-for-sustainable-supply-chains

48 Kyle Zimmer, "Nonprofit Collaboration: Finding Common Ground to Accelerate Social Sector Progress," *Forbes*, April 13, 2023, https://www.forbes.com/councils/forbesnonprofitcouncil/2023/04/13/nonprofit-collaboration-finding-common-ground-to-accelerate-social-sector-progress/

49 National Human Genome Research Institute, "The Human Genome Project," https://www.genome.gov/human-genome-project?utm_source=chatgpt.com

50 OpenAI, Response to "What is a good process for identifying an opportunity for a pre-competitive space?" *ChatGPT-4o*, 2025.

51 OpenAI, Response to "Consider the following situation. A small group of people is organizing a problem-solving effort. The problem is complex and therefore requires a multi-disciplinary team to solve it. But because the problem is so complex, it's hard to know all the disciplines that will be required to solve

it. The organizers intend to use generative AI to help them identify the needed disciplines. What is the best way for them to do so?" *ChatGPT-4o*, 2025.

52 Timothy Collins, Maureen Kearney, and David Maddison, "The Ideas Lab Concept, Assembling the Tree of Life, and AVAToL," *PLoS Currents*, March 7, 2013, https://doi.org/10.1371/currents.tol.0fdb85e1619f313a2a5a2ec3d7a8df9e

53 OpenAI, Response to "As you consider what you know about the process variously referred to as a 'Sandbox' or 'Ideas Lab,' how should the prospective members of a multi-disciplinary team be evaluated to assess how well they will work with others." *ChatGPT-4o*, 2025.

54 Anita Williams Wooley, Margaret E. Gerbasi, Christopher F. Chabris, Stephen M. Kosslyn, and J. Richard Hackman, "Bringing in the Experts: How Team Composition and Collaborative Planning Jointly Shape Analytic Effectiveness," *Small Group Research*, June 2008, 39(3), 352–371.

55 See again the definition of a problem given in the previous chapter.

56 OpenAI, Response to "Describe a hypothetical business situation in which managers must determine what will happen based on various scattered and incomplete pieces of evidence, and they use the foregoing seven steps to make the determination." *ChatGPT-4o*, 2025.

57 OpenAI, Response to "Describe a hypothetical situation in which a multi-disciplinary team must determine the causes of a social problem based on various scattered and incomplete pieces of evidence, and they use the foregoing seven steps to make the determination." *ChatGPT-4o*, 2025.

58 SCNAT Knowledge Website, "Methods and Tools for Co-Producing Knowledge," *td-net Toolbox*, https://scienzenaturali.ch/co-producing-knowledge-explained/methods/td-net_toolbox/about_td_net_toolbox

59 For details, see https://zenodo.org/records/4627136#.YHfnzGhCTBI.

60 Sibylie Studer and Theres Paulsen, "Co-Producing Knowledge: Phases, Issues, and the td-net Toolbox," *Integration and Implementation Insights Blog*, October 10, 2023, https://i2insights.org/2023/10/10/co-producing-knowledge-td-net-toolbox/

61 OpenAI, Response to "Explain the different ways in which evidence can be integrated. In other words, the different ways to combine insights from different sources. Use the example of youth crime to illustrate each of the ways." *ChatGPT-4o*, 2025.

Chapter 3

Processes

Group Methods, Problem-Solving Methods, and AI

In the previous chapter, I explained that a team's collective intelligence is the product of cognitive diversity, effective communication, and a strategy for working together. But there's more to the equation than that. Teams are also made smarter by processes that guide and stimulate their thinking. In this chapter we'll examine four kinds of processes—meeting, group, problem-solving, and task-specific processes. As you read through them, remember that the different kinds of processes can and should be combined. The meeting process should specify group processes that implement the problem-solving process that includes task-specific processes.

Meeting Processes

The first thing you need to do when planning a meeting is to get clear on the *objective(s)* and *desired outcome(s)* for the meeting. There are all kinds of possible meeting objectives (e.g., sharing information, coordinating schedules), but because the focus of this book is problem-solving, I'm limiting this discussion to the objectives that relate to it. Depending on the complexity of the problem, the objective of the meeting will be to complete one or more of the elements of the problem-solving process listed below (see also Figure 3.6). The desired outcome for each objective might be as simple as specifying the desired number of ideas to be generated for the objective(s) or as complex as a document that details what's been identified, generated, selected, detailed, or planned.

- Identify and clarify the undesired effect or state.
- Identify the cause(s) of the undesired effect or state.
- Generate alternative ways of acting on the cause(s).
- For each cause, select one of the ways as best.
- Detail the nature of the solution (i.e., the transformed causes).
- Plan the implementation of the solution.

DOI: 10.4324/9781003654407-4

The next step in planning a meeting is to establish the *activities* that will be used to accomplish the objective(s) and desired outcome(s). The activities will consist of a combination of group, problem-solving, and task-specific processes. For example, the group might use breakout groups (a group process) to generate alternative ways of acting on a cause (part of the problem-solving process) by using analogical thinking (a task-specific process).

The objectives, desired outcomes, and activities are used to create the *agenda*.[1] A sample agenda is shown in Figure 3.1. I suggest that the meeting start no sooner than 9:00 am and that it end no later than 4:00 pm. This gives the participants time to travel to and from the meeting, respond to emails, make phone calls, and so on. And it acknowledges the fact that a person's energy level declines over the course of the day to the point where they are worn out by 4:00 pm. Fred Dust goes so far as to insist that instead of scheduling one all-day meeting, his clients agree to several shorter meetings that end at 2:00 pm.[2] For the same reason (energy management), you should schedule a 15-minute break every 90 minutes, a 45- to 60-minute lunch, and the most energy-demanding activities, such as brainstorming, in the morning. Studies on the default mode network (DMN) indicate that periods of rest and relaxation promote creative insights.[3] The DMN is a network of interconnected brain regions that becomes active when the brain is at rest and not engaged in goal-directed tasks. It engages in the sort of subconscious mind-wandering that contributes to creative problem-solving. You can find a more elaborate description of the DMN in my book *Differentiation Strategy: Winning Customers by Being Different*.[4]

For several reasons, I keep the doors to the meeting room locked until 8:50 am. The first reason is that it makes it difficult to set up the room when people drift in early, place their things on the table, and ask me questions. The second reason is that it makes a poor first impression for participants to find that the room is only partially set up and that I'm too busy to talk to them. The third reason is that it gives the participants the opportunity to mingle and engage in small talk before entering the meeting room. Research by the psychology professor Joseph Allen and his colleagues found that pre-meeting small talk is a significant predictor of meeting effectiveness.[5] They propose that the talk increases meeting effectiveness by setting the tone for the actual meeting, by enabling the participants to settle in, and by enabling them to gather information about others' intentions for the meeting or opinions concerning specific meeting topics. When the meeting participants don't know one another, rather than leave it to them to introduce themselves to each other, assign one or more of the meeting organizers to play "party host" and catalyze the conversations.

Good Works Company
Strategy Workshop Agenda
Date

Objective: Create a strategy for responding to our most important challenges
Desired Outcome: A workshop report that outlines the strategy

Activities

8:00 AM	**Registration and breakfast buffet** • Pick up your name badges, enjoy the breakfast buffet, and mingle with your fellow workshop participants.
8:50 AM	**Doors to the workshop open** • Look for your tent card to find your seat.
9:00 AM	**Introduction** • Ms. CEO welcomes everyone. • Mr. Facilitator explains the agenda. • Electronic brainstorming practice question.
9:30 AM	**What are our most significant external challenges?** • Brainstorm the external threats and opportunities (challenges) we need to respond to. • Discuss which ones are most important for us to respond to in the next 12–18 months and why. • Vote to select the three most important challenges.
10:30 AM	**Break**
10:45 AM	**What are all the things that make it difficult for us to respond to the challenges?** • Brainstorm the things that make it difficult for us to respond to each challenge. • Discuss why each thing makes it difficult.
11:45 PM	**Lunch**
12:45 PM	**What are all the ways of responding to this challenge?** • Form three breakout groups. • Each breakout group is assigned one of the challenges. • Each breakout group brainstorms ways of responding to the challenge and chooses one as best. • Make sure to use analogical thinking. • Create a general (vs. detailed) action plan for the chosen way of responding.
2:15 PM	**Break**
2:30 PM	**What are all the ways this way of responding to the challenge can be improved?** • The plenary group reconvenes. • Each breakout group presents their way of responding to the challenge. • The other two breakout groups suggest ways it can be improved. • The improvements are incorporated in each response.
4: 00 PM	**Adjourn**

Figure 3.1 A sample meeting agenda showing the meeting objective, desired outcome, and activities.

Note that the activities on the sample agenda are phrased as questions. Phrasing the activities as questions has several benefits:

- *It improves clarity and focus*: Questions define the purpose of each activity more clearly and prevent vague discussions by specifying what needs to be done. For example, it's better to say, "What specific negative effects are we experiencing?" than "Identify the undesired effect." This question focuses discussion on observable effects rather than vague descriptions, and it promotes a shared understanding of the effect.
- *It encourages engagement and participation*: Questions invite active contributions rather than passive listening. They also encourage the participants to think critically and to start thinking of responses in advance of the meeting. Rather than say "Discuss the causes of the undesired effect," say something like, "What are all the things that are causing this effect to exist and how do they interact?" This phrasing encourages deeper exploration of the issue.
- *It drives decision-making and action*: Questions naturally lead to answers, which then lead to decisions and action items. It's better to ask, "What are all the things we can do to eliminate or mitigate the causes?" than "Brainstorm solutions."
- *It encourages efficient use of time*: Questions set a clear endpoint for each discussion item. Once a question is answered, the group is psychologically prepared to move on. This minimizes unnecessary tangents and keeps the meeting on track. Instead of "Next Steps," ask "What are the top three priorities we need to focus on before the next meeting?"

Note that I began two of the foregoing questions with the phrase "What are all the ways . . ." rather than the usual "How can we . . ." way of starting the questions. Asking "What are all the ways . . ." implicitly implies the existence of multiple answers, whereas asking "How can we . . ." subtly suggests there is only one answer. Another way to encourage people to think more expansively is to ask them to think far into the future. According to *construal level theory*, the further something is in the future, the more abstractly the brain processes it.[6] This abstraction stimulates big-picture thinking and makes it easier to generate novel, non-obvious ideas. Future-oriented thinking also encourages people to view problems within a larger system, leading to more innovative and interconnected solutions.[7] I asked ChatGPT for other ways to phrase questions to stimulate people to think more expansively.[8] This is what it had to say:

Prompt

What are all the ways questions can be phrased or preceded in order to get people to break free of constraints and limitations?

ChatGPT's Response

1. *Use "What If?" Questions*
    - "What if?" questions challenge assumptions and open doors to radical possibilities.
    - They shift the focus from current limitations to explorative thinking.
    - Examples:
        - *What if we had unlimited resources to solve this problem?*
        - *What if this problem didn't exist—what would we be focusing on instead?*
        - *What if we had to solve this challenge in 24 hours?*
2. *Reframe Questions to Shift Perspectives*
    - Changing the point of reference can unlock new insights.
    - Encourages looking at the problem from a different angle.
    - Examples:
        - *Instead of "How can we improve customer service?" → "If we were our customers, what would we want changed the most?"*
        - *Instead of "How do we increase efficiency?" → "What are we doing now that's holding us back?"*
        - *Instead of "How do we improve our product?" → "If a startup were trying to disrupt us, what would they do differently?"*
3. *Introduce Artificial Constraints to Force Creativity*
    - Paradoxically, imposing new (but artificial) constraints can help break out of existing ones.
    - Encourages creative problem-solving by forcing adaptation.
    - Examples:
        - *If we had only $1,000 to launch this idea, how would we do it?*
        - *If we had to implement this with half our team, what would change?*
        - *If we could only solve this problem using technology from 50 years ago, what approach would we take?*

4. *Use Reverse Thinking*
    - Instead of solving the problem directly, flip the question to think about its opposite.
    - Encourages counterintuitive insights that might lead to new solutions.
    - Examples:
        - *How could we make this problem worse instead of better?*
        - *If we wanted to lose customers as quickly as possible, what would we do?*
        - *What would have to happen for this idea to fail completely?*
5. *Frame It as a Science Fiction or Fantasy Scenario*
    - Encourages thinking outside the bounds of reality and then working backward to practical solutions.
    - Examples:
        - *If we had magic powers to fix this, what would we do first?*
        - *If we lived in a world where time travel existed, how would that change our industry?*
        - *If aliens landed and wanted to solve this problem, what unconventional approach might they take?*
6. *Use Extreme or Exaggerated Cases*
    - Forces thinking beyond incremental improvements and into radical changes.
    - Examples:
        - *How would we solve this if we had infinite money?*
        - *If we had to 10x our results in one year, what would we change?*
        - *What if failure was not an option—what would we do differently?*
7. *Pretend You're Someone Else*
    - Encourages stepping into the mindset of different individuals or groups.
    - Examples:
        - *How would a 5-year-old solve this problem?*
        - *If Elon Musk/Leonardo da Vinci/a medieval monk were in charge of this, what would they do?*
        - *If we were designing this for an audience from another culture, what would we change?*

8. *Make It a Game or Challenge*
    - Gamifying the question lowers inhibitions and encourages playfulness.
    - Examples:
        - *If this were a heist movie, how would we "steal" the best idea?*
        - *If this were a survival challenge, how would we hack our way to a solution?*
        - *Let's compete: Who can come up with the weirdest (but still somewhat plausible) idea?*
9. *Ask "What's the Bigger Question?"*
    - Sometimes the real constraint is the question itself—zooming out leads to a more powerful inquiry.
    - Examples:
        - *We're asking how to fix X . . . but is that the right problem to solve?*
        - *What's the bigger issue we're not addressing?*
        - *If we had to completely redefine this problem from scratch, what would we ask instead?*

Conclusion

By reframing, exaggerating, reversing, or shifting the way questions are asked, you can unlock deeper creativity and help people break free from existing mental constraints. Different techniques work better depending on the team, the problem, and the context—but all of them help move beyond the obvious into breakthrough thinking.

I next asked ChatGPT how to prompt it to generate useful questions for problem-solving.[9] Here is how it responded:

Prompt

Tell me what people should tell you to do to get you to generate useful questions. What prompts should they use?

ChatGPT's Response

To get high-quality, diverse, and thought-provoking questions, users should structure their prompts in ways that maximize creativity, depth, and specificity. Below is a guide on what to ask ChatGPT to get the best results.

1. Generate Open-Ended, Expansive Questions
Prompt:

> "Generate a list of open-ended questions that will help us explore [problem/topic] from multiple angles."
>
> This encourages broad thinking and prevents premature narrowing of ideas.

Example Use Case:

> "Generate a list of open-ended questions to explore why employee engagement is declining in our company."

2. Frame Questions to Imply Multiple Answers
Prompt:

> "Give me a list of 'What are all the ways . . .' questions to explore solutions for [problem/topic]."
>
> This expands idea generation by implying multiple solutions rather than a single answer.

Example Use Case:

> *What are all the ways we could improve customer retention in a subscription business?*

3. Reframe the Problem in Multiple Ways
Prompt:

> "Reframe the question '[original question]' in five different ways to encourage more creative answers."
>
> This helps avoid tunnel vision and find fresh perspectives.

Example Use Case:

Reframe the question 'How can we make meetings more productive?' in five different ways.

4. Use "What If?" to Challenge Assumptions
Prompt:

"Generate 'What if . . .?' questions that challenge assumptions about [problem/topic]."

This helps break mental constraints and open up innovative ideas.
Example Use Case:

"Generate 'What if . . .?' questions that challenge assumptions about how we do project management in a remote team."

5. Reverse the Question for Unexpected Insights
Prompt:

"Create reverse-thinking questions for [problem/topic] to help us see blind spots and hidden assumptions."

This helps uncover hidden weaknesses, counterproductive habits, and overlooked factors.
Example Use Case:

Create reverse-thinking questions for why customers might stop using our product.

6. Generate Analogical Thinking Questions
Prompt:

"Create questions that compare [problem/topic] to a completely different field or system (e.g., nature, sports, technology)."

This encourages cross-disciplinary insights and breakthrough thinking.
Example Use Case:

Create analogy-based questions to improve teamwork by comparing it to how an orchestra operates.

7. Generate Implementation-Focused Questions
Prompt:

"Generate practical 'How might we . . .?' questions that focus on actionable solutions for [problem/topic]."

This ensures that questions lead to tangible steps and strategies.
Example Use Case:

Generate practical 'How might we . . .?' questions to make remote work more engaging for employees.

8. Ask for Contradictions and Tensions in the Problem
Prompt:

"What are contradictory or paradoxical questions we should ask about [problem/topic]?"

This helps identify tensions that might lead to innovative resolutions.
Example Use Case:

What are contradictory or paradoxical questions we should ask about how we balance innovation with efficiency?

9. Use Future-Scenario Questions to Think Long-Term
Prompt:

"Generate future-oriented questions that help us imagine what [problem/topic] will look like in 10+ years."

This encourages long-term, transformative thinking.
Example Use Case:

Generate future-oriented questions to explore how education will evolve in 20 years.

10. Generate Questions Based on Cognitive Biases
Prompt:

"What are cognitive biases that might affect our thinking about [problem/topic], and what questions can we ask to counteract them?"

This helps prevent flawed reasoning and expand decision-making clarity.

Example Use Case:

What are cognitive biases that might affect our thinking about AI adoption in our company, and what questions can we ask to counteract them?

Final Takeaways: How to Prompt ChatGPT for the Best Questions

- Asking for multiple versions of the question encourages variety.
- Using expansive phrasing such as *What are all the ways . . .?* instead of *How can we . . .?* leads to more comprehensive exploration.
- Leveraging different thinking modes, such as "*What if . . .?*", "*Reverse the problem*", or "*Use analogies*", results in deeper insights.
- Targeting specific goals like discovery, innovation, or implementation ensures that questions remain relevant. Incorporating biases, tensions, and contradictions helps avoid shallow thinking and uncover hidden challenges.

The agenda should be sent to the meeting participants seven to ten days before the meeting. If you send it sooner than that, chances are it will be misplaced or forgotten, and if you send it later than that, the participants may not have time to read it. Along with the agenda, you should send the materials (e.g., reports, articles, videos) the participants need to review to prepare for the meeting. The agenda should also be given to each of the participants at the meeting itself.

If you're facilitating the meeting, your next step is to create a facilitator's guide. A partial example is provided in Figure 3.2. This is what you'll use to guide you through the details of implementing each agenda item. The guide should contain the following columns, from left to right: (1) time block, (2) person responsible, (3) topic and details of the process that will be used to answer the question, and (4) the materials needed to implement the process. Note that the guide should also specify the timing of the calendar invitation and the pre-meeting email in which you send the agenda and reading materials.

Good Works Company Workshop: Date

Time/Minutes	*Person*	*Topic*	*Details*	*Materials and Tools*
30 days prior	MO	Calendar invitation	• Send calendar invitation to the participants	• List of participants • Email addresses
7 days prior	KH	Meeting email	• Send meeting email with details about the meeting location, agenda, list of participants and reading materials	• List of participants • Mtg. detail information • Agenda • Reading materials
8:00–8:50 50"	MO	Registration and breakfast buffet	• MO gives participants their name badges • MO mixes with and introduces the participants to each other	• Breakfast buffet items • Name badges
8:50–9:00 10"	MO and KH	Entry & seating	• Doors to the meeting room open at 8:50 • MO and KH greet the participants as they enter • Participants are instructed to sit by their tent cards	• Tent cards • Agenda at each seat
9:00–9:15 15"	MO	Welcome & introduction	• MO welcomes and thanks group for participating • MO explains logistics (restrooms, snacks, stretch when you want) • MO explains the purpose of the meeting • MO introduces KH	• MO slide deck loaded on KH computer • Remote control
9:15–9:30 15"	KH	Meeting overview	• KH introduces self • KH explains the agenda • KH explains the behaviors that contribute to a successful meeting • KH explains electronic brainstorming technology (EB) and generative AI (AI) and leads the group through a practice question	• Slide deck loaded on KH computer • Remote control • Flipchart page with meeting behaviors listed
9:30–10:30 60"	KH	External challenges	• Group and AI brainstorm the external challenges • Group votes to select the top three challenges	• Elec, brainstorming tech • Generative AI tech
10:30–10:45 15"	All	Break	• Group breaks for 15"	• Beverages and snacks at back of room
10:45–11:45 60"	KH	Challenge difficulties	• Group and AI brainstorm the things that make it difficult to respond to the challenges • Group votes to select the top three challenges or opportunities	• Elec, brainstorming tech • Generative AI tech
11:45–12:45 60"	All	Lunch	• Group breaks for lunch	• Box lunches

Figure 3.2 A sample facilitator's guide setting forth the details of the meeting process.

There are more things for a meeting facilitator to consider than the series of activities that constitute the meeting process. Managing the conversation was addressed in Chapter 2, and the meeting room and tools will be addressed in Chapter 4. Addressing the rest of the issues (e.g., inviting the participants, establishing ground rules, opening and closing the meeting, meeting minutes) is beyond the scope of this book. Some useful resources are provided in this end note.[10]

One step up from creating the process for a single meeting is to create the process for a series of meetings. This involves planning the output (e.g., meeting minutes, data dashboards) that will serve as the input for the next meeting. In cases where some form of research is done between the meetings, the process should also include feeding the research results into the next meeting. As Geoff Mulgan points out, a good series of meetings on the same topic is visibly cumulative.[11]

Group Processes

A group process consists of the steps the group members take to interact with each other. An interaction occurs when two people exchange their thoughts during one or more conversations. Ideally, to take full advantage of a cognitively diverse group's cognitive repertoires and thereby maximize the group's collective intelligence, every member of the group should interact with every other member at least once. A handy equation for calculating the total number of interactions is: $(n \times (n-1))/2$, where n is the number of people in the group. For example, maximizing the collective intelligence of a 20-person group (or 19 humans and one artificial intelligence) would require $(20 \times (20-1))/2 = 190$ interactions.

That's a lot of interactions, or conversations, to have in a single day. What's more, considering that taking full advantage of the group's knowledge is likely to require two people to engage in multiple conversations with each other, the number of interactions can easily increase to thousands. Clearly, enabling everybody in a 20-person group to have the optimal number of conversations with each other (i.e., conversations in which they're able to exchange most of their cognitive repertoires pertaining to the focal topic) during a one- or two-day workshop ranges from extremely difficult to impossible. Most of the following group processes, while acknowledging that fact, work to get as close to the ideal as is realistically possible. For example, if the group members can't optimally interact, they can at least listen to what others have to say or vote on what they have to say. It's important to understand this idea, so I'm going to say it again. To take full advantage of a cognitively diverse group's cognitive repertoires and thereby maximize its collective intelligence, you need to employ group processes that enable the group members to "mine" each other's minds as much as is realistically possible.

Something else to note about the following processes is the way they increase the probability of asking Einstein's "right questions" and Nielsen's "ingenious questions," as described in Chapter 1 and as will be considered again in Chapter 4. This is especially true when generative AI is incorporated into the processes.

Traditional Brainstorming

The traditional brainstorming process is a structured group technique designed to generate a large number of ideas in a short period of time. It was popularized by advertising executive Alex Osborn in the 1940s. The process typically unfolds as follows:

Preparation Stage: A facilitator defines the problem or challenge to be addressed. Participants are briefed on the brainstorming rules and objectives. A comfortable, non-judgmental environment is established to encourage participation.

Idea Generation Stage: Participants freely verbalize ideas as they come to mind. The focus is on quantity over quality. The more ideas, the better. No criticism or judgment is allowed; all ideas are considered valid. Participants are encouraged to build on each other's ideas by refining, elaborating, or extending them. Wild and unconventional ideas are welcome, as they may spark novel solutions. The ideas are captured on a flipchart, on real or virtual sticky notes, in a word processing software, or using electronic brainstorming technology.

Idea Categorization Stage: The themes in the ideas are identified.[12] The ideas are categorized by theme.

Idea Addition, Expansion, and Combination Stage: Each theme is examined to determine if additional ideas can be added to it. The ideas are reviewed, refined, and in some cases, combined.

Evaluation and Selection Stage: After the brainstorming session, the group assesses ideas based on selected criteria, such as feasibility. Voting, ranking, or clustering methods may be used to prioritize the ideas. The best ideas are further developed into actionable strategies or solutions.

Despite its widespread use, traditional brainstorming has been criticized for the earlier-described process losses. This has led to refinements, like the nominal group technique, 1–2–4-All method, and brainwriting methods described below and the development of the electronic brainstorming technology described in Chapter 4.

I asked ChatGPT to describe a creative way to incorporate generative AI into the traditional brainstorming process.[13] It responded with the following:

Prompt

Describe a creative way to incorporate generative AI into the traditional brainstorming process as it is described in the foregoing text.

ChatGPT's Response

Generative AI can augment the traditional brainstorming process by mitigating process losses, enhancing creativity, and accelerating idea synthesis. Below is a structured integration of AI into each phase of brainstorming:

1. *Preparation Stage—Enhancing Problem Definition & Contextual Understanding*
    - AI-Powered Problem Framing & Prompt Engineering
        - Use AI to analyze past solutions, industry trends, and case studies related to the problem statement.
        - AI can generate alternative ways of framing the challenge (e.g., rewording the problem in different perspectives).
        - AI chatbots can engage participants in structured conversations to refine the problem definition.
    - Pre-Session Briefing Enhancement
        - AI-generated idea prompts or pre-brainstorming exercises can warm up participants' creativity.
        - AI can suggest relevant analogies, metaphors, or cross-industry inspirations related to the problem.
2. *Idea Generation Stage—AI as a Creativity Catalyst*
    - AI as a Non-Judgmental Idea Generator
        - AI can generate random, unexpected, or wild ideas that participants might not consider.
        - AI can provide opposite, extreme, or paradoxical solutions to challenge assumptions.
        - AI-driven reverse brainstorming: Generate bad ideas first, then AI helps flip them into good ones.

- AI-Augmented Ideation & Expansion
  - As participants verbalize ideas, AI can:
  - Suggest related ideas or conceptual extensions.
  - Reframe ideas in different industries or problem spaces.
  - Generate counterfactuals (e.g., "What if X didn't exist?").
- AI-Supported Real-Time Documentation & Visualization
  - AI can transcribe and summarize spoken ideas in real time.
  - AI-powered mind maps or concept graphs can dynamically visualize connections between ideas.

3. *Idea Categorization Stage—AI for Thematic Analysis*
   - AI-Assisted Clustering of Ideas
     - AI can use natural language processing (NLP) to detect patterns and group similar ideas.
     - AI-generated semantic maps can help visualize emerging themes.
   - Automated Sentiment & Feasibility Analysis
     - AI can analyze the sentiment of ideas (e.g., optimistic vs. skeptical).
     - AI can quickly assess feasibility based on historical data and predictive modeling.
4. *Idea Addition, Expansion & Combination Stage—AI for Synergy & Refinement*
   - AI-Supported Expansion & Combination of Ideas
     - AI can propose variations and extensions to existing themes.
     - AI can generate hybrid solutions by combining unrelated ideas (e.g., "How might we merge Idea A and Idea B?").
   - AI-Generated Role-Playing & Scenario Testing
     - AI can simulate how different stakeholders (e.g., customers, competitors) might react to an idea.
     - AI can generate "What if" scenarios for evaluating the potential impact of an idea.
5. *Evaluation & Selection Stage—AI for Prioritization & Decision-Making*
   - AI-Assisted Scoring & Ranking

- AI can use multi-criteria decision analysis (MCDA) to rank ideas based on feasibility, impact, and novelty.
- AI can simulate future trends to assess the long-term viability of certain ideas.

- AI-Powered Collaborative Voting & Justification

  - AI can facilitate anonymous voting while providing rationale-based scoring (e.g., "This idea ranks high because it aligns with market trends").
  - AI-generated pro-con lists for each idea can help decision-making.

- AI for Implementation Roadmaps

  - AI can suggest next steps, project plans, and potential challenges for top-selected ideas.
  - AI-generated risk assessments can highlight implementation barriers.

Beyond Traditional Brainstorming: Addressing Process Losses

Generative AI can eliminate key weaknesses of traditional brainstorming:

- Prevents Production Blocking—AI enables asynchronous ideation via AI-enhanced brainwriting or chatbot-facilitated discussions.
- Reduces Social Loafing—AI keeps track of individual contributions, ensuring everyone's ideas are considered.
- Mitigates Groupthink—AI can introduce contrarian perspectives and challenge group biases.
- Enhances Remote Collaboration—AI-powered brainstorming boards enable seamless virtual collaboration.

Conclusion: AI as a Brainstorming Augmenter, Not a Replacement

AI should complement human creativity, not replace it. It serves as a:

- Stimulus provider (offering novel perspectives).
- Pattern recognizer (helping with idea categorization).
- Synthesizer (combining ideas into new possibilities).
- Evaluator (ranking and assessing idea viability).
- By integrating AI into each phase, brainstorming becomes more dynamic, inclusive, and efficient, ensuring better ideas with less cognitive friction.

Nominal Group Technique

The nominal group technique (NGT) is a group process designed to maximize participation, minimize dominance by individuals, and overcome the previously described phenomenon known as *anchoring*, or *anchoring bias*. Again, anchoring occurs when the group members moor on the initial idea, opinion, or piece of information that is contributed (the "anchor"). The anchor limits the group's dialogue because subsequent contributions are subconsciously adjusted to align with, support, or contest the anchor rather than considering a broader range of possibilities, including the relevant parts of the group member's cognitive repertoires. The steps for implementing the NGT are these:

Step 1: Pose the Question: The group members are given the question they are to answer. For example: What are the key features we need in our next AI-powered collaboration tool?

Step 2: Silent Idea Generation: Each group member writes down their ideas individually without discussion. This prevents the participants from anchoring on each other's ideas.

Step 3: Round-Robin Sharing of Ideas: Each member takes turns sharing one idea at a time until everyone's ideas are voiced. The ideas are recorded on a whiteboard, flipchart, or digital tool for everyone to see.

Step 4: Discussion for Clarification: The facilitator leads a discussion in which participants can ask for clarifications, elaborate on unclear ideas, combine similar ideas, and possibly eliminate or modify ideas based on other's critiques. This ensures that all ideas are fully elaborated and understood before prioritization.

Step 5: Individual Ranking of Ideas: If the ideas are to be prioritized, the group members vote to rank or score the ideas based on importance, feasibility, or other relevant criteria. Alternative voting methods are described later in this chapter.

Step 6: Aggregation and Decision: The facilitator tallies the scores to determine the group's collective priorities. The highest-ranking ideas are selected for further discussion, decision-making, or action.

I asked ChatGPT to describe a creative way to incorporate generative AI into the nominal group technique.[14] Here is how it responded:

Prompt

Describe a creative way to incorporate generative AI into the Nominal Group Technique process.

ChatGPT's Response

Step 1: AI-Assisted Independent Idea Generation

How It Works:

- Participants submit their initial ideas anonymously into an AI-powered platform.
- The AI expands, refines, or prompts alternative perspectives for each participant.
- This encourages broader and more diverse ideas, preventing cognitive fixation or narrow framing.

AI Benefit: Overcomes cognitive inertia by suggesting variations, counterpoints, or unseen connections.

Example:

- Human: "Use blockchain for secure collaboration."
- AI Expands: "How might blockchain enhance privacy in AI-assisted teamwork?"
- AI Contrasts: "Would decentralized federated learning be a better approach?"

Step 2: AI-Moderated Round-Robin Idea Collection

How It Works:

- AI presents ideas in a randomized order to prevent primacy effects or social anchoring.
- AI clusters similar ideas, allowing for automatic categorization before human discussion.
- Participants see AI-generated summaries that highlight key themes.

AI Benefit: Minimizes bias by depersonalizing and restructuring idea presentation.

Example Output:

- *"AI has grouped 4 variations* of decentralized collaboration: blockchain, federated learning, hybrid models, and privacy-first architectures."

Step 3: AI-Enhanced Discussion and Clarification

How It Works:

- AI suggests questions to probe deeper into ideas based on linguistic analysis.
- AI provides contrasting viewpoints based on prior knowledge and external sources.
- AI visualizes interconnections between ideas using concept mapping tools.

AI Benefit: Encourages critical thinking and non-obvious linkages between ideas.

Example:

- AI: "This idea relates to previous discussions on digital sovereignty—should we consider policy implications?"
- AI: (Auto-generates a concept map showing how *'trustless systems' relate to 'scalability in AI governance'*.)

Step 4: AI-Assisted Voting & Ranking

How It Works:

- AI offers adaptive ranking criteria based on the group's goals (e.g., feasibility, impact, novelty).
- AI predicts potential biases in voting patterns (e.g., recency bias, popularity bias).
- AI suggests alternative ranking methods, such as pairwise comparisons or Bayesian scoring.

AI Benefit: Prevents heuristic bias, making rankings more balanced and informed.

Example:

- AI: "Your votes show recency bias—do you want to review early ideas before finalizing?"
- AI: (Auto-ranks based on a combination of *feasibility & innovation*, offering weighted results.)

Step 5: AI-Guided Consensus & Decision Support

How It Works:

- AI synthesizes top-ranked ideas into an executive summary with supporting arguments.
- AI generates future projections (e.g., impact scenarios, risk factors).
- AI provides actionable next steps using decision-tree modeling.

AI Benefit: Transforms group insights into structured, actionable knowledge.

Example Output:

- AI: "Based on ranked priorities, the top initiative is 'Privacy-first AI collaboration tools'. Here are projected benefits and implementation challenges."
- AI: (Auto-generates a strategic roadmap with milestones.)

1-2-4-All Method

The 1–2–4-All method builds on the nominal group technique.[15] In a 20-person group, the group would be divided into five four-person groups. Groups larger than 20 people require more four-person groups. There are four steps to the process. The suggested timing of each step is optional.

1. *Individual Reflection (1 minute)*: Each person considers the question alone and jots down their ideas or thoughts.
2. *Pair Discussion (2 minutes)*: The group members pair up to share and refine their ideas.
3. *Group of Four Discussion (4 minutes)*: The pairs pair up to form groups of four to share and refine the ideas developed in the pair discussions.

4. *All (5 minutes or more)*: Each group of four shares one of their ideas with the rest of the 20-person group. The four-person groups can share additional ideas in round-robin style.

Note that this method aligns well with what is known as *Bayesian updating through dialogue*.[16] This refers to the process by which individuals or groups revise their beliefs based on new information. In essence, it models conversation as an iterative updating of prior beliefs in light of new evidence, leading to more refined, probabilistically informed perspectives.

I asked ChatGPT to describe useful ways that generative AI can be incorporated into the 1–2–4-All method.[17] It responded as follows:

Prompt

Describe useful ways that generative AI can be incorporated in the 1–2–4-All method.

ChatGPT's Response

1. *Individual Reflection—AI as a Cognitive Stimulus*
    - AI-Powered Thought Prompts:
        - AI can generate divergent thinking prompts to challenge assumptions and stimulate deeper individual reflection.
        - Example: Instead of a generic question, AI can reframe it dynamically—e.g., "What would this problem look like in a completely different industry?"
    - Personalized Knowledge Retrieval:
        - AI can summarize relevant information from past discussions, literature, or datasets to augment individual priors before they engage in dialogue.
    - Simulation of Opposing Views:
        - AI can present counterarguments or alternative perspectives, forcing individuals to preemptively refine their reasoning.
2. *Pair Discussion—AI as a Mediator & Amplifier*
    - AI-Powered Socratic Questioning:
        - AI can guide the pair conversation with adaptive questioning, nudging participants toward deeper insights.

- Example: "Your ideas seem to be focusing on efficiency—what about resilience? How might this work in an unstable environment?"

- Idea Comparison & Contradiction Spotting:
  - AI can compare inputs from both participants and highlight contradictions, missing assumptions, or potential synergies.
  - Example: If one person emphasizes automation while the other emphasizes human oversight, AI can suggest hybrid solutions.

- Instant Feedback & Summarization:
  - AI can summarize key insights from the conversation, ensuring efficient synthesis before moving to the group of four.

3. *Group of Four Discussion—AI as a Pattern Recognizer*
   - Real-Time Idea Clustering:
     - AI can analyze contributions from all pairs and automatically cluster overlapping themes.
     - This prevents redundancy and helps the group focus on emergent insights rather than rehashing the same points.
   - Generative Scenario Exploration:
     - AI can create simulated "what-if" scenarios based on the group's discussion, helping participants test their ideas dynamically.
     - Example: "If your proposed solution were implemented, AI models suggest these three potential consequences. Does this align with your expectations?"
   - Knowledge Expansion via External Context:
     - AI can pull in relevant case studies, analogies, or expert insights to broaden the discussion.

4. *(All) Whole-Group Sharing—AI as a Collective Intelligence Amplifier*
   - AI-Powered Synthesis & Visualization:
     - AI can automatically generate a structured summary of the group discussions, highlighting key insights, disagreements, and innovative ideas.

- Example Outputs:
    - A concept map connecting key discussion points.
    - A consensus vs. divergence heatmap.
    - A real-time AI-generated report for future reference.
- Sentiment & Perspective Analysis:
    - AI can analyze sentiment patterns to highlight areas of strong consensus or tension.
    - Example: "Most groups converged on X, but there's a significant divergence on Y. Do we need to explore this further?"
- AI-Augmented Decision-Making:
    - AI can suggest prioritized action items, ensuring that discussions translate into concrete outcomes.
    - Example: "Based on the group discussions, here are three possible next steps—vote on which to pursue."

Meta-Level Uses: AI as a Continuous Feedback & Learning System

- Longitudinal Learning & Iteration:
    - AI can track discussion evolution over multiple sessions, helping groups build cumulative knowledge rather than starting from scratch.
- Bias & Blind Spot Detection:
    - AI can analyze linguistic and conceptual patterns to flag cognitive biases and groupthink risks.
- Adaptive Facilitation Assistance:
    - AI can dynamically adjust the structure of 1–2–4-All based on group engagement levels and discussion flow.

Final Thought: AI as an Augmenter, Not a Replacement

AI should not replace human intuition, creativity, or deep discussion but should act as a catalyst for deeper engagement, faster synthesis, and more informed decision-making. The key is to balance AI augmentation with human judgment, ensuring that AI serves as an enhancer of collective intelligence rather than a deterministic decision-maker.

Brainwriting Method

Brainwriting is a structured idea-generation technique that enhances group creativity by having participants write down their ideas rather than speaking them aloud. This method reduces process losses resulting from production blocking and cognitive interference. One study found that brainwriting groups produce 20 percent more ideas and ideas that are 42 percent more original as compared to traditional brainstorming methods.[18] The steps in the brainwriting process are set forth below.

1. *Define the Problem or Topic*: Clearly state the problem, challenge, or opportunity that needs innovative solutions. Ensure that all participants understand the scope and constraints.
2. *Individual Idea Generation (Silent Phase)*: Each participant writes down a set number of ideas (e.g., three ideas per round) on a piece of paper, digital document, or a shared collaborative tool. No discussion occurs at this stage to prevent premature evaluation.
3. *Idea Exchange*: Participants pass their written ideas to another group member, either in sequence or randomly. The receiver reads the ideas and builds upon them by refining them or adding new thoughts.
4. *Iteration (Multiple Rounds)*: This cycle continues for a predetermined number of rounds, ensuring that diverse perspectives are integrated. Typically, three to five rounds are conducted to maximize idea evolution.
5. *Review and Consolidation*: After several rounds, the group reviews the accumulated ideas. Similar ideas are clustered, redundant ones are removed, and the most promising ideas are selected for further development.
6. *Discussion and Evaluation*: The participants now engage in open discussion to evaluate the selected ideas.

The foregoing method is referred to as a *rotational brainwriting* method. The optimal group size for rotational brainwriting typically falls between four and seven people. This size ensures a balance between idea diversity and manageability while preventing cognitive overload. One way to implement this in a 20-person group is to divide it into four five-person groups, have the groups conduct the rotational brainwriting, and then have each group report out to the whole group.

An alternative to rotational brainwriting is the *gallery brainwriting* method:

1. *Define the Problem or Topic*: Clearly state the problem, challenge, or opportunity that needs innovative solutions. Ensure all participants understand the scope and objectives.

2. *Initial Idea Generation (Individual Contribution)*: Each participant writes down one or more ideas on a large sheet of paper, a whiteboard, or a digital collaborative tool. Each idea is written on a separate sheet or virtual board section such that it is visible to others.
3. *Display of Ideas (Gallery Setup)*: The sheets, sticky notes, or digital posts are arranged in a way that enables the participants to easily walk around (physically or virtually) and view each contribution. This setup mimics an art gallery where each idea is treated as an exhibit.
4. *Idea Expansion and Iteration (Silent or Collaborative Review)*: Participants move around the "gallery" to review the displayed ideas. They annotate, comment, or expand upon existing ideas directly on the sheets, adding new insights, improvements, or alternative perspectives.
5. *Multiple Rounds of Refinement (Optional)*: The group might conduct multiple rounds in which ideas are further refined and expanded upon by different participants.
7. *Discussion and Prioritization*: After several rounds, the group reviews the accumulated ideas. Similar ideas are clustered, redundant ones are removed, and the most promising ideas are selected for further development.

I asked ChatGPT to describe how generative AI could be used to enhance rotational brainwriting.[19] Here is what it had to say.

Prompt

Describe how generative AI could be used to enhance the rotational brainwriting method described in the foregoing text.

ChatGPT's Response

1. *AI-Augmented Idea Generation*

- Enhancing Individual Contributions:
  - AI can suggest variations, refinements, or expansions of ideas participants write down, helping those who may struggle with idea generation.
  - AI can use semantic clustering to suggest related ideas, ensuring diversity while avoiding redundancy.
- Pre-Round AI Ideation Boost:
  - Before participants start, AI can generate a set of seed ideas based on previous successful solutions or domain knowledge to inspire creativity.

- Example: If working on a product innovation challenge, AI can generate trend-based or cross-industry analogies as inspiration.

2. *AI-Assisted Idea Rotation & Refinement*

   - Automated Summarization & Context Retention:
     - As ideas rotate, AI can provide concise summaries of previous contributions, reducing cognitive load.
     - Example: Instead of participants reading through long responses, AI generates bullet-point summaries highlighting key insights.
   - Personalized Idea Expansion Suggestions:
     - AI can tailor suggestions to different participants based on their prior contributions.
     - Example: If a participant leans toward technical solutions, AI might suggest feasibility improvements, whereas a more creative participant might get wild idea prompts.
   - Preventing Idea Stagnation:
     - If ideas start becoming repetitive, AI can detect patterns and prompt participants to explore alternative directions.
     - Example: "This idea focuses on cost-efficiency. How might we adapt it for sustainability?"

3. *AI-Powered Group Optimization*

   - Dynamic Round Structuring Based on Engagement Data:
     - AI can track engagement levels via digital platforms and suggest adjustments, such as:
       - Shortening/lengthening rounds based on contribution density.
       - Splitting ideas into thematic clusters for deeper exploration.
       - Identifying low-engagement areas and prompting specific participants to contribute.
   - Adaptive Grouping for Large Teams:
     - If there are 8+ participants, AI can automatically form subgroups based on complementary thinking styles or expertise.
     - Example: AI detects a cluster of engineering-focused ideas and groups participants who can enhance technical feasibility.

4. *AI-Driven Synthesis & Prioritization*

- Automated Thematic Clustering:
    - AI can analyze all ideas in real-time, grouping similar ones and surfacing emerging themes.
    - Example: Instead of manually clustering post-session, AI automatically organizes ideas into categories like "cost-saving," "user experience," and "new technology."
- Smart Ranking of Ideas:
    - AI can analyze which ideas receive the most engagement, refinement, or unique contributions and highlight the most promising ones.
    - Example: AI ranks top ideas based on a weighted score of uniqueness, feasibility, and engagement.
- AI-Generated Executive Summary:
    - At the end of the session, AI can produce a structured report summarizing key ideas, themes, and next steps.
    - Example: "The top three ideas are X, Y, and Z. Based on feasibility analysis, X is most viable. Suggested next steps: A/B testing."

5. *AI-Powered Digital Facilitation & Accessibility*

- Chatbot or Voice-Activated AI as a Facilitator:
    - AI can act as a virtual facilitator, guiding participants through rounds, keeping time, and offering gentle nudges (e.g., "Let's explore a more radical idea next!").
- Multimodal Idea Input (Voice, Sketch, Text):
    - AI can transcribe spoken ideas or convert rough sketches into structured text for digital whiteboards, making participation easier.
- Language Translation & Inclusivity:
    - AI-powered real-time translation allows global teams to contribute in their native language while ensuring seamless idea exchange.

Alternating Between the Plenary Group and Small Breakout Groups

Consistent with this book's focus on small groups, assume that the plenary group consists of 20 people and that there are four five-person breakout groups. As detailed in the following five steps, each of the breakout groups is assigned a different task to divide up the labor. The alternative is to assign the same task to all the breakout groups to obtain different perspectives on it. Regardless of which way of assigning tasks is used, after discussing their task, the breakout groups reform into the plenary group, where each breakout group presents its ideas and the members of the other three breakout groups comment on the ideas. See Figure 4.1 for a floor plan that supports this process.

1. Plenary Session (Initial Phase)
    - The full group meets to introduce the topic, frame the objectives, and provide necessary instructions or background information.
    - The facilitator may set guidelines, pose key questions, or outline the specific tasks to be addressed in the breakout groups.
2. Breakout Groups
    - The participants are divided into smaller groups.
    - Each group works independently, either focusing on the same issue as the other groups or focusing on a subset of the larger issue.
    - Roles may be assigned, such as a facilitator, scribe, and reporter.
    - The groups may be instructed to follow a structured group process (e.g., the nominal group technique) and a task process (e.g., use a decision matrix). If so, they should be given instructions and templates for implementing the methods.
3. Return to Plenary (First Integration)
    - The small groups reconvene as a full group.
    - Each breakout group shares its findings, proposals, or key discussion points.
    - The plenary group discusses patterns, integrates ideas, and refines the collective understanding by asking questions, expanding on the ideas, or identifying problems and opportunities.
    - The plenary group might vote to select one or more alternatives. (See the later section on voting for details.)
4. Iterative Rounds (Optional)
    - The cycle repeats, if necessary.
    - New breakout groups may be formed to refine ideas, address unresolved issues, or work on specific action plans.

- The process continues, alternating between small groups and the plenary until a solution, decision, strategy, or shared understanding is reached.

5. Final Plenary Session

   - The group synthesizes insights from all the breakout groups.
   - Consensus-building, action planning, or formal decision-making takes place.
   - Next steps, responsibilities, and follow-up actions are determined.

Note that in Step 3, one of the options is for the plenary group to vote to choose one or more of the ideas. This is a good time to recall the earlier discussion of *group judgment* and the idea that a group is more likely to choose the best idea because the individual errors in judgment tend to cancel each other out. It's best to have the plenary group do the voting because the more voters there are, the more effective will be the error canceling.

The breakout groups, on the other hand, are better able to engage in *group reasoning* because they are more appropriately sized for deliberation. A study by the conversation researcher Gus Cooney and his colleagues concludes that the optimal group size for effective deliberation is four to five people.[20] They explain that this size enables:

- *Balanced Participation*: Each member has sufficient airtime to contribute without the conversation becoming too fragmented.
- *Effective Turn-Taking*: Turn-taking is more manageable, reducing the likelihood of interruptions and ensuring smoother transitions between speakers.
- *Adequate Feedback*: Listeners can provide timely and relevant feedback, enhancing the quality of the discussion and supporting speakers during disclosures.
- *Minimized Social Risk*: The social risk of disclosure (evaluation apprehension) is lower compared to larger groups, making participants more willing to share personal or sensitive information.

Because the breakout groups will have focused on different aspects of the topic, a more complete picture of it will emerge during the plenary discussion as insights from the different breakout groups are addressed and synthesized. Consider, for example, how a team selecting a new software platform would benefit from the collective insights of technical staff (who evaluate system compatibility), finance staff (who assess cost), and end-users (who consider usability). No single individual has all this knowledge alone.

A plenary discussion also reduces bias and groupthink. The breakout groups may develop localized biases or get locked into a particular way of thinking. The plenary session provides a check and balance mechanism where ideas are challenged, refined, or reconsidered. A larger, more diverse group is more likely to spot logical inconsistencies, hidden assumptions, or oversights. For example, a breakout group may strongly favor an AI-driven solution for customer support, but reconsider their position when concerns about ethical risks and implementation are raised in the plenary discussion.

I asked ChatGPT to create a plenary and breakout group process that integrates generative AI.[21] It responded as follows:

Prompt

Describe how generative AI can enhance a process whereby there are breakout groups that return to the plenary and discuss the alternatives they have created, then jointly create a set of alternatives, and finally vote to select the best alternative.

ChatGPT's Response

1. Initial Breakout Group Discussions (Divergence Phase)
Objective: Each breakout group develops diverse alternatives, supported by AI for brainstorming and structuring ideas.
Actions (with AI Enhancements):

- AI-Assisted Problem Framing:
  - Before starting, AI generates a custom problem brief for each group, providing context, historical insights, and potential framing questions.
  - AI chatbots (e.g., GPT-powered assistants) answer real-time questions about industry trends or best practices.
- AI-Generated Brainstorming Prompts:
  - Each group receives AI-generated idea sparks based on the topic.
  - AI-powered tools like Miro AI or ChatGPT brainstorming assistants help groups diverge into multiple directions.
- AI-Assisted Structuring of Alternatives:
  - Once ideas are generated, AI categorizes alternatives into clusters (e.g., "high-risk/high-reward," "low-cost/quick implementation").
  - AI provides instant SWOT analysis on each alternative.

AI Output: Each group has at least one structured alternative, enriched by AI-powered insights and categorized for easy comparison.

2. Return to Plenary for Group Presentations (Convergence Phase, Round 1)

Objective: The plenary reviews, compares, and discusses alternatives using AI-assisted analysis.

Actions (with AI Enhancements):

- AI-Synthesized Group Summaries:
    - Each breakout group inputs their alternative into an AI system that generates one-page structured summaries (Problem, Solution, Benefits, Risks).
    - AI-powered transcription tools (e.g., Otter.ai, Whisper) record and summarize live presentations for later reference.
- AI-Generated Visualizations:
    - AI maps similarities and overlaps between group alternatives using concept clustering.
    - A shared AI-generated mind map visualizes the relationship between alternatives, making it easier to identify common themes.
- AI-Powered Q&A Support:
    - AI suggests critical discussion questions to challenge assumptions.
    - AI sentiment analysis highlights controversial points needing deeper discussion.

AI Output: The plenary has AI-driven insights, structured presentations, and visual maps, making it easier to synthesize the best ideas.

3. Refinement & Joint Alternative Creation (Convergence Phase, Round 2)

Objective: The plenary merges, refines, and synthesizes alternatives into a final AI-assisted decision set.

Actions (with AI Enhancements):

- AI-Facilitated Alternative Merging:
    - AI identifies redundant or overlapping alternatives and suggests potential combinations.
    - AI-powered writing tools generate combined alternative descriptions automatically.
- AI-Generated Feasibility Scoring:
    - AI provides scoring models for each refined alternative, analyzing feasibility based on historical data, industry benchmarks, and expert knowledge.

    - AI-powered risk analysis tools predict potential challenges and highlight trade-offs.

- Real-Time AI Discussion Assistance:

    - AI summarizes key points from the plenary discussion in real time, ensuring that the conversation remains focused.
    - AI sentiment analysis identifies emerging consensus or areas of disagreement needing resolution.

AI Output: The plenary now has a refined, AI-enhanced set of 3–5 alternatives, optimized for feasibility, risk, and impact.

4. AI-Driven Voting & Selection (Decision Phase)
Objective: The plenary votes on the best alternative using AI-powered decision support tools.
Actions (with AI Enhancements):

- AI-Generated Comparison Matrix:

    - AI creates a decision matrix that compares alternatives across feasibility, risk, impact, and innovation.
    - AI applies weighted scoring models to highlight top-ranked options based on objective factors.

- AI-Powered Voting System:

    - Anonymous, AI-assisted voting ensures fairness and prevents social pressure.
    - AI supports multiple voting methods:

        - Majority Voting (Simple selection of the most popular option).
        - Ranked Choice Voting (Each participant ranks options; AI tallies weighted results).
        - AI-Assisted Consensus Modeling (AI detects near-consensus and suggests refinements before finalizing).

- AI-Generated Decision Rationale Report:

    - AI instantly summarizes the reasoning behind the chosen alternative, ensuring documentation and buy-in.
    - AI visualizes how each voting method impacted the final decision, making the process transparent.

AI Output: The plenary selects the best alternative, backed by AI-driven insights, structured evaluations, and transparent voting results.

5. Final Wrap-Up & AI-Generated Action Plan
Objective: Ensure the selected alternative is ready for implementation.
Actions (with AI Enhancements):

- AI-Summarized Decision Report:
    - AI generates an automated final report, capturing key decisions, discussion points, and voting outcomes.
    - AI extracts actionable insights and generates a follow-up strategy.
- AI-Assigned Action Steps:
    - AI suggests who should lead implementation based on past contributions and expertise.
    - AI helps structure a timeline and accountability plan to ensure follow-through.
- AI-Facilitated Post-Decision Review:
    - AI schedules automated progress check-ins and sends reminders about action steps.
    - AI continuously monitors key metrics related to the decision's success.

AI Output: The plenary leaves with a documented decision, clear action steps, and AI-powered implementation tracking.

The composition of the breakout groups depends on the task at hand. The usual way of composing each group is to maximize its cognitive diversity by including members with different and complementary kinds of expertise, such as people from different departments (e.g., operations, design, finance, HR, manufacturing) or people who are trained in different disciplines (e.g., chemistry, physics, mathematics, biology, plastics engineering). As shown in Figure 3.3, a twist on this approach is to form research teams comprised of the same discipline. The research teams are responsible for conducting background research in their discipline prior to the workshop. Then, during the workshop, the research team members are assigned to different breakout teams.

Another technique is to change the composition of the breakout groups during each iteration of the process. For example, in the second breakout session, C1 moves to the breakout group to his right, C2 to the breakout

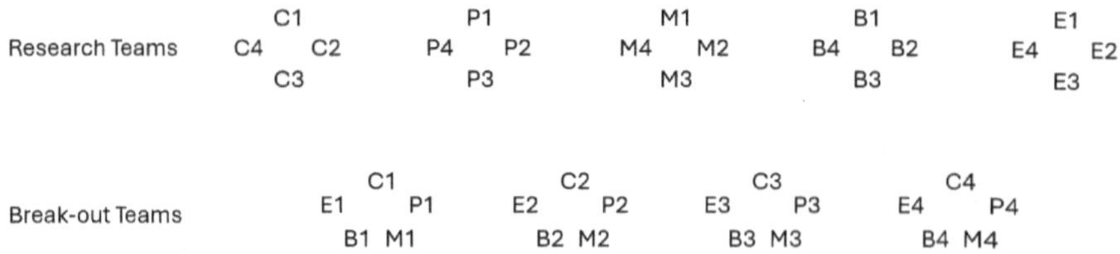

Figure 3.3 Teams comprised of chemists (C), physicists (P), mathematicians (M), biologists (B), and plastics engineers (E) first conduct background research. Then, the research team members are assigned to different breakout teams.

group to her right, C3 to the breakout group to his right, and C4 to the left-most breakout group. In this way, the new members pollinate their new groups with ideas from their old groups. A potential drawback of this approach is the time it takes to get the new member(s) up to speed on the existing members' deliberations.[22]

Team Syntegrity Method

The Team Syntegrity Method is a group process created by the mathematician and cybernetician Stafford Beer.[23] Beer employed the mathematics of the icosahedron to formulate a method in which as much as 96 percent of the relevant knowledge people possess on the focal topic is shared among them. Beer's full process, called a *syntegration*, involves 30 people meeting over a three- to five-day period. Modifications of the process enable it to be conducted with as few as 12 people over two days.[24] The books cited in the foregoing two end notes explain the process in detail. An overview of the method is this:

- *The Participants*: Because the method is designed to address complex problems, the participants are as cognitively diverse as possible. For example, the group might include people from the following corporate functions[25]:
    - Finance
    - IT
    - Expert
    - CXO
    - Service
    - Operations
    - Customer Care
    - Communications

Figure 3.4 Participants play the role of *member* in 2 of the 12 topic sessions, *critic* in another 2 of the 12 topic sessions, and *observer* in the remaining 8 topic sessions.

Source: David Holt Design

- Legal
- Market Research
- Sales
- Logistics
- Business Development
- Consultant
- Partner
- General Manager
- R&D

- *Identify the Topics*: The first steps involve proposing topics pertaining to the focal problem, then distilling them down to the 12 topics the group considers most important.
- *Topic Sessions*: Topic sessions are conducted two at a time. Three sessions are devoted to each of the 12 topics. There is a plenary session at the close of the process.
- *Topic Assignments*: A mathematical algorithm is used to assign the participants to the topic sessions. As shown in Figure 3.4, the participants play different roles in the sessions:
  - *Member*: In two of the 12 topics, they play the role of member. Members actively discuss the topic among themselves. The discussion is managed by a facilitator. In a 20-person group, there are five members in the member group. They sit at a table, facing the facilitator.
  - *Critic*: In another two of the 12 topics, they play the role of critic. Critics can contribute brief comments to the members' discussion

(e.g., something they know about the topic), but they cannot engage in interactive dialogues with the members. In a 20-person group, there are five members in the critic group. They sit in a row behind the member group.

- *Observer*: In the remaining 8 of the 12 topics, the participants play the role of observer. They can listen to the discussion but cannot contribute to it. Observers can choose which of the two simultaneous sessions they want to attend. If equally split, this would mean that there are five observers in each of the two topic sessions. They stand or sit behind the critic group.

In summary, *members* exchange knowledge with each other and jointly reason about it, they convey it to the critics and observers (who are listening to the discussion), and they take the knowledge to the sessions in which they are critics, where they may share some of it with the session's members and observers. *Critics* convey knowledge to the members, to each other, and to the observers, but they do not reason with anyone during the session. They also capture knowledge to take back to the sessions in which they are members. And *observers* capture knowledge from the members and the critics to take back to the sessions in which they are members or critics.

I asked ChatGPT to comment on how generative AI could be used to enhance the Team Syntegrity Method.[26] Here is how it responded. (Keep in mind, as previously described, not all of its suggestions are technologically feasible at this time.)

Prompt

How could generative AI be used to enhance the Team Syntegrity Method?"

ChatGPT's Response

1. Pre-Syntegration: AI-Augmented Preparation
Participant & Topic Selection

- AI-Driven Sentiment & Expertise Analysis
  - Use NLP (Natural Language Processing) to analyze participant backgrounds and past discussions to ensure diverse, relevant expertise in the group.
  - Identify potential biases or knowledge gaps that may affect discussions.

- AI-Assisted Thematic Clustering
  - Use generative AI to analyze participant inputs (pre-event surveys, interviews, or previous meeting data) and suggest emerging themes for discussion.
  - AI can recommend key topics based on real-time trends, domain knowledge, or organizational needs.

Simulating the Process in Virtual Environments

- Digital Twin of the Syntegration
  - AI-driven simulation can model different participant interactions in the icosahedral structure before the event.
  - This helps optimize seating arrangements and ensure evenly distributed expertise and diversity across topics.

2. Problem Jostle: AI for Dynamic Knowledge Synthesis
Real-Time AI-Assisted Facilitation

- AI suggests connections between topics based on concept clustering algorithms.
- Intelligent summarization tools extract key themes from conversations, preventing redundancy and enhancing topic convergence.
- AI-generated visualizations (knowledge graphs, mind maps) map idea evolution in real-time.
- AI-Powered Idea Validation & Clustering
- AI analyzes sentiment, relevance, and coherence of participants' Statements of Importance (SI) to refine key issues faster.
- AI-assisted semantic clustering identifies redundant, overlapping, or highly interconnected topics, reducing cognitive overload.
- Generative AI suggests alternative phrasings for ideas to ensure clarity and shared understanding.

3. Hexadic Reduction: AI for Efficient Prioritization
AI-Enhanced Voting & Prioritization

- AI detects patterns in participant votes, identifying latent connections between issues that may need integration.
- AI-generated decision trees simulate potential topic outcomes, helping participants visualize impact before selecting final topics.
- AI dynamically proposes alternative groupings for discussions based on inferred relationships between issues.

4. Outcome Resolve: AI-Augmented Discussion & Cross-Team Learning

AI-Generated Meeting Summaries & Knowledge Diffusion

- AI listens to conversations (via speech-to-text) and provides real-time summaries, allowing participants to:
  - Quickly catch up on discussions from parallel teams.
  - Identify key themes emerging across teams.
  - Flag contradictions or knowledge gaps that need addressing.
- AI-assisted multi-document summarization integrates insights across all 12 topics, ensuring information flows seamlessly across the icosahedral structure.
- AI-Powered Critique & Counterarguments
- AI can act as a "virtual critic", offering counterpoints based on:
  - External knowledge sources (e.g., academic papers, industry reports).
  - Contradictions between team discussions.
  - Historical insights from past Syntegrity sessions.

AI-Assisted Visualization & Emergent Knowledge Mapping

- AI creates dynamic knowledge graphs to track how ideas evolve across iterations.
- NLP-based clustering tools detect shifts in group consensus and visualize emerging themes, aiding adaptive learning.

5. Closing Plenary & Action Planning: AI-Driven Implementation

AI-Generated Action Plans & Commitments

- AI converts final Outcome Resolve statements into structured action plans with:
  - Milestones, KPIs, and responsible stakeholders.
  - Potential risks and mitigations based on past data.
- AI can suggest customized implementation strategies by integrating organizational constraints, resources, and goals.
- AI-Powered Reflexive Analysis & Future Forecasting
- AI models simulate the long-term impact of proposed decisions.
- AI provides feedback loops by tracking how past Syntegrity sessions translated into action, helping improve future iterations.

6. Hybrid & Virtual Syntegrity: AI for Scalability

AI-Powered Virtual Syntegration Platforms

- AI facilitates remote Syntegrity through:

- Virtual assistants guiding participants through structured discussions.
- Automated discussion synthesis across breakout rooms.
- AI-driven translation tools enabling multilingual participation.

Asynchronous AI-Enhanced Syntegrity

- AI enables asynchronous participation, allowing:
  - Stakeholders to contribute outside scheduled sessions.
  - AI to synthesize and integrate new insights into ongoing discussions.

Conclusion: AI as a Catalyst for Collective Intelligence

By integrating Generative AI into the Team Syntegrity method, we can:

- Enhance knowledge synthesis & cross-pollination of ideas.
- Reduce cognitive overload while preserving emergent intelligence.
- Improve the efficiency of decision-making without imposing hierarchy.
- Scale Syntegrity beyond physical constraints for global participation.

AI doesn't replace human collective intelligence—it amplifies and accelerates it. The future of Syntegrity + AI is a powerful augmented decision-making model, where self-organizing human teams collaborate dynamically with AI as an enabler, not a decision-maker.

Ideas Lab

While the Ideas Lab concept was conceived to foster cross-disciplinary innovation among scientists, I believe it is adaptable to nonprofits seeking solutions to social problems and companies looking for innovative ways to solve problems and identify new offerings. An Ideas Lab is a workshop in which a multi-disciplinary group of 20–30 scientists work to develop novel and potentially transformative approaches to a grand challenge.[27] The structured, five-day process brings together participants from diverse fields to tackle complex, large-scale problems that require pushing the boundaries of science to solve them. Unlike traditional research funding mechanisms, which require pre-formed teams and fully developed proposals, an Ideas Lab encourages the spontaneous formation of new research teams around novel ideas, which are refined through an iterative process that includes continuous feedback from peers, provocateurs, and mentors.

The Ideas Lab concept was first introduced by the National Science Foundation (NSF) in the United States. It was inspired by the "Sandpits" methodology created by the Engineering and Physical Sciences Research Council (EPSRC) in the United Kingdom. Both methods are intended to break down disciplinary silos and foster cross-disciplinary research. A key distinction, however, is that where Sandpits do not place an emphasis on immediate funding, Ideas Labs have a direct funding component, meaning selected projects can transition immediately into full-scale research. Another distinction is that Ideas Labs, unlike Sandpits, employ an iterative approach where, over the course of the five days, teams form, dissolve, and reconfigure multiple times until the most promising project ideas emerge.

There are multiple players in an Ideas Lab, each playing a critical role in the process:

- *Participants*: The 20–30 participants include researchers, technologists, and experts from various disciplines, selected based on their openness to collaboration and ability to think beyond traditional academic boundaries. They must be willing to work on new, high-risk research directions without being overly invested in pre-existing projects.
- *Mentors*: The mentors are three to five experts from diverse backgrounds who guide discussions, provide feedback, and evaluate emerging ideas. Their role is to challenge assumptions and ensure that the proposed research is transformative.
- *Facilitators*: The facilitation team consists of three to four professional meeting facilitators. They are responsible for keeping the discussions on track.
- *Organizational Psychologist*: An organizational psychologist provides insights into participant selection by identifying individuals who are likely to contribute productively to interdisciplinary collaboration.
- *Provocateurs*: There are several provocateurs. They are experts or thought leaders who introduce disruptive ideas and challenge conventional wisdom. Their role is to push participants out of their comfort zones and encourage bold thinking.
- *Funders*: The funders are representatives of interested funding agencies. They provide real-time feedback on ideas and ensure that the most promising projects receive support. Unlike traditional grant applications, funders play an active role throughout the Ideas Lab.

The Ideas Lab follows a structured process that unfolds before, during, and after the workshop:

- *Pre-event Preparation*: A private online networking platform enables participants to introduce themselves, discuss potential ideas, and start forming connections before the event. This ensures that the participants arrive having some familiarity with each other, which makes the initial brainstorming sessions more effective.

- *Day 1–2: Defining the Challenge and Exploring Ideas*: The facilitators lead exercises to define the problem space, encouraging creative and open-ended thinking. A knowledge map is created that captures all the major challenges and opportunities related to the research topic. Small breakout sessions enable the participants to brainstorm ideas, identify key obstacles, and propose possible solutions.
- *Day 3–4: Developing and Refining Ideas*: Teams begin to form around specific research challenges. The membership of the teams remains fluid, enabling participants to change groups based on evolving interests and expertise. Continuous feedback from the mentors and provocateurs helps to shape and refine the ideas. Teams pitch their preliminary ideas multiple times, receiving real-time feedback from peers, mentors, provocateurs and funders.
- *Day 5: Proposal Development and Selection*: Each team submits a short proposal outlining their research idea, methodology, and budget. Mentors evaluate the proposals and provide their final feedback to the funders. The most promising teams are invited to submit full proposals no later than two months after the Ideas Lab concludes. The proposals are evaluated for funding by NSF staff, with input from the mentors.

The Ludwig Boltzmann Gesellschaft (LBG), a German research funding organization, used two interesting methods in an Ideas Lab, one to identify the topic of the lab and the other to identify prospective participants.[28] To identify the topic, they launched the *Tell Us!* initiative, a crowdsourcing project in which they used a specially created online platform to solicit mental health research questions from patients, families, and healthcare professionals. More than 400 high-quality contributions were submitted from in excess of 80 countries. The submissions were analyzed, clustered, and rated by a jury of experts to identify the most pressing research needs. The primary research focus emerging from this effort was children of mentally ill parents, including questions on early intervention, digital health tools, environmental influences, and destigmatization.

LBG and its partner organization *winnovation* used pyramiding contacts to reach a cognitively diverse range of researchers. Pyramiding is a search process based on the idea that people with a strong interest in a topic or field know others who are more expert than themselves.[29] They identified 775 researchers, who were asked to share the call with colleagues, thereby acting as "multiplicators." They sorted the total set of researchers into three discipline zones—core, linked, and distant—based on their conceptual distances from the field of Mental Health of Children and Adolescents.

The four disciplines in the *core zone* were pediatric psychology, pediatric psychiatry, pediatric neuroscience, and child sociology. In the *linked zone*, the 11 disciplines included public health, nursing, nutrition, medical physics, immunology, and social work. And examples of the 12 disciplines in the *distant zone* were dance, theater, poetry, educational science, and system theory. Approximately one-third of the researchers in each of the three zones were invited to apply. A total of 127 applied, of which 30 were selected to participate in the Ideas Lab.

I asked ChatGPT how generative AI could be used to enhance the Ideas Lab process.[30] Here is its response:

Prompt

First read the foregoing text. Then describe the ways generative AI could be used to enhance the Ideas Lab process.

ChatGPT's Response

Generative AI could enhance the Ideas Lab process in several ways, spanning from participant selection and ideation to iterative development and proposal refinement. Below are key areas where AI could provide significant benefits:

1. *Enhancing Pre-Event Preparation*
   - AI-Enhanced Participant Selection: Generative AI can analyze candidate backgrounds, prior work, and interdisciplinary potential based on their published research, patents, and collaboration history. By leveraging natural language processing (NLP), AI could suggest a balanced mix of participants from diverse disciplines.
   - AI-Driven Networking & Icebreakers: An AI chatbot or virtual assistant could help participants engage before the event by suggesting potential collaborations based on shared interests, expertise, and knowledge gaps. AI could also summarize past work of participants and provide topic-relevant insights.
   - Automated Topic Refinement: Building on LBG's crowdsourcing method, AI could synthesize large volumes of public input (such as from surveys or social media discussions) into structured themes, identifying emerging research areas through topic modeling.

2. *Augmenting Idea Generation (Day 1–2)*

   - AI-Assisted Knowledge Mapping: Instead of manually building a knowledge map, AI could use semantic analysis to generate a dynamic visual knowledge graph that maps key challenges, research gaps, and potential solutions in real time.
   - Generative Brainstorming Support: AI could act as a "provocateur" by generating novel research questions or hypothetical scenarios based on interdisciplinary literature reviews, expanding participants' perspectives.
   - AI-Supported Breakout Sessions: AI models could generate customized discussion prompts, suggest related research papers, and provide real-time summaries of discussions for each breakout group.

3. *Strengthening Idea Refinement & Iteration (Day 3–4)*

   - Dynamic Team Formation Assistance: AI can recommend optimal team formations based on participants' evolving interests, expertise, and contributions. It could help ensure cognitive diversity by flagging potential echo chambers or disciplinary silos.
   - Real-Time Idea Evolution Tracking: AI could analyze discussion transcripts, extract key insights, and provide a summary of idea evolution, ensuring teams don't lose track of earlier breakthroughs.
   - AI as a Continuous Feedback Tool: AI-powered critique models can analyze pitches and proposals to highlight weak points, contradictions, and opportunities for strengthening arguments.

4. *Improving Proposal Development & Selection (Day 5)*

   - AI-Assisted Proposal Drafting: AI can generate structured proposal templates, suggest methodologies, and refine problem statements based on best practices from funded research.
   - Real-Time Proposal Evaluation: AI can compare emerging proposals against funding criteria, previously successful projects, and even real-time mentor feedback to predict funding potential and suggest improvements.
   - Ethical & Feasibility Analysis: AI can flag potential ethical concerns, suggest missing research dimensions (e.g., equity considerations), and help teams refine feasibility assessments.

5. *Post-Lab Knowledge Retention & Scaling*

- AI-Driven Knowledge Repository: AI can organize all workshop discussions, presentations, and proposals into a searchable knowledge base, providing ongoing access to insights generated in the Ideas Lab.
- Tracking Research Impact: AI can track the long-term impact of funded projects by monitoring citations, collaborations, and real-world applications of Ideas Lab-funded research.
- AI as a Collaboration Continuation Tool: AI-powered virtual co-working spaces could help teams stay engaged after the event, facilitating cross-institutional collaboration.

Conclusion

By integrating generative AI into the Ideas Lab process, the event could become more inclusive, dynamic, and iterative, ensuring that the best ideas emerge efficiently. AI would not replace human creativity but rather amplify the collective intelligence of participants, funders, and mentors.

Dialogue Decision Process

The Dialogue Decision Process—so called because it supports a decision-focused dialogue—was developed by General Motors in the 1980s.[31] In this process, diagrammed in Figure 3.5, a decision board (aka steering committee) interacts with a cross-functional project team (aka working group) in a series of workshops. Swimlane diagrams like the one in Figure 3.5 are a useful tool for planning the interactions of two or more groups. A third swim lane would be added to the bottom of the diagram if the project team planned to interact with others (e.g., various departments in the company or a customer focus group) to gather information.

Voting Processes

There are several ways for a group to vote to rank-order a set of alternatives. Each method has different strengths and is suited to different decision-making contexts. As you read through the following voting methods, bear in mind that if a voting method introduces bias, cognitive overload, or forced trade-offs, it distorts rather than enhances *group judgment*. (See again the discussion of group judgment in Chapter 2.) By selecting the optimal voting

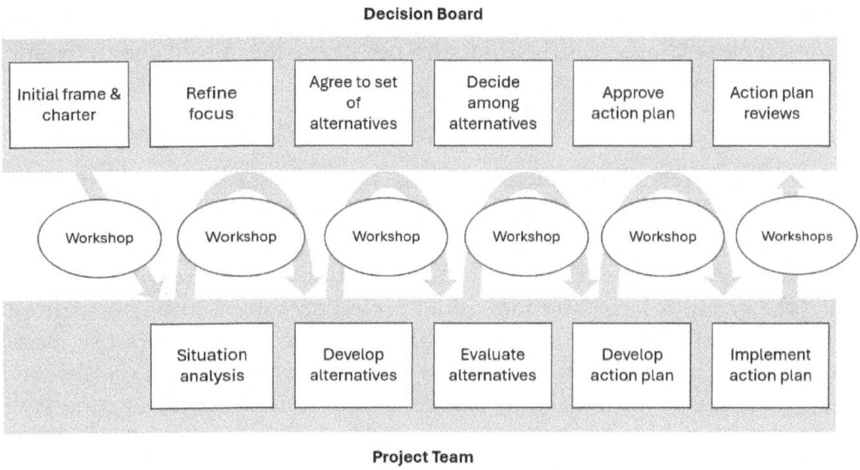

Figure 3.5 A two-lane swim lane diagram showing how the two teams interact during the Dialogue Decision Process.

method for the decision at hand, you preserve the benefit of aggregating the judgments of the group members. Also note that you will need a software app to implement the voting methods. Other than pairwise voting and influence allocation voting, the XLeap electronic brainstorming technology, which will be explained in Chapter 4, supports each type of voting.

Likert Rating Scale: When using Likert rating scales, each participant rates each alternative on a scale (e.g., 1–5, 1–7, 1–10), indicating their level of agreement with the alternative, preference for the alternative, or the perceived quality, performance, importance, or feasibility of the alternative.

- Odd-numbered Likert scales have the advantage of a neutral midpoint, so voters aren't pressured to lean positive or negative. The disadvantage is that some respondents may default to the "safe" middle option rather than making a genuine choice.
- Even-numbered Likert scales have the advantage of forcing respondents to lean positive or negative on the alternative. Because they identify a clearer direction, they are better when a decision or preference is needed. Their disadvantage is that some respondents may feel neutral but are forced to choose a side, which introduces noise in the results.
- Small 3- and 5-point scales impose less cognitive load on the respondents. They suffice when only broad categories are needed. Large 7- and 9-point scales enable respondents to express gradual intensity of preference. They are more statistically powerful because the fine-grained responses improve statistical analysis (e.g., mean, variance, correlations).

- An absolute zero in a Likert scale (e.g., 0–10) means that one response option clearly indicates the total absence of the measured characteristic. This enables a ratio-level measurement, which enables you to say, for example, "Option A is twice as important as Option B."

Scores are averaged or summed across voters to rank the alternatives. Likert ratings are best used when evaluating subjective qualities (e.g., satisfaction, importance, feasibility), when seeking to capture the intensity of preference for the alternatives rather than just rank ordering them, or when the group is large and individual preferences need to be normalized. Normalization helps account for differences in how the voters use rating scales—some may consistently give high scores, while others consistently give low scores. Normalization ensures that no single voter's rating style disproportionately influences the final results.

Allocating Points (Score Voting or Borda Count): In the allocating points method, the participants are given a fixed number of points to distribute among the alternatives based on their preference for each alternative. There are various ways to decide how many points are to be allocated.

- One way is to assign each voter 100 points no matter how many alternatives there are. This works best when using a percentage-based approach, such as using point allocation to distribute 100 percent of available budget dollars.
- Another way to decide how many points are to be allocated is to divide the number of alternatives by 3 and round up the answer. For example, if there are 15 alternatives, dividing by 3 would yield 5 points to allocate. This method forces voters to focus on their top choices because they cannot allocate points to every alternative, and it prevents them from spreading points too thinly across too many alternatives.

There are two ways for the voters to allocate points, unconstrained and constrained, which are explained in the following list:

- Unconstrained voting allows voters to allocate their points freely, as long as they do not exceed a specified total. There are no restrictions on how many points must be assigned to each alternative, meaning a voter could give all their points to one option or spread them evenly or unevenly across multiple options. Say, for example, a team is given 100 points to distribute among five potential product features to indicate the importance of each feature. One voter might choose to assign all 100 points to a single feature; another voter might split them across three features (e.g., 50, 30, 20); and another voter might allocate 20 points to each of the five features.

- Constrained voting imposes specific rules on how points must be distributed. The rules might require voters to give a minimum number of points to each alternative, allocate at least some points to every option, or distribute points in a fixed manner. Constraints ensure a baseline level of consideration for all alternatives and prevent voters from heavily skewing the results toward a single option. For example, using the same 100-point system, a constrained rule might require voters to allocate at least 10 points to each of the five product features. This ensures that every option receives some level of support and prevents extreme favoritism toward a single feature (like the foregoing voter who allocated 100 points to a single feature). Another possible constraint would be to mandate that no single alternative receives more than 50 points, forcing a more balanced distribution.

The sum of allocated points determines the ranking. It's best to use point allocation when prioritization is necessary, such as resource allocation or budgeting, when you want participants to indicate the relative importance of options, or when precise differentiation among alternatives is required.

Rank-Ordering (Ordinal Voting): In rank-ordering, each voter ranks all alternatives in order of preference (e.g., 1st, 2nd, 3rd). There are various ways to aggregate the rankings, including the Borda Count (assigning points based on rank position), the Condorcet Method (comparing each option pairwise—see below), and Instant Runoff (eliminating the least popular until a winner emerges). With the Borda Count, where N is the number of alternatives, the way to assign points to the alternatives is to give $N - 1$ points to the 1st-ranked alternative, $N - 2$ points to the 2nd-ranked alternative, and so on down to 0 points for the last-ranked alternative. The Borda Count rewards broad support rather than just majority preference. In other words, the top-ranked alternative wins not because it was ranked 1st by the most voters but because it consistently received high rankings across multiple voters.

Rank-ordering is best used when clear ordinal preferences are needed rather than intensity of preference, when a final ranking is needed but not precise scores, or when working with a relatively small number of alternatives. It's best not to use rank-ordering when there are more than ten options because ordering a large number is mentally exhausting. As a result, voters tend to rank the few they most prefer at the top, the few they least prefer at the bottom, then arbitrarily order of the rest of the alternatives.

Multiple Selection (Approval Voting): With this method, voters select any of the alternatives they approve of without ranking them. All approved alternatives receive one point per voter. The alternative with the most total approvals wins, or multiple top choices move forward. Multiple selection is best used when seeking a broad consensus on acceptable options, when there are many acceptable solutions and the group seeks to narrow down the list, or when simplicity is a priority.

An alternative is limited-selection voting where instead of allowing voters to select any number of choices, they can only pick up to a fixed number of choices (e.g., three choices). This forces prioritization while still allowing for multiple selections. Limited-selection voting is best used to prevent voters from choosing too many options indiscriminately, to encourage stronger preferences rather than broad approval, or to filter options before a ranked or head-to-head decision.

Another alternative is threshold voting, where instead of picking a single highest-scoring option, an alternative must reach a predefined approval threshold (e.g., 60 percent) to be considered. If multiple options meet the threshold, they proceed to the next round. This option avoids low-support winners (e.g., preventing a winner with just 25 percent support) and ensures broad consensus before advancing choices.

Multi-Criteria Voting (Weighted Criteria Voting): This is a decision-making method that enables voters to evaluate alternatives based on several criteria rather than just ranking or selecting a single winner. Instead of choosing one option outright, voters rate or score alternatives across different criteria that contribute to the overall decision. The rating can be done using a Likert scale, a percentage score, or a binary yes/no. Each criterion is assigned a predefined weight. A weighted sum is computed, where scores are multiplied by criterion weights. Multi-criteria voting is best used when decisions must balance multiple factors (e.g., importance and feasibility), when objective and subjective criteria must be combined, or where transparency in decision-making is crucial. For a comprehensive description of the different ways to implement this method and associated software, see the sources cited at this end note.[32]

Pairwise Rating (Pairwise Comparison or Tournament Voting): In the pairwise rating method, alternatives are compared two at a time and voters indicate which one they prefer. This means that each head-to-head matchup is treated as a binary outcome—either an alternative wins or loses against another. The ranking is determined using the Condorcet Method (alternative that wins the most pairwise matchups), Elo Rating (used in competitive ranking systems like chess), or Bradley-Terry Model (statistical modeling of comparisons). In the Condorcet Method, the winner of each matchup receives 1 point, and the loser receives 0 points; if there is a tie (equal number of votes for both options), each receives 0.5 points.

The number of pairwise comparisons that voters are required to make is calculated using the formula you encountered above: $(n \times (n-1))/2$. Consider that as few as 10 alternatives requires $(10 \times (10-1))/2 = 45$ comparisons, which is a burdensome number of comparisons to make. Thus, pairwise rating should only be used when the number of alternatives is small, when head-to-head comparisons are more intuitive than ranking all options at once, and when seeking to find the most broadly preferred option rather than a full ranking.

Influence Allocation Voting: Influence allocation processes are voting methods that allow the voters to distribute some or all of their decision-making influence to other voters. For example, in the point voting method, a voter would distribute some or all of their 100 points to one or more other voters. Influence allocation voting exploits both the group's knowledge of the alternatives and the group's knowledge of the relative expertise of each of the other voters (i.e., its knowledge of itself).[33] A voter may wish to give power to another who is more qualified to evaluate a particular topic, or to another who is more qualified to choose who is expert on the topic and will, presumably, pass the power on to the person. Two influence allocation methods are SPAN and RCON, though I know of no voting software that implements the methods.[34]

Ray Dalio employs a form of influence allocation voting he calls *believability weighting* for making major decisions at his hedge fund Bridgewater Associates.[35] As compared to autocratic decision-making and democratic decision-making, he says, "It is far better to weight the opinions of more capable decision makers more heavily than those of less capable decision makers."[36] At Bridgewater, they determine who is most capable of making a correct decision by keeping track of those who have previously made the most accurate decisions on the topic and by considering who can logically explain the cause-effect relationships behind their conclusions.

I asked ChatGPT to explain how generative AI can enhance group voting.[37] Following is its response:

Prompt

Read the foregoing text. Then explain ways generative AI can enhance group voting.

ChatGPT Response

Generative AI can enhance group voting by optimizing decision-making processes, improving accessibility, reducing bias, and increasing efficiency. Based on the previous discussion on AI's role in voting and the different voting methods described in the provided text, here are specific ways AI can augment group voting:

1. Optimizing the Selection of the Voting Method
Since different voting methods suit different decision contexts, AI can analyze the nature of the decision and recommend the most appropriate voting method.

How AI Helps:

- Dynamic Method Selection: AI can suggest the best method based on group size, the number of alternatives, and decision importance.
  - If the group has many alternatives, AI can recommend Likert scaling or multi-criteria voting instead of rank-ordering, which suffers from cognitive overload.
  - If a compromise solution is needed, AI might suggest Borda Count instead of a simple plurality vote.
  - If broad consensus is required, AI can suggest Approval Voting or Influence Allocation Voting.
- Predicting Voting Complexity: AI can simulate voting scenarios and estimate cognitive load on voters. If a proposed method is too demanding, AI can suggest an alternative.

2. *Enhancing the Voting Experience*
AI can improve usability, accessibility, and engagement in group voting.
How AI Helps:

- Smart Ballots: AI can adjust the interface dynamically based on voter behavior, highlighting relevant alternatives to prevent decision fatigue.
- Conversational Voting Assistants: AI-powered chatbots can answer questions about voting rules, methods, or criteria.
- Real-Time Error Prevention: AI can detect and alert voters if they:
  - Accidentally skip ranking an option in a rank-order vote.
  - Distribute more points than allowed in a point allocation system.
  - Make contradictory choices in pairwise voting.

3. *Reducing Bias & Improving Decision Integrity*
Generative AI can mitigate biases that distort collective intelligence by helping voters make more rational, unbiased choices.
How AI Helps:

- Identifying & Correcting Cognitive Biases:
  - AI can detect patterns of bias, such as recency bias (favoring recently seen alternatives) or status quo bias (favoring familiar choices).

    - AI can suggest randomized ballot orders to prevent positional bias (where alternatives listed first receive more attention).

- Preventing Strategic Voting:

    - In Borda Count, AI can detect if voters are exaggerating rankings to manipulate the outcome.
    - In Approval Voting, AI can detect if voters are selecting too many or too few options in a way that skews results.

- Ensuring Fair Influence Allocation:

    - In Influence Allocation Voting, AI can assess decision-maker credibility using historical data and help voters allocate their influence optimally.

4. Automating Vote Aggregation & Real-Time Analysis
Generative AI can automate complex vote calculations and provide instant insights into voting trends.
How AI Helps:

- Automatic Score Computation:

    - AI can instantly aggregate Likert-scale scores, Borda counts, and multi-criteria weighted sums, providing real-time rankings.
    - In pairwise voting, AI can build Condorcet matrices and identify cycles (e.g., when no clear winner exists).

- Live Feedback & Simulations:

    - AI can show real-time projections (e.g., "If five more voters select B, it will move ahead of A").
    - AI can simulate alternative outcomes (e.g., "If a different voting method were used, the ranking would change as follows . . .").

5. Improving Multi-Criteria Voting
Multi-criteria voting requires careful weighting of criteria, which can be difficult for voters. AI can simplify and refine this process.
How AI Helps:

- Auto-Suggesting Criteria Weights:

    - AI can analyze past decisions or stakeholder priorities to suggest rational weight distributions.

  - AI can simulate outcomes using different weight configurations, helping decision-makers adjust criteria dynamically.
- Adaptive Criterion Scaling:
  - AI can identify when a criterion is overly dominant and suggest rebalancing the weights.
  - If voters struggle with criteria definitions, AI can generate clear descriptions and example use cases.

6. Assisting Pairwise Comparisons
Pairwise voting can become burdensome when there are too many alternatives, as it requires many comparisons.
How AI Helps:

- Reducing Comparison Workload:
  - AI can pre-screen unlikely winners to reduce the number of required matchups.
  - AI can prioritize head-to-head comparisons that are most influential, reducing cognitive load.
- Predicting Voting Outcomes:
  - AI can forecast likely Condorcet winners before all comparisons are made, helping decision-makers focus on crucial matchups.
- Detecting Cycles & Resolving Ties:
  - AI can identify cycle issues (e.g., A > B, B > C, but C > A) and suggest alternative tie-breaking methods like the Schulze method.

7. Enhancing Group Consensus in Influence Allocation Voting
Influence Allocation Voting is complex because voters transfer their influence based on expertise. AI can help voters make informed delegation choices.
How AI Helps:

- Tracking Decision Accuracy:
  - AI can maintain a reputation system that tracks the accuracy of past decision-makers.
  - AI can recommend influence distribution based on historical correctness and expertise alignment.
- Explaining Delegation Choices:
  - AI can generate rationale explanations for why a voter might want to delegate influence to a particular person.

- Ensuring Fair Power Distribution:
  - AI can detect over-concentration of power and suggest redistribution strategies to maintain diversity in decision-making.

8. Integrating Generative AI for Post-Vote Insights
Once a vote is complete, AI can generate reports, predict satisfaction levels, and suggest next steps.
How AI Helps:

- Generating Decision Summaries:
  - AI can create narrative-style summaries explaining why a particular alternative won.
  - AI can highlight key voting trends, such as why certain alternatives performed better than expected.
- Predicting Voter Satisfaction:
  - AI can analyze voting patterns to predict which voters are likely to be dissatisfied.
  - AI can suggest follow-up actions (e.g., running a second vote, negotiating a hybrid solution).
- Enhancing Decision Implementation:
  - AI can suggest policy adjustments or budget allocations based on multi-criteria vote results.
  - AI can track real-world outcomes and recommend adjustments to future voting systems.

Conclusion

Generative AI can greatly enhance group voting by:

1. Optimizing the choice of voting methods based on decision context.
2. Improving usability and accessibility for voters.
3. Reducing cognitive bias and manipulation risks.
4. Automating complex vote aggregation and analysis.
5. Enhancing multi-criteria and pairwise voting methods.
6. Supporting more intelligent Influence Allocation Voting.
7. Providing real-time feedback and decision insights.
8. Predicting voter satisfaction and improving post-vote decision-making.

By integrating AI with collective intelligence, group voting can become more efficient, fair, and data-driven, ensuring that decisions reflect the true wisdom of the group rather than being distorted by bias, complexity, or strategic manipulation.

Problem-Solving Process

I defined a problem and overviewed the problem-solving process in Chapter 1, where I also included a figure, reproduced here as Figure 3.6. A step-by-step approach to the problem-solving process is this:

1. *Define the undesired effect/state*: Describe what is happening that you don't want to be happening or what is not happening that you do want to be happening. This is often referred to as framing the problem.
2. *Identify the cause(s) of the undesired state*: Identify the cause or causes of the undesired state. A cause can be something that exists or is occurring or something that does not exist or is not occurring. If you do not know what's causing the undesired state, you will have to hypothesize possible causes, then do some form of research to validate or invalidate each of your hypotheses.
3. *Determine how to act on the causes*: Determine the best way to act on each cause so as to transform it into a cause of the desired effect/state by first generating alternative actions (diverging), then voting to select one of them as the best (converging).
4. *Test the selected solution*: You never know for sure if a solution will work until you test it. The best way to test a solution is to create a "quick and dirty" prototype, test it, use what you learn to improve the prototype, test it again, and so on until you're certain your solution will work.

For a detailed description of the problem-solving process, see my book *Differentiation Strategy: Winning Customers by Being Different*, which

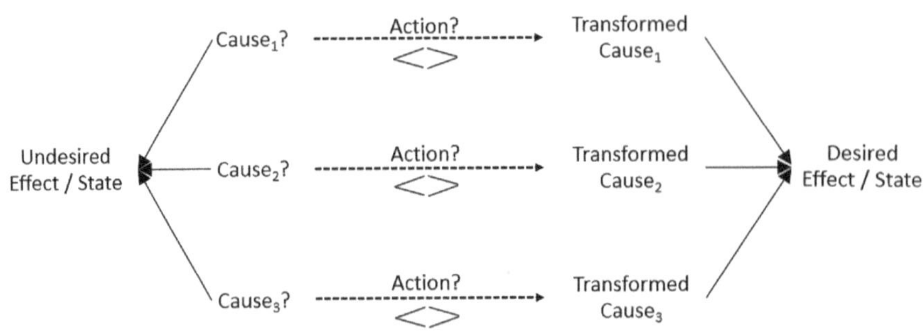

Figure 3.6 Problem-solving is thinking of ways to act on the causes of the undesired effect (or state) to transform them into the causes of the desired effect (or state).

includes a 32-page chapter on the following creative problem-solving methods—expertise, logic, analogy, and conceptual combination.[38] You can find a book-length explanation of the first three methods in *Creativity: Understanding Innovation in Problem Solving, Science, Invention and the Arts*, authored by the psychology professor Robert Weisberg.[39] And the book titled *Logical Creative Thinking Methods* written by the business professor Min Ding provides a book-length treatment of conceptual combination.[40] Note that my book also contains an 11-page chapter on research methods.

I asked ChatGPT to generate three examples of the foregoing problem-solving process, one for a business problem, one for a social problem, and one for an engineering problem. There are two lessons to be learned from these examples. First is to understand the various ways the process can be applied. Second is to realize that you can instruct generative AI to apply the four-step process to your problems.

I asked ChatGPT to generate an example of the problem-solving process applied to a business problem.[41] Here is what it created:

Prompt

Describe an example of problem solving using the steps and methods set forth in the foregoing text.

ChatGPT's Response

A manufacturing company is experiencing high defect rates in its production line for precision-engineered automotive parts. The company wants to reduce the number of defective parts to improve efficiency and customer satisfaction.

Step 1: Define the Undesired Effect/State
Undesired Effect:

- The company's defect rate is 12%, which is significantly above the industry standard of 5%. This leads to increased costs due to waste, rework, and customer dissatisfaction.

Framing the Problem:

- The problem can be framed as:

"How can we reduce the defect rate in our production line from *12% to below 5%?*"

Step 2: Identify the Cause(s) of the Undesired State
A cross-functional team (quality engineers, production supervisors, and machine operators) analyzes potential causes. They hypothesize that defects could be caused by:

1. Equipment Calibration Issues—Machines may not be precisely calibrated, leading to dimensional errors.
2. Material Quality Variation—Inconsistent material properties may cause defects.
3. Operator Errors—Employees may not be following standard operating procedures correctly.
4. Environmental Factors—Temperature or humidity fluctuations may be affecting production.

Validation of Hypotheses:

- A statistical process control (SPC) analysis of recent production data reveals that defects spike immediately after machine recalibration.
- A materials analysis shows some variation in supplier batches.
- Observation of the production process identifies occasional procedural deviations.
- Findings: The primary cause appears to be equipment calibration inconsistencies, but material variation and operator errors also contribute.

Step 3: Determine How to Act on the Causes
Generating Alternatives:

1. Implement automated calibration checks before production starts each day.
2. Introduce a real-time monitoring system for machine performance.
3. Train operators on precision handling and quality control procedures.
4. Establish stricter supplier quality control processes.

Selecting the Best Solution:
The team votes and selects a combined approach:

- Implement automated calibration checks to address the primary cause.
- Conduct training sessions for operators to reduce human errors.

Step 4: Test the Selected Solution

1. Prototype Implementation:
   - A pilot program is run on one production line for two weeks with automated calibration checks and enhanced operator training.
   - Data is collected on defect rates before and after implementation.
2. Results & Iteration:
   - The defect rate drops from 12% to 6% in the test line.
   - Operators report improved confidence in machine adjustments.
   - Some issues remain, particularly with raw material variation.
3. Refinement:
   - The company decides to expand the solution to all production lines and implement stricter material quality standards with suppliers.

Outcome

After full implementation and further refinements, the defect rate drops to 4.8%, meeting the company's goal.

Key Takeaways:

- The structured problem-solving approach helped diagnose root causes rather than treating symptoms.
- Prototyping and iteration ensured the solution was validated before scaling.
- A combination of technological and human interventions was more effective than a single approach.
- This case illustrates how a systematic, hypothesis-driven approach using expertise, logic, and research methods can drive real-world improvements in organizational problem-solving.

I asked ChatGPT to generate another example of the problem-solving process, this time applied to a social problem.[42] Here is what it created:

Prompt

Describe an example of problem solving using the steps and methods set forth in the foregoing text. This time describe a social problem.

ChatGPT's Response

A mid-sized city is experiencing a rise in youth homelessness, which has increased by 20 % over the past three years. Community leaders, social workers, and local government officials want to address this issue and reduce the number of unhoused young people.

Step 1: Define the Undesired Effect/State
Undesired Effect:
The number of homeless youth (ages 16–24) in the city has risen from 500 to 600 over the past three years. Many young people are living on the streets, couch-surfing, or staying in shelters, and they struggle with access to stable housing, employment, and mental health services.
Framing the Problem: "How can we reduce youth homelessness in our city and provide sustainable pathways to stable housing and employment?"

Step 2: Identify the Cause(s) of the Undesired State
A coalition of community organizations conducts surveys, interviews, and data analysis to determine the root causes. They identify several key factors:

1. Aging out of Foster Care—Many young people become homeless after turning 18 and leaving the foster care system.
2. Family Conflict & Abuse—A large percentage of homeless youth cite family conflict, domestic violence, or rejection (especially among LGBTQ+ youths) as the reason for leaving home.
3. Lack of Affordable Housing—The rising cost of rent and limited access to transitional housing programs make it difficult for youth to find stable homes.
4. Barriers to Employment—Many homeless youth lack job experience, identification documents, or access to job training programs.

Validation of Hypotheses:

- City shelter records confirm that a significant portion of homeless youth aged out of foster care.

- Surveys show that over 40% of respondents left home due to family conflict or domestic violence.
- A review of housing data confirms a lack of affordable rental units for low-income individuals.
- Focus groups highlight the challenges youth face in securing stable employment.

Findings: The primary causes of youth homelessness are aging out of foster care, family conflict, and lack of affordable housing, with employment barriers also playing a role.

Step 3: Determine How to Act on the Causes
Generating Alternatives:

1. Expand transitional housing programs for youth aging out of foster care.
2. Create a family mediation program to prevent youth from leaving home due to conflict.
3. Develop a rental assistance program and increase investment in affordable housing units.
4. Launch a job training and mentorship initiative for homeless youth.

Selecting the Best Solution:
Community stakeholders vote and decide on a multi-pronged approach:

- Expand transitional housing programs to support youth aging out of foster care.
- Pilot a job training and mentorship program to help homeless youth gain employment.
- Create a crisis mediation program to assist families in resolving conflicts before youth become homeless.

Step 4: Test the Selected Solution

1. Prototype Implementation:
    - A six-month pilot program is launched with 20 transitional housing units, providing support services for youth exiting foster care.
    - A small-scale job training program partners with local businesses to offer apprenticeships.
    - A mediation hotline is created to offer family counseling and crisis intervention.

2. Results & Iteration:

   - 85% of youth in transitional housing remain housed after six months.
   - 60% of participants in the job training program secure stable employment.
   - The mediation program prevents 30% of at-risk youth from becoming homeless by helping families resolve conflicts.

3. Refinement:

   - The city secures additional funding to expand the transitional housing program to 50 units.
   - The job training initiative partners with more businesses to increase employment opportunities.
   - The mediation program is integrated into local schools to reach at-risk youth earlier.

Outcome

After scaling up the solutions, youth homelessness in the city declines by 15% over two years. The combination of housing support, employment training, and family mediation proves effective in addressing the root causes of homelessness.

Key Takeaways:

- A systematic, data-driven approach helped identify the true causes of the problem.
- Testing and iteration allowed for refinement before full-scale implementation.
- Addressing multiple contributing factors simultaneously was more effective than a single solution.
- This example demonstrates how a structured problem-solving framework can be applied to social issues, combining expertise, community engagement, and evidence-based solutions to create lasting change.

Finally, I asked ChatGPT to generate an example of the problem-solving process applied to an engineering problem.[43] Here is its response:

Prompt

Generate another example. This time use an engineering problem.

ChatGPT's Response

A chemical manufacturing plant produces high-purity ethanol for pharmaceutical applications. However, recent quality control tests show an increasing trend in contamination levels, leading to batches being rejected due to failing to meet the required purity of 99.9% ethanol.

Step 1: Define the Undesired Effect/State
Undesired Effect:
The ethanol production process is yielding contaminated batches that fail to meet purity standards. This leads to increased production costs, delays in supply chain delivery, and loss of revenue.
Framing the Problem: "How can we identify and eliminate the cause of contamination in our ethanol production process to consistently achieve *99.9% purity?"*

Step 2: Identify the Cause(s) of the Undesired State
A team of chemical engineers and quality control specialists investigates the issue by examining potential sources of contamination. They hypothesize several possible causes:

1. Inefficient Distillation Process—The fractional distillation column may not be separating impurities effectively.
2. Raw Material Impurities—The fermentation feedstock (sugar-based raw materials) could contain higher-than-expected levels of non-ethanol byproducts.
3. Equipment Contamination—Biofilm buildup, residual solvents, or corrosion in pipelines could be introducing contaminants.
4. Solvent Handling Issues—Cross-contamination in storage tanks or transfer lines could be affecting purity.

Validation of Hypotheses:

- Distillation column efficiency analysis shows that the column is operating within expected parameters. Hypothesis #1 is invalidated.
- Raw material impurity testing indicates higher-than-usual concentrations of acetaldehyde and methanol in the feedstock, suggesting potential fermentation inefficiencies. Hypothesis #2 is partially validated.

- Equipment inspection reveals residual buildup in the stainless steel piping that could be leaching contaminants into the ethanol stream. Hypothesis #3 is validated.
- Storage and handling audits do not show evidence of cross-contamination. Hypothesis #4 is invalidated.

Findings:
The primary causes of contamination appear to be:

1. Impurities in the raw material feedstock, leading to increased byproducts.
2. Buildup of contaminants in the piping system, which could be introducing unwanted chemicals into the ethanol stream.

Step 3: Determine How to Act on the Causes
With the root causes identified—impurities in the raw material feedstock and buildup of contaminants in the piping system—the engineering team now develops and evaluates possible solutions.
Generating Alternative Solutions:
The team explores multiple ways to address each cause:
Cause 1: Impurities in the Raw Material Feedstock

1. Change Feedstock Supplier: Source higher-purity raw materials from a different supplier with stricter quality control.
2. Pre-Treatment of Feedstock: Implement an additional filtration or purification step before fermentation to remove excess impurities.
3. Optimize Fermentation Conditions: Adjust pH levels, temperature, and nutrient balance to reduce the formation of by-products like acetaldehyde and methanol.

Cause 2: Contaminant Buildup in Piping System

1. Increase Cleaning Frequency: Introduce a more rigorous cleaning-in-place (CIP) protocol with optimized chemical cleaning agents.
2. Material Upgrade: Replace older stainless steel pipelines with corrosion-resistant alloys to prevent contamination.
3. Inline Monitoring System: Install real-time sensors to detect contamination buildup in pipelines before it affects ethanol purity.

Selecting the Best Solution:
The team evaluates each option based on cost, feasibility, and expected effectiveness and votes on the best combination of solutions. They decide to:

- Optimize fermentation conditions to minimize impurity formation.
- Implement an enhanced CIP protocol with more frequent cleanings and stronger solvent-based cleaning agents.
- Monitor impurity levels in the feedstock and work with the supplier to ensure raw material consistency.

These solutions are expected to eliminate contamination at the source while also ensuring that any residual contaminants are regularly cleaned from the system.

Step 4: Test the Selected Solution
Since it is uncertain whether these solutions will fully resolve the issue, the team initiates a pilot testing phase using an iterative "quick & dirty" prototyping approach to refine the solutions before full-scale implementation.
Prototype Testing Plan:

1. Fermentation Optimization Pilot:
    - A small batch of ethanol is produced using adjusted pH levels and optimized fermentation parameters to see if it reduces unwanted byproducts.
    - Result: The concentration of acetaldehyde and methanol is reduced by 30%, validating this approach.
2. Cleaning Protocol Trial:
    - The new CIP protocol is tested on a single processing line to observe its impact on contamination levels.
    - Result: After two cleaning cycles, ethanol purity increases from 99.7% to 99.9%, confirming effectiveness.
3. Raw Material Testing:
    - A more rigorous quality check is applied to new feedstock shipments to ensure impurity levels remain within acceptable limits.
    - Result: A new supplier is found that provides more consistent purity, reducing variability in ethanol production.

Iterate and Scale:

- Based on successful pilot results, the optimized fermentation and enhanced CIP process are implemented across the entire production line.

- Real-time monitoring is introduced to detect any future contamination risks.
- The company establishes a long-term supply agreement with the new feedstock provider to maintain consistent raw material quality.

Outcome & Long-Term Impact:

- Ethanol purity is restored to 99.9%, eliminating batch rejections.
- Production efficiency improves, reducing material waste and costs associated with reprocessing.
- A proactive contamination monitoring system is established, preventing future quality issues.
- The company secures stronger supplier relationships and higher confidence in process control.
- This structured problem-solving approach ensures that solutions are data-driven, validated through testing, and continuously improved, allowing the company to maintain high product quality and operational efficiency in ethanol production.

Task-Specific Processes

There are all manner of task-specific processes, or methods, that provide structured approaches to solving complex problems, innovating products and services, and improving social systems. Many of them are interdisciplinary, drawing from design, business strategy, behavioral science, and systems thinking. Depending on the nature of the challenge, the best approach may be to combine several of them. A sampling of these methods is given below, though comprehensive descriptions are beyond the scope of this book. Each includes an end note that references additional sources of information about the method. All the examples were generated by ChatGPT.

Design Thinking Method

The design thinking method is a human-centered, iterative approach to problem-solving that prioritizes empathy, creativity, and experimentation.[44] It consists of five stages: (1) Empathize (understanding user needs); (2) Define (framing the problem); (3) Ideate (brainstorming solutions); (4) Prototype (creating testable versions of solutions); and (5) Test (refining based on feedback).

Unlike traditional problem-solving approaches that focus primarily on logic and feasibility, design thinking emphasizes deep user research, reframing problems, and rapid iteration.

- *Business Example*: A financial services company uses design thinking to make mobile banking more accessible for elderly customers. Research reveals that seniors struggle with complex app navigation and security verification. Through prototyping and testing, they develop an intuitive banking interface with voice commands and simplified authentication to better serve this demographic.
- *Social Example*: A global health organization applies design thinking to improve access to affordable prosthetics in low-income regions. By observing how people interact with existing prosthetic options, they develop lightweight, modular prosthetic limbs that can be easily adjusted without specialized tools.

Systemic Design Method

The systemic design method integrates systems thinking and design thinking to tackle complex, interconnected problems by considering broad systemic relationships, long-term consequences, and interdependencies.[45] Instead of solving problems in isolation, systemic design looks at how various factors interact within a larger ecosystem to find more sustainable and scalable solutions.

- *Business Example*: A global fashion retailer applies systemic design to create a circular economy in clothing production by incorporating recycled materials, optimizing supply chains, and providing customers with incentives for returning used clothing for repurposing.
- *Social Example*: A city struggling with homelessness uses systemic design to integrate housing, employment, mental health, and addiction services rather than treating homelessness as an isolated issue. This results in a "housing-first" approach with wraparound services that improve long-term outcomes.

Jobs-to-Be-Done (JTBD) Method

The JTBD method focuses on identifying the fundamental "jobs" that people are trying to get done by buying a product or service.[46] It focuses on the functional jobs and emotional jobs that drive a purchase decision. The method helps organizations design solutions that truly align with customer intent rather than just improving existing features.

- *Business Example*: Traditional vacuum cleaners require manual operation, which is time-consuming and physically demanding. iRobot's Roomba isn't just selling a robotic vacuum. It is solving the job of keeping floors clean without having to invest physical effort and time.
- *Social Example*: A nonprofit organization working to reduce youth unemployment applies the JTBD method to understand why young people struggle to find jobs. Research reveals that the primary job they need to get done is gaining work experience and professional connections, rather than just applying for jobs. This insight leads to the development of apprenticeship programs and mentorship initiatives that provide young people with both skills and industry networks.

Consumption Chain Method

The consumption chain method is a systematic approach to analyzing every step in a customer's interaction with a product or service, from initial awareness to final disposal or discontinuation.[47] In other words, the consumption chain maps the steps the customer takes before, during, and after using the product or service. The objective of mapping the chain is to optimize each step of the consumption process for efficiency, differentiation, and value creation.

- *Business Example*: A luxury hotel chain applies the consumption chain method by mapping guests' entire guest experience, from the booking process and arrival at the hotel to in-room services, dining, and check-out. By analyzing these steps, the hotel identifies pain points, such as slow check-in times and lack of personalized room preferences, leading to the development of mobile check-in and AI-driven customization of guest experiences.
- *Social Example*: A city government seeks to improve public transportation usage. By mapping the consumption chain of a commuter, from route planning and ticket purchasing to boarding, riding, and exiting the system, they identify pain points like long ticket queues and unclear transfer information. As a result, they implement contactless payments and real-time transit tracking to enhance user experience.

Journey Mapping Method

The journey mapping method is a technique used to visualize and analyze the end-to-end experience of a customer or user interacting with a service, product, or system.[48] While the two methods are similar, journey mapping focuses more on the customer's emotional experience (e.g., frustrations), whereas the consumption chain method emphasizes efficiency, differentiation, and value creation.

- *Business Example*: An e-commerce retailer creates a journey map to analyze the online shopping experience. They track each step, from searching for a product and navigating the website to making a purchase and receiving post-sale support. Through this process, they discover that many customers abandon their carts due to unexpected shipping fees, leading the company to introduce free shipping for orders over a certain amount to increase conversions.
- *Social Example*: A public health initiative uses journey mapping to understand the experience of patients seeking mental health services. The map reveals barriers such as long wait times for appointments, difficulty navigating insurance coverage, and stigma-related concerns. In response, policymakers create a telehealth service with simplified booking and anonymous counseling options to improve access to care.

Root Cause Analysis (RCA) Method

The RCA method is a structured problem-solving technique that seeks to identify and eliminate the underlying causes of issues rather than merely addressing their symptoms.[49] RCA often employs tools such as the 5 Whys method (asking "why" multiple times to uncover deeper causes), Fishbone Diagrams (Ishikawa diagrams that map out possible causes), and Fault Tree Analysis (visual representations of failure points).

- *Business Example*: A manufacturing plant experiencing frequent machine breakdowns uses RCA to investigate the root cause. The 5 Whys analysis reveals that poor lubrication schedules lead to premature wear on machine parts. The company implements an automated lubrication system, reducing downtime.
- *Social Example*: A school district suffering from high dropout rates applies RCA and finds that a lack of reliable transportation and after-school support are significant contributing factors. To address this, they implement free bus services and community tutoring programs to reduce dropout rates.

TRIZ (Theory of Inventive Problem-Solving) Method

TRIZ (the Russian acronym for Theory of Inventive Problem-Solving) is a structured innovation framework that analyzes patterns of invention across different industries to solve technical and creative problems.[50] The method is based on the idea that most problems have already been solved in some form in another field, so existing solutions can be adapted.

- *Business Example*: A battery manufacturer applies TRIZ to solve the issue of overheating lithium-ion batteries by adapting a cooling system used in spacecraft technology to regulate temperature.
- *Social Example*: A rural infrastructure project applies TRIZ to design low-cost, disaster-resistant bridges, drawing inspiration from lightweight yet strong biological structures found in nature.

Scenario Planning Method

The scenario planning method is a strategic foresight approach that involves creating multiple plausible future scenarios to prepare for uncertainty and make better long-term decisions.[51] Instead of predicting a single future, organizations develop different narratives based on potential economic, technological, regulatory, and social changes.

- *Business Example*: A large retail chain is planning its five-year strategy and wants to prepare for major shifts in consumer behavior, technology, and market dynamics. The company develops four distinct future scenarios based on two key uncertainties: consumer adoption of digital shopping (low vs. high) and economic conditions (boom vs. recession).
- *Social Example*: A city government is developing a long-term climate resilience plan for rising sea levels and extreme weather events. They create four possible futures based on two major uncertainties: rate of climate action (strong vs. weak global policies) and technology advancements in climate resilience (slow vs. fast).

Prototyping Method

The prototyping method involves creating preliminary versions or models of a product, service, or system to test key functionalities, gather user feedback, and create iterative improvements before final development.[52] Prototyping helps reduce risk by identifying potential issues early in the design process and ensuring that solutions align with user needs.

- *Business Example*: A software company developing a new mobile banking app creates a low-fidelity wireframe prototype to test with potential users before proceeding with full development. They discover that customers find the payment process confusing, leading them to redesign the interface for greater simplicity before investing in full-scale coding.
- *Social Example*: A disaster relief organization wants to create temporary shelters for displaced families. Instead of mass-producing a design, they build several prototypes and invite affected communities to provide

feedback. This process reveals that privacy and climate adaptability are key concerns, leading to design modifications such as modular partitions and better ventilation systems.

Lean Startup Method

Similar to prototyping, the lean startup method is an iterative approach to developing products and services by rapidly testing hypotheses, gathering user feedback, and refining solutions to reduce the risk of failure.[53] The process follows a Build-Measure-Learn cycle: entrepreneurs build a Minimum Viable Product (MVP), test it in the real world, collect data, and adjust their strategy based on user feedback before investing in full-scale development.

- *Business Example*: A subscription meal service startup uses the lean startup approach by first launching a small-scale pilot program with limited menu options. Customer feedback highlights the demand for more customizable meal plans, leading the company to expand its offerings before a full market rollout.
- *Social Example*: A municipal government develops a citizen reporting app for urban infrastructure issues. Instead of launching a full-featured app, they first test a simple MVP in one neighborhood. The feedback reveals the need for real-time tracking of issue resolutions, leading to a more refined final product.

Living Labs Method

The living labs method is an open innovation approach where prototypes are tested in real-life environments and user communities are actively involved in co-developing, testing, and refining solutions.[54] Unlike traditional R&D conducted in isolated labs, living labs integrate real-world feedback loops to create user-centered innovations in fields like urban development, healthcare, and digital transformation.

- *Business Example*: A smart home technology company creates a living lab where real families test connected home devices such as AI-powered thermostats, voice assistants, and security cameras. By observing how users interact with these technologies in their daily lives, the company refines the designs to improve usability, energy efficiency, and security features.
- *Social Example*: A sustainable urban development initiative establishes a living lab in a low-income neighborhood to test affordable smart energy solutions. Residents participate in designing and testing solar-powered

microgrids, energy-efficient appliances, and real-time consumption monitoring apps. Their feedback helps fine-tune the technologies before broader implementation, ensuring that solutions are both practical and accessible.

Blue Ocean Strategy Method

The blue ocean strategy method focuses on creating entirely new market spaces (blue oceans) rather than competing in existing crowded markets (oceans red with the competitors' blood).[55] It involves identifying unmet needs, eliminating unnecessary features, and redefining value in an industry. For more on this method, see my book *Differentiation Strategy: Winning Customers by Being Different*.[56]

- *Business Example*: A fitness company creates a VR-based interactive workout experience, targeting individuals who dislike traditional gyms and creating an entirely new market segment.
- *Social Example*: A public transportation department develops on-demand micro-transit services to reach underserved communities, filling a transportation gap that traditional bus routes don't cover.

Action Planning Method

The action planning method is a structured approach to outlining specific steps, responsibilities, and timelines to achieve a desired goal.[57] It ensures that a strategy moves beyond conceptualization and into practical implementation by defining objectives, allocating resources, setting milestones, and monitoring progress. Action plans often include contingencies to adapt to changing circumstances.

- *Business Example*: A retail company wants to expand its presence in international markets. Using action planning, they break down the process into key steps, including market research, regulatory compliance, supply chain development, and localized marketing strategies. A timeline and responsible teams are assigned to each phase, ensuring an organized and coordinated expansion effort.
- *Social Example*: A city government wants to reduce food waste by 30% within three years. An action plan is developed with specific initiatives, such as educational campaigns, food redistribution partnerships, incentives for composting, and supermarket waste reduction policies. By assigning deadlines and accountability measures, the city ensures that initiatives are executed effectively.

Summary

In this chapter, we looked at meeting processes, groups processes, the problem-solving process, and several task-specific processes. The four types of processes can and should be integrated. The meeting process should include group processes that carry out the problem-solving process, which may include one or more of the task-specific processes. In the next chapter, we're going to look at technologies that can be used to support the processes.

Notes

1 Jeff Shannon, *Lead Engaging Meetings* (Rabble Studio Press, 2023), 38. This format is similar to the one described by Shannon.

2 Fred Dust, *Making Conversation: Seven Essential Elements of Meaningful Communication* (New York, NY: HarperCollins Publishers, 2020), 157.

3 Jessica R. Andrews-Hanna, "The Brain's Default Network and Its Adaptive Role in Internal Mentation," *Neuroscientist*, June 2012, 18(3), 251–270, https://doi.org/10.1177/1073858411403316. Epub June 15, 2011. PMID: 21677128; PMCID: PMC3553600.

4 Kevin Holt, *Differentiation Strategy: Winning Customers by Being Different* (New York, NY: Routledge, 2022), 155–156.

5 Josheph A. Allen, Nale Lehmann-Willenbrock, and Nicole Landowski, "Linking Pre-Meeting Communication to Meeting Effectiveness," *Journal of Managerial Psychology*, 2014, 29(8), 1064–1081.

6 Yaacov Trope and Nira Liberman, "Construal-Level Theory of Psychological Distance," *Psychological Review*, 2010, 117(2), 440–463, https://doi.org/10.1037/a0018963

7 Peter M. Senge, *The Fifth Discipline: The Art & Practice of the Learning Organization* (New York, NY: Doubleday, 1990), chapter 4.

8 OpenAI, Response to "What are all the ways questions can be phrased or preceded in order to get people to break free of constraints and limitations?" *ChatGPT-4o*, 2025.

9 OpenAI, Response to "Tell me what people should tell you to do to get you to generate useful questions. What prompts should they use?" *ChatGPT-4o*, 2025.

10 Jeff Shannon, *Lead Engaging Meetings: A Practical Guide to Maximize Participation and Effectiveness* (Amazon Digital Services LLC, 2023). This is a concise and eminently practical book on meeting facilitation. Jolie Bain Pillsbury, *Results Based Facilitation: Introduction, Book 1 & Book 2* (Sherbrooke Consulting, 2015). These three books give a deep and extensive treatment of meeting facilitation. Dan M. Brown, *Designing Together: The Collaboration and Conflict Management Handbook for Creative Professionals* (Indianapolis, IN: New Riders, 2013), which is a great book on facilitating designers and design meetings, with emphasis on managing disagreements and conflict.

11 Geoff Mulgan, *Big Mind: How Collective Intelligence Can Change Our World* (Princeton, NJ: Princeton University Press, 2018), 139.

12 H. William Dettmer, *Brainpower Networking; Using the Crawford Slip Method* (New Bern, NC: Trafford Publishing, 2003). This book explains the theming method developed by Professor Claude C. Crawford.

13 OpenAI, Response to "Describe a creative way to incorporate generative AI into the traditional brainstorming process as it is described in the foregoing text." *ChatGPT-4o*, 2025.
14 OpenAI, Response to "Describe a creative way to incorporate generative AI into the Nominal Group Technique process." *ChatGPT-4o*, 2025.
15 Henri Lipmanowicz and Keith McCandless, *The Surprising Power of Liberating Structures: Simple Rules to Unleash a Culture of Innovation* (Liberating Structures Press, 2013), 167–168.
16 Richard C. Jeffrey, *The Logic of Decision* (Chicago, IL: University of Chicago Press, 1990). Explores how belief updates happen probabilistically. See also Cass R. Sustein, *Infotopia: How Many Minds Produce Knowledge* (Oxford, UK: University of Oxford Press, 2006), which describes how groups aggregate information and refine collective knowledge.
17 OpenAI, Response to "Describe useful ways that generative AI can be incorporated in the 1–2–4-All method." *ChatGPT-4o*, 2025.
18 Steven G. Rogelberg, *The Surprising Science of Meetings: How You Can Lead Your Team to Peak Performance* (Oxford University Press, 2019), 110.
19 OpenAI, Response to "Describe how generative AI could be used to enhance the rotational brainwriting method described in the foregoing text." *ChatGPT-4o*, 2025.
20 Gus Cooney, Adam M Mastroianni, Nicole Abi-Esber, and Alison Wood Brooks, "The Many Minds Problem: Disclosure in Dyadic Versus Group Conversation," *Current Opinion in Psychology*, February 2020, 31, 22–27, https://doi.org/10.1016/j.copsyc.2019.06.032
21 OpenAI, Response to "Describe how generative AI can enhance a process whereby there are breakout groups that return to the plenary and discuss the alternatives they have created, then jointly create a set of alternatives, and finally vote to select the best alternative." *ChatGPT-4o*, 2025.
22 Paul R. Paulus and Bernard A. Nijstad (Eds.), *The Oxford Handbook of Group Creativity and Innovation* (New York, NY: Oxford University Press, 2019), 300.
23 Stafford Beer, *Beyond Dispute: The Invention of Team Syntegrity* (West Sussex, UK: John Wiley & Sons, 1994). Beer provides a lengthy and dense description of the full Team Syntegrity method.
24 David Benjamin and David Komlos, *Cracking Complexity Now: The Breakthrough Formula for Solving Just About Anything, from Anywhere, Fast* (Boston, MA: Nicholas Brealey Publishing, 2019). The authors, who are consultants specializing in the Team Syntegrity Method, give a much easier-to-understand account of the method and more abbreviated versions of the full method.
25 David Benjamin and David Komlos, *Cracking Complexity Now: The Breakthrough Formula for Solving Just About Anything, from Anywhere, Fast* (Boston, MA: Nicholas Brealey Publishing, 2019), 140.
26 OpenAI, Response to "How could generative AI be used to enhance the Team Syntegrity Method?" *ChatGPT-4o*, 2025.
27 Timothy Collins, Maureen Kearney, and Davide Maddison, "The Ideas Lab Concept, Assembling the Tree of Life, and AVAToL," *PLoS Currents Tree of Life*, March 7, 2013, https://doi.org/10.1371/currents.tol.0fdb85e1619f313a2a5a2ec3d7a8df9e.
28 "Research Groups on Mental Health of Children & Adolescents: A Novel Approach to Form Research Groups," *Ludwig Boltzmann Gesellschaft*, July 2017, https://ois.lbg.ac.at/wp-content/uploads/sites/24/2024/03/Beispielablauf-fuer-ein-IdeasLab_en.pdf

29 Eric von Hippel, Nikolaus Franke, and Reinhard Prügl, "Pyramiding: Efficient Search for Rare Subjects," *Research Policy*, November 2009, 8(9), 1397–1406, https://doi.org/10.1016/j.respol.2009.07.005
30 OpenAI, Response to "First read the foregoing text. Then describe the ways generative AI could be used to enhance the Ideas Lab process." *ChatGPT-4o*, 2025.
31 David Matheson and Jim Matheson, *The Smart Organization: Creating Value Through Strategic R&D* (Boston, MA: Harvard Business School Press, 1998), 177–179.
32 Alessio Ishizaka and Philippe Nemery, *Multi-Criteria Decision Analysis: Methods and Software* (Hoboken, NJ: John Wiley & Sons, 2013); Thomas L. Saaty, *Fundamentals of Decision Making and Priority Theory*, 2nd Edition (Pittsburgh, PA: RWS Publications, 2013).
33 Pierre A. Balthazard, William R. Ferrell, and Dorothy L. Aguilar, "Influence Allocation Methods in Group Decision Support Systems," *Group Decision and Negotiation*, July 1998, 7(4), 347–362, https://doi.org/10.1023/A:1008638222056
34 M.C. Stanley and J.E. Marlow, "Making N Heads Beter Than One: Integrating Opinions of Experts," The pre-publication article, provided to me by the authors in the early 2000s, describes a software implementation of the SPAN and RCON voting methods called N_Heads. I don't believe the article was ever published. The two methods are also described in the article cited in the preceding Note #33.
35 Ray Dalio, *Principles* (New York, NY: Avid Reader Press, 2017), 371–383.
36 Ray Dalio, *Principles* (New York, NY: Avid Reader Press, 2017), 371.
37 OpenAI, Response to "Read the foregoing text. Then explain ways generative AI can enhance group voting." *ChatGPT-4o*, 2025.
38 Kevin Holt, *Differentiation Strategy: Winning Customers by Being Different* (New York, NY: Routledge, 2022), chapters 10–11.
39 Robert W. Weisberg, *Creativity: Understanding Innovation in Problem Solving, Science, Invention, and the Arts* (Hoboken, NJ: John Wiley & Sons, 2006).
40 Min Ding, *Logical Creative Thinking Methods* (New York, NY: Routledge, 2020).
41 OpenAI, Response to "Describe an example of problem solving using the steps and methods set forth in the foregoing text." *ChatGPT-4o*, 2025.
42 OpenAI, Response to "Generate another example. This time use a social problem." *ChatGPT-4o*, 2025.
43 OpenAI, Response to "Generate another example. This time use an engineering problem." *ChatGPT-4o*, 2025.
44 Tim Brown, *Change by Design: How Design Thinking Transforms Organizations and Inspires Innovation* (New York, NY: Harpers Business, 2009); Hartmut Esslinger, *A Fine Line: How Design Strategies Are Shaping the Future of Business* (San Francisco, CA: Jossey-Bass, 2009); John Kolko, *Exposing the Magic of Design: A Practitioner's Guide to Methods & Theory of Synthesis* (Oxford, UK: Oxford University Press, 2011); Vijay Kumar, *101 Design Methods: A Structured Approach for Driving Innovation in Your Organization* (Hoboken, NJ: John Wiley & Sons, 2013). The books are listed in order from those that focus more on the general design process to those that focus on specific design methods.
45 David Peter Stroh, *Systems Thinking for Social Change: A Practical Guide to Solving Complex Problems, Avoiding Unintended Consequences, and Achieving Lasting Results* (White River Junction, VT: Chelsea Green Publishing, 2015). See also the website of the Systemic Design Association for Multiple Resources, https://systemic-design.org/

46 Anthony W. Ulwick, *What Customers Want: Using Outcome-Driven Innovation to Create Breakthrough Products and Services* (New York, NY: McGraw-Hill, 2005); Anthony W. Ulwick, *Jobs to Be Done: Theory to Practice* (Idea Bite Press, 2016). Ulwick's books focus on applying the JTBD method to product innovation. Lance A. Bettencourt, *Service Innovation: How to Go from Customer Needs to Breakthrough Services* (New York, NY: McGraw-Hill, 2010). Bettencourt applies the JTBD method to different aspects of service innovation. Sandra M. Bates, *The Social Innovation Imperative: Create Winning Products, Services, and Programs That Solve Society's Most Pressing Challenges* (New York, NY: McGraw-Hill, 2012). Bate's focus is on applying the JTBD method to social problems.

47 Rita Gunther McGrath and Ian C. MacMillan, *Market Busters: 40 Strategic Moves That Drive Exceptional Business Growth* (Boston, MA: Harvard Business School Press, 2005), chapter 2; Ian MacMillan and Rita Gunther McGrath, "Discovering New Points of Differentiation," *Harvard Business Review*, July–August 1997.

48 Jim Kalback, *Mapping Experiences: A Complete Guide to Creating Value Through Journeys, Blueprints & Diagrams* (Boston, MA: O'Reilly, 2016). This book explains various ways of mapping experiences. Nathan Shedroff, *Experience Design* (Indianapolis, IN: New Riders, 2001), which explains multi-disciplinary ways of designing experiences.

49 Dean L. Gano, *Apollo Root Cause Analysis: Effective Solutions to Everyday Problems* (Yakima, WA: Apollonia Publications, 1999). This is a very good, very concise book on the topic that includes a comparison of common RCA methods.

50 Kalevi Rantanen, David W. Conley, and Ellen Domb, *Simplified TRIZ: New Problem Solving Applications for Technical and Business Professionals*, 3rd Edition (Boca Raton, FL: CRC Press, 2018); Darrell Mann, *Hands on Systematic Innovation* (Bideford, UK: IFR Press, 2007).

51 Peter Schwartz, *The Art of the Long View: Planning for the Future in an Uncertain World* (New York, NY: Currency-Doubleday, 1991); Woody Wade, *Scenario Planning: A Field Guide to the Future* (Hoboken, NJ: John Wiley & Sons, 2012).

52 Kathryn McElroy, *Prototyping for Designers: Developing the Best Digital and Physical Products* (Boston, MA: O'Reilly, 2017); Todd Zaki Warfel, *Prototyping* (Brooklyn, NY: Rosenfeld, 2009); Bjarki Hallgrimsson, *Prototyping and Modelmaking for Product Design* (London, UK: Laurence King Publishing, 2012). Each of these books provides a useful and somewhat different perspective on prototyping.

53 Eric Ries, *The Lean Startup: How Today's Entrepreneurs Use Continuous Innovation to Create Radically Innovative Businesses* (New York, NY: Currency, 2011).

54 David V. Keyson, Olivia Guerra-Santin, and Dan Lockton (Eds.), *Living Labs: Design and Assessment of Sustainable Living* (Cham, Switzerland: Springer Publishing, 2017); Zaid Hassan, *The Social Labs Revolution: A New Approach to Solving Our Most Complex Challenges* (San Francisco, CA: Barrett-Koehler Publishers, 2014). See also the European Network of Living Labs Website, https://www.enoll.org

55 W. Chan Kim and Renee Mauborgne, *Blue Ocean Strategy: How to Create Uncontested Market Space and Make the Competition Irrelevant* (Boston, MA: Harvard Business School Press, 2005); W. Chan Kim and Renee Mauborgne,

Blue Ocean Shift Beyond Competing: Proven Steps to Inspire Confidence and Seize New Growth (New York, NY: Hachette Books, 2017).

56 Kevin Holt, *Differentiation Strategy: Winning Customers by Being Different* (New York, NY: Routledge, 2022).

57 Susan B. Wilson and Michael S. Dobson, *Goal Setting: How to Create an Action Plan and Achieve Your Goals* (New York, NY: Harper Collins Leadership, 2008).

Chapter 4

Platforms

Meeting Rooms, Thinking Tools, and AI

In their 1976 book *How to Make Meetings Work*, organizational consultants Michael Doyle and David Strauss predicted that the need to solve complex problems would give rise to a new kind of facility which, they said, "may be called 'problem-solving centers' and will exist inside large organizations as well as in major urban areas at large."[1] The problem-solving centers, they elaborated, would support group problem-solving and decision-making by providing people a neutral place to meet, new kinds of meeting rooms and technologies, and meeting facilitators to help plan and manage the meetings. They asked readers to imagine themselves inside a problem-solving center in the year 2000, where a 25-person community task force is meeting in an octagonal-shaped room, sitting in futuristic-looking chairs, using light pens to write and draw on television screens, and surrounded by display screens on each of the eight walls.

Well, I'm writing this in the year 2025 and the authors' vision of wide-spread urban problem-solving centers has yet to occur, though there has been some progress. A handful of organizations, like Arizona State University, have installed sophisticated decision theaters. And others, like Google and IKEA, have built innovation laboratories where employees collaborate to create new products and services. But the sad fact is that, save for substituting flat screens for flipcharts, most meeting rooms are little changed from the way they were in 1976. If organizations want to take full advantage of collective intelligence and artificial intelligence, the meeting rooms and technologies—together, the *platforms*—they use have got to change. I'll start with meeting rooms, then talk about analog technologies, and then digital technologies, with a focus on dialogue mapping, generative AI, and electronic brainstorming (EBS) technology.

Meeting Rooms

In the foreword to *Make Space: How to Set the Stage for Creative Collaboration*, David Kelley, the co-founder of the design firm IDEO and now

DOI: 10.4324/9781003654407-5

a professor at Stanford University's design school (the "d.school"), says, "Space matters. We read our physical environment like we read a face. Consciously or not, we feel and internalize what the space tells us about how to work. . . . Regardless of whether it's a classroom or the offices of a billion-dollar company, space is something to think of as an instrument for innovation and collaboration."[2] Following are key issues to consider, whether you're choosing a space in which to meet, modifying an existing space, or building a new one from scratch.

Seating and Floor Plans

Seating and floor plans should support what you're doing, not work against it. In other words, you want them to enable what you're trying to accomplish, not prevent it. Let's start with seating plans.

U-Shaped Seating: A U-shaped seating arrangement, like the one shown in the left half of Figure 4.1, is best for problem-solving and decision-making meetings. It supports this type of meeting by leveraging

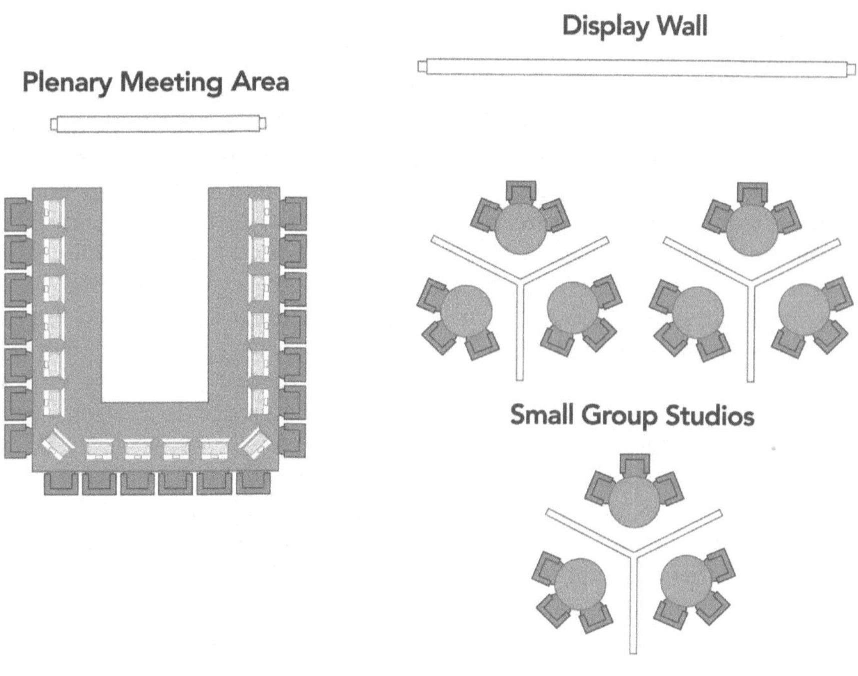

Figure 4.1 Small-group floor plan with a plenary space, small group studios for breakout groups, and a display wall.

Source: David Holt Design

the cognitive and communicative factors that enhance group dynamics and collective intelligence:

- *Encourages Psychological Safety*: A U-shaped seating arrangement minimizes the hierarchical feel of traditional boardroom setups where the highest-status person sits at the head of the table. This encourages more inclusive participation by increasing the sense of psychological safety.
- *Facilitates Active Discussion and Collaboration*: The U-shape provides a natural focal point at the open end, where the people with clearly defined roles (the facilitator, presenter, or key speaker) can guide the discussion. This helps to ensure a more orderly discussion. The U-shape also permits people on opposite sides to have a direct line of sight to one another. And for those sitting on the same side, it enables them to keep more participants in their peripheral vision. The better lines of sight enable the participants to observe facial expressions, gestures, and body language, which supports more fluid conversational turn-taking and reduces miscommunication. Note, however, that having two sides facing each other, as is done in the British parliament, promotes debate rather than deliberation. So, if your group has two warring factions, make sure the faction members are intermingled on both sides of the U.
- *Improved Visibility of Shared Space*: The U-shape ensures that all the participants have an unobstructed view of the flipchart, whiteboard, or projection screen at the open end of the U. This is no small matter, for as Michael Schrage explains, a key to group problem-solving is to have a *shared space*.[3] The shared space, be it an analog whiteboard or the display of a digital software tool, is where ideas are contributed, moved, and linked together, says Schrage, "to become parts of hierarchies, priorities, and networks of meaning . . . [and where] comments can be ranked and grouped together in appropriate categories or linked into a discussion map that can be edited instantaneously." The fundamental benefit of a shared space, he emphasizes, is to cause the group members to shift their focus from each other to the knowledge artifact they are building together.
- *Optimized for Hybrid and Digital Collaboration*: In hybrid meetings (some in-person, some remote), the open structure allows for better camera angles, ensuring that virtual participants see faces rather than just the backs of people's heads. The shape also facilitates better microphone placement for improved audio clarity.

Circular Seating: Like U-shaped seating arrangements, circular (round table) arrangements deemphasize hierarchy by making sure no one is seated at the head of the table. Fishbowl seating is a modified form of circular seating in which there is an inner circle of people who participate in the discussion and an outer circle of people who listen to it. Circular seating is good for discussions characterized by shared power, mutual respect, and inclusivity and where all the participants are given an equal opportunity to contribute, regardless of status, hierarchy, or authority. The disadvantage of a purely circular arrangement is that, as compared to U-shaped seating, the role of the meeting facilitator is less clearly defined. Circular seating is also less well suited for problem-solving and presentations.

Theater-Style Seating: With theater-style seating, shown in the lower right quarter of Figure 4.2, the chairs are arranged in rows. Usually there are no tables, though there may be. This seating arrangement is best for large audiences listening to presentations and panel discussions. Other than (perhaps) a limited question and answer session at the end of the presentation, there is no discussion between the audience and the presenter(s).

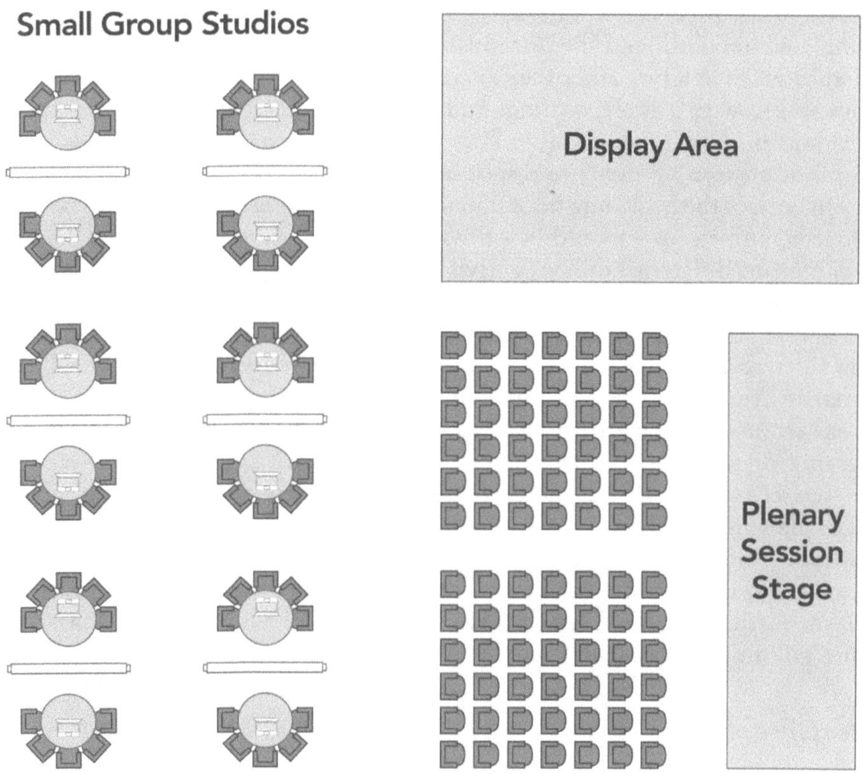

Figure 4.2 Large-group floor plan with a plenary space, small group studios for breakout groups, and a display area.

Source: David Holt Design

It makes sense to use theater-style seating when a problem needs to be presented before breaking into discussion groups and when the entire group votes to select an alternative.

Now let's move on to floor plans. Most small-group meetings take place in a conference room. If the meeting involves breakout activities, the breakout groups are dispersed into separate, smaller rooms. Illustrated in Figure 4.1 is an alternate way of accommodating small groups that alternate between the whole group and breakout groups. The floor plan has three areas—the *plenary area* in which the participants sit at a U-shaped table optionally equipped with a computer at each seat; *breakout studios*, with or without tables and with or without computers, separated by three whiteboards, as also shown in the left half of Figure 4.3; and a *display wall* for photos, diagrams, and other materials that are to be displayed.

The same three areas can be set up for larger groups. In this case, as shown in Figure 4.2, the *plenary area* consists of theater-style seating in front of a raised platform (dais), the *breakout studios* are divided by a single whiteboard, and the *display area* consists of a section of floor space dedicated to exhibits and other displays. Options are to equip each breakout studio with a table, seating, and a computer and to provide each participant in the plenary area with a voting tool. (See the following section for a discussion of audience response systems.)

In both of the foregoing floor plans, everything—the tables, chairs, whiteboards, and so on—should be on wheels so that the room can be quickly adapted to different kinds of activity. For example, with the small-group floor plan, to implement a different plenary arrangement, the whiteboards might be rearranged end-to-end in a curvilinear shape like the one shown on the right half of Figure 4.3 and the chairs moved in front of the whiteboards. And in the large-group format, the seating and whiteboards could be rearranged into separate clusters for discussing different topics, perhaps again using the curvilinear shape shown in the right half of Figure 4.3.

In all cases, whether a traditional conference room or creative floor plans like the foregoing case, the room should be the right size for the group, meaning big enough for the participants to comfortably move around, but not so big as to dwarf the group, disperse their energy, and compromise the acoustics. The ideal venue has an outdoor space where people can walk and talk in pairs or small groups, or they can sit alone to relax and reflect.

Sensory Cues

Let's start with the location of the meeting space. Ideally you want to meet off-site, away from the place where the group members usually work. Removing the group from their regular workplace(s) creates a sense of psychological distance, or separation, which has the effect of reducing the habitual thinking and emotional patterns tied to that environment. New settings activate different cognitive associations and emotional states. A second reason for meeting off-site is that it minimizes interruptions, thereby enabling deeper engagement and sustained discussions. Finally, off-site meetings remove the participants from the hierarchical structures of their workplace, which fosters a more level playing field where everyone feels comfortable contributing their thoughts.

The emerging field of *neuroarchitecture* studies the way architecture impacts the way we think and behave. Among its findings is the *cathedral effect*, which explains that high ceilings tend to evoke a sense of openness and freedom, promoting abstract thinking and creativity.[4] Research using functional magnetic resonance imaging (fMRI) has shown that high ceilings activate brain regions associated with spatial exploration and creative cognition. In the absence of high ceilings, vertical lines and uplighting contribute to the cathedral effect. By contrast, low-ceiling environments and small, walled-in spaces create a sense of confinement, which encourages more detailed task-focused thinking and focused discussions.

Other neuroarchitecture research pertains to what is known as *biophilia*, the innate human tendency to connect with other life forms and nature. Plants and animals have shapes made of curved lines (curvilinear shapes), whereas man-made artifacts tend to be made of straight lines (rectilinear shapes). Biophilia research demonstrates that views of nature (e.g., trees, flowers, a garden) and curvilinear shapes cause people to be happier, less stressed, and more creative.[5] The reason is that curves activate brain systems that have evolved to detect natural (biological) stimuli that confer selective advantage for survival and reproduction.[6] Neuroarchitectural design incorporates curvilinear shapes in everything from curved walls to curved table corners and armrest corners to curved patterns in the carpet.[7]

Natural light and colors are also linked to the way we think and feel. Studies show that individuals working in environments with ample natural light experience improved alertness, better performance on tasks requiring sustained attention, and elevated mood states.[8] This is attributed to natural light's role in regulating hormones such as serotonin, which influences mood stabilization. Colors also influence mood and cognitive performance.[9] For instance, blue hues are known to foster calmness and focus, whereas green stimulates creativity and relaxation. Choosing appropriate colors can create a meeting space conducive to the desired type of work.

Visual cues even extend to the pictures on the walls. The social psychologist Sapna Cheryan discovered a phenomenon she calls *ambient belonging*, which she defines as an individual's sense of fit with the environment and the people in it.[10] Her research focuses on the degree to which women and minorities experience a sense of fit in environments normally dominated by men and majorities.[11] Cheryan explains that a person's sense of belonging can be determined by as little as a cursory glance at a few objects. There are a number of ways to acknowledge and enhance a sense of belonging in a meeting space. Visual cues include pictures of diverse role models and leaders and avoiding décor that reinforces traditional power dynamics, such as all the images showing male leaders or leaders from other dominant groups. Another visual cue is to use warm, inviting colors and natural elements that are associated with inclusivity and openness rather than the dark woods, deep blues, and rigid structures that characterize a masculine design. And yet another visual cue is to rotate facilitators so as to include women and minorities.

Our other senses also play a role in determining the way we think and feel. In the meetings I facilitate, I play music at the beginning and ending of the meeting and at the start and stop of each of the breaks. One reason I do it is because music signals transitions. Consider, for example, the clever ways the *Morning Edition* and *All Things Considered* shows on National Public Radio use music to signal transitions between different stories. Music also stirs energy levels and emotions. High-energy music typically falls within the range of 120–150 beats per minute (BPM), so I play it at the start of the meeting and at the conclusion of lunch and the breaks. Music in the 40–80 BPM range relaxes people, which is why I play it at the start of lunch and each break. An upbeat, celebratory type of music in the BPM range between these two scales is a great way to end the day.

Another reason to use music relates to creative thinking. A key finding of one research study is that passively listening to music before a cognitive task boosts creativity.[12] Two experiments found that listening to music improved creative cognition as measured by the Remote Associates Test (RAT), an associative thinking task requiring participants to think of a fourth word that is somehow related to each of the first three words (e.g., ____ is related to room, blood, and salts),[13] and by a semantic memory task in which the participants listed as many words as possible from a given category (e.g., animals, supermarket items). The researchers discovered that after listening to hip-hop music, RAT creativity scores were significantly higher and participants generated larger clusters of related words in the semantic fluency task, suggesting deeper searches within semantic memory. Classical music and background babble noise, by contrast, did not produce these effects.

Proper sound management is also important. Minimizing external noise reduces distractions. Microphones and good acoustics enable people to hear and understand what others are saying, which is no small matter. I've participated in multiple meetings where you couldn't hear what soft-spoken people were saying because there were no microphones to amplify their voices. In other cases, even though you could hear the people, it was difficult to understand them because the room's acoustics distorted sound. The acoustics of a room distort sound when sound waves reflect off hard-surfaced walls and floors so that they arrive at the listener's ears at slightly different times. This results in "muddy" or uneven sound quality, with certain frequencies being amplified or dampened depending on the room's size and shape. The moral of the story is to make sure your meeting room has microphones and good acoustics.

The sense of smell is another way to impact thought and emotion.[14] Lemon scent elicits stimulation and activation, while lavender scent elicits relaxation and sedative effects. I put this fact to work by distributing lemon-scented nasal inhaler tubes at the start of the meeting and encouraging the participants to periodically take a whiff, especially when they feel the need for an energy boost. Another way to distribute scents (which I've yet to try) is to use an essential oil diffuser.

Food and Refreshments

The brain's 100 billion neurons consume about 20 percent of the body's energy. Keeping them working at peak capacity requires that they be fed. For this reason, food and refreshments should be available all day long, not just during the morning and afternoon breaks. After consulting with nutritionists, Margot Bloomstein, a brand consultant who frequently leads workshops, has the following suggestions for feeding the brain.[15] Avoid simple carbohydrates like juice, soda, and refined sugars in pastries that cause a sugar rush followed by a crash (made worse by coffee jitters) unless they are accompanied by fat and proteins that slow their absorption. For breakfast and morning breaks, it's best to skip the pastries altogether in favor of foods like breakfast burritos that combine carbohydrates, protein, and fat. Yogurt with no added sugar also combines carbohydrates, protein, and fat. Avoid white bread at lunch in favor of whole wheat, which contains more complex carbohydrates that break down slower. In the afternoon, skip the cookies and offer trail mix and yogurt instead.

Analog Tools

Analog tools include everything from name tags, notepads, sticky notes, dry erase markers, chalk, colored pens, and index cards to timers, chimes, prompt cards, building blocks, craft supplies, graph paper, and posters. In this section, I'm going to focus on just a few of them.

Whiteboards

Whiteboards figure prominently in both the small-group and large-group floor plans. Flipcharts don't. That's because a flipchart page provides little space to write on, which limits the group's thinking. Yes, you can arrange multiple flipchart pages on a wall, but it's clumsy and most meeting rooms aren't designed for it. It's also impossible to erase or rearrange what's been written on a flipchart page.

Analog whiteboards offer several comparative advantages over digital whiteboards. One advantage pertains to what researchers refer to as *embodied cognition* and *kinesthetic engagement*.[16] Research shows that physical movement enhances thinking. Writing, drawing, and erasing on an analog whiteboard and standing, moving, and gesturing while explaining ideas require physical, whole-body engagement. This engagement, along with the spatial structuring of ideas, activates spatial and motor cognition that causes deeper cognitive processing. Deeper cognitive processing refers to understanding, analyzing, and integrating information at a more complex and meaningful level, as contrasted with the shallow processing that focuses on surface-level details, such as memorization without understanding. Whole-body engagement also activates spatial memory and visual anchoring. The physicality of writing and drawing on an analog whiteboard enables users to intuitively track where information is written, which enhances recall.

A second way in which analog whiteboards are superior to digital whiteboards is that they enable *faster and more intuitive input*.[17] Writing with a marker on a whiteboard enables instant, uninterrupted transitions between writing, pointing, and erasing, whereas digital interfaces introduce intermediary steps like switching from pen to eraser, selecting colors, and resizing elements, all of which disrupt the fluidity of thought.

Larger and more flexible workspaces are a third advantage of analog whiteboards. The large workspace of a whiteboard enables expansive ideation, sketching, and mapping unimpeded by digital screen size limitations. Users can write freely in any direction without concerns about screen boundaries, zooming, or panning. Larger whiteboards also make it possible for multiple people to write, draw, and erase simultaneously, fostering a more immersive and collaborative environment.

One of my pet peeves is meeting rooms equipped with whiteboards barely big enough to write "Welcome!" Whiteboards should be as large as possible. Vertically, they should be as low and as high as a person can conveniently write or draw, possibly with the help of a step stool. Horizontally, they should be as wide as the space permits. In offices and meeting rooms, it's an excellent idea to turn entire walls, including hallway walls, into whiteboard surfaces. This is a good point at which to recall my earlier mention of CEOs like Jeff Bezos and Elon Musk who prize functionality over aesthetics.[18]

It also makes sense to equip meeting rooms with whiteboards on wheels, as illustrated in Figure 4.3. By equipping the whiteboards with wheels,

Figure 4.3 Two ways of setting up three whiteboards.

Source: David Holt Design

it's possible to arrange them in various configurations. The whiteboards should extend almost to the floor (to maximize space and minimize the transmission of sound from one side to the other) and they should extend above the person's head, again to maximize space. (Just make sure you can get them through the door.) It's also important that they be sturdy enough to prevent them from jiggling when someone is writing or drawing on the other side.

Tables

U-shaped setups, like the one shown in Figure 4.1, should be formed by fitting together tables that comfortably accommodate two people, each of whom is using a computer, which means you will need ten tables for a 20-person group. Even better are one-person tables that can be wheeled together to create the U or to create other configurations in the room, such as the "periodic tables" that are the core horizontal surfaces in the teaching areas of Stanford University's d.school. The design specifications for periodic tables are given in Scott Doorley and Scott Witthoft's book *Make Space: How to Set the Stage for Creative Collaboration.*[19]

Round tables, as I said, are good for the breakout groups because they eliminate the implicit hierarchy of a table where somebody sits at the head of the table. Another option is to use high-top tables large enough to accommodate 4–6 people, like the one shown in Figure 4.4. High-top tables offer several advantages for group problem-solving and design. Standing at high-top tables encourages shorter, more focused discussions, preventing stagnation in brainstorming sessions. They also make it easier to physically engage with the whiteboard or with a physical prototype or template (see the following discussion of templates) on the table. And high-top tables

Figure 4.4 A design team working at a high-top table.

Source: David Holt Design

promote more dynamic discussions by enabling group members to reposition themselves and gesture more easily, thereby enabling embodied cognition. Note that the height of the d.school's periodic tables can be adjusted so that 2–4 of them can be configured to create a high-top table.

Design Tools

Doorley and Witthoft's book provides an encyclopedic listing and description, including design specifications, of the many other analog tools used at the d.school. Thus, it serves as a useful resource for outfitting your meeting room. Among the d.school's tools are z-rack whiteboards, whiteboard sliders, foam cubes, flip stools, flip-top tables, quick component tables, prototyping tables, prototyping toolkits, hanging screens, see-through walls, T-walls, mini-screens, aesthetic panels, signage, bleacher blocks, wall displays, short board displays, transit trolleys, and storage towers. Their book also provides an equally lengthy list of room configurations, ranging from those that require nothing more than rearranging the furniture to those that require construction. In short, you have many more floorplans and analog tools to choose from than the ones I've described.

Templates

It's a good idea to equip breakout groups with ideation templates (analog or digital), especially when two or more of the groups are assigned the same task. Doing so ensures clarity, consistency, and comparability across the groups' discussions. Clarity is improved when participants spend more energy on generating insights than they do on figuring out how to organize their thoughts. It's also improved by the fact that the templates keep the participants on track, reducing the risk of tangents and unstructured debates. When the breakout groups reconvene in the plenary and present their results, the uniform format of the templates standardizes their output, making it easier for others to understand it and to compare and synthesize the groups' insights. Rather than a simple list of topics, it's best to create graphic templates that visually organize the topics. This makes them easier to understand and use and forces all the breakout groups to place information in the same geographic space on the template, thereby enhancing comparability. Following are five examples generated by ChatGPT.[20]

Prompt

Imagine that you are a meeting facilitator. It is a good meeting practice to give the breakout group participants templates to follow so that all the breakout groups can make apples-to-apples comparisons when they reconvene. Describe the format of five hypothetical templates.

ChatGPT's Response

1. *SWOT Analysis Template*

Purpose: Analyzes Strengths, Weaknesses, Opportunities, and Threats for a given topic.

Structure:

- Strengths: Internal advantages and capabilities.
- Weaknesses: Internal limitations or challenges.
- Opportunities: External factors that could be beneficial.
- Threats: External risks or obstacles.
- Key Takeaways: Prioritize the most critical insights.

2. *Root Cause Analysis (5 Whys) Template*

Purpose: Helps groups systematically identify the root cause of a problem using the "5 Whys" technique.

Structure:

- Problem Statement: Clearly define the issue.
- Why #1: Identify the first cause.
- Why #2: Dig deeper—why did that cause happen?
- Why #3: Continue drilling down.
- Why #4: Uncover deeper layers of causation.
- Why #5: Identify the core issue.
- Root Cause Summary: Final explanation of the fundamental issue.
- Recommended Solutions: Propose ways to address the root cause.

3. Risk Assessment Template
Purpose: Helps teams evaluate risks associated with a project, decision, or strategy.
Structure:

- Risk Description: Identify the potential risk.
- Likelihood (Low/Medium/High): Estimate probability.
- Impact (Low/Medium/High): Assess potential consequences.
- Mitigation Strategies: Outline ways to reduce or eliminate risk.
- Contingency Plan: Define actions if the risk materializes.
- Overall Risk Level (RAG Rating): Red (high), Amber (medium), Green (low).

4. Empathy Map Template
Purpose: Helps teams understand user needs and perspectives when designing solutions.
Structure:

- Who is the User? Describe the target audience.
- What Do They Think & Feel? Internal thoughts, worries, and motivations.
- What Do They See? Environment, influences, and experiences.
- What Do They Hear? Conversations, advice, and media exposure.
- What Do They Say & Do? Actions, statements, and behaviors.
- Pain Points: Challenges and frustrations.
- Gains: Desired outcomes and needs.

5. Action-Reflection Cycle Template
Purpose: Encourages iterative learning and improvement through reflection and action planning.

Structure:

- Action Taken: What was done?
- Observations: What happened as a result?
- Successes: What worked well?
- Challenges: What obstacles arose?
- Lessons Learned: Key takeaways.
- Next Steps: What changes or improvements should be made?

Digital Tools

In the last section, I explained the comparative advantages of analog whiteboards over digital whiteboards. In the spirit of "turnabout is fair play," I asked ChatGPT to describe the comparative advantages of digital tools over analog tools.[21] It responded in the following way:

Prompt

Describe the comparative advantages of digital tools (e.g., diagramming software) over analog tools (e.g., whiteboards).

ChatGPT's Response

1. *Persistence and Editability*

    - Digital Tools: Allow for easy modifications, version control, and undo/redo functionality. Changes can be made without erasing or starting over, preserving the evolution of ideas.
    - Analog Tools: Once written or drawn, modifications can be cumbersome (e.g., erasing or redrawing manually). Past versions are difficult to retrieve.

2. *Scalability and Space Efficiency*

    - Digital Tools: Offer virtually infinite canvas space, zooming, and layering options. Complex diagrams, notes, and mind maps can be scaled without spatial constraints.
    - Analog Tools: Limited by the physical size of the whiteboard or paper, making large-scale visualization difficult.

3. *Collaboration and Accessibility*

   - Digital Tools: Enable remote, real-time collaboration with multiple users editing the same document from different locations. Cloud storage ensures access across devices.
   - Analog Tools: Require physical presence, limiting remote teamwork. Information can be lost if erased or not documented separately.

4. *Integration with Other Tools and Data Sources*

   - Digital Tools: Can integrate with databases, AI tools, spreadsheets, and automation software to dynamically update content.
   - Analog Tools: Require manual updates and cannot link to external information sources.

5. *Multimedia and Rich Content*

   - Digital Tools: Support text, images, videos, hyperlinks, and interactive elements (e.g., simulations, AI-assisted design).
   - Analog Tools: Limited to what can be drawn or written manually; cannot include dynamic or multimedia content.

6. *Searchability and Organization*

   - Digital Tools: Content is searchable and can be categorized, tagged, and indexed for easy retrieval.
   - Analog Tools: Finding specific information requires scanning manually, which is time-consuming.

7. *Automation and AI Assistance*

   - Digital Tools: AI can suggest improvements, auto-format diagrams, transcribe handwriting, and offer real-time analytics.
   - Analog Tools: No automation; requires full manual effort.

8. *Environmental and Economic Impact*

   - Digital Tools: Reduce paper waste and the need for physical storage, making them more sustainable in the long run.
   - Analog Tools: Require consumables (markers, erasers, paper), leading to recurring costs and waste.

When Analog Tools Still Have an Edge

- While digital tools dominate in flexibility, analog tools may still have advantages in certain scenarios:

- Low-tech simplicity: No need for power, software, or internet access.
- Physical engagement: Writing by hand can improve memory and cognitive processing.
- Spontaneity: Quick, unstructured brainstorming is often more fluid on a physical whiteboard.

Conclusion

Digital tools provide superior functionality in terms of collaboration, storage, searchability, and scalability, making them indispensable for modern workflows. However, analog tools still hold value for rapid, in-person ideation and low-tech settings. The best approach often involves a hybrid model, where digital tools enhance but do not entirely replace analog methods.

Groups function most effectively when supported by both analog and digital tools. In the following subsections, with the help of ChatGPT, I identify the major kinds of digital tools and provide a sampling of the tools in each category. In the sections that follow this Digital Tools section, I give more elaborate explanations of three of the technologies that I use extensively when facilitating meetings—dialogue mapping, electronic brainstorming, and generative AI. As you read through the following subsections and sections, keep in mind that oftentimes the best approach is to combine several of the tools.

Audience Response Systems

Real-time polling devices (audience response systems) that enable an audience to vote and immediately see the vote results are often used in meetings, classrooms, and conferences. Note that audience response systems can be used to enable the plenary session participants to vote for ideas generated in the breakout groups. As detailed below, some of the systems require that each person be equipped with a voting keypad. Others enable the voters to use their mobile phones to vote.

Keypad-Based Voting Tools:

- Standalone voting devices (keypads) that allow live audiences to submit responses quickly and anonymously include *Ombea*, *Turning Technologies*, *iClicker*, *EZ-VOTE*, and *Option Power*.

Mobile-Phone-Based Voting Tools:

- Voting platforms that enable audiences to vote using their smartphones via apps, SMS, or web-based interfaces include *Slido*, *Mentimeter*, *Poll Everywhere*, *Voatz*, and *Democracy Live*.

Speech Recognition and Transcription Tools

In multiple places in this book, you've read about the idea of generative AI generating real-time responses to what the group is talking about. For generative AI to do so, the group members' spoken words must first be converted to text. The digital tools in this category facilitate the capture and conversion of speech into text. Note that microphones are needed to capture the spoken words. In smaller rooms, a good quality omnidirectional microphone will do. Other rooms might call for separate microphones at each station. As meeting rooms become more sophisticated, there may even come a time when each group member is wearing a headset with a microphone so that, for example, each of them can interact with generative AI separately.

Real-Time Transcription:

- *Otter.ai*: Provides live transcription services for meetings and lectures, offering features like collaborative notetaking and integration with platforms such as Zoom and Microsoft Teams.
- *Fireflies.ai*: An AI assistant that joins meetings to record and transcribe conversations in real time, supporting platforms like Google Meet, Teams, and Zoom.

Post-event Transcription:

- *Google Cloud Speech-to-Text*: Utilizes machine learning models to convert audio files into text, supporting a wide range of languages and audio formats.
- *Whisper by OpenAI*: An open-source speech recognition system capable of transcribing audio files and translating multiple languages into English.

Dictation Software:

- *Dragon Speech Recognition*: Offers speech-to-text capabilities for creating documents and controlling desktop applications through voice commands, enhancing productivity for professionals.

- *Braina*: A virtual assistant that provides speech recognition and dictation features, allowing users to control their computer and transcribe speech in multiple languages.

Communication and Collaboration Tools

Effective problem-solving starts with seamless communication and collaboration. The tools in this category support synchronous and asynchronous communication.

Synchronous Communication (Real-Time Interaction):

- Video Conferencing and Virtual Meetings: Platforms like *Zoom*, *Microsoft Teams*, and *Google Meet* enable real-time discussions with video, audio, and chat functions. Features like breakout rooms support parallel discussions, while polling and Q&A tools ensure active participation.
- Live Chat and Instant Messaging: Tools such as *Slack* and *Discord* enable fast, informal communication with threaded discussions, topic-specific channels, and integrations with other productivity tools.

Asynchronous Collaboration (Non-Real-Time Interaction):

- Discussion Forums and Message Boards: Platforms like *Discourse*, *Loomio*, and *Google Groups* enable groups to hold structured debates over time, with threaded conversations, voting features, and long-form deliberation.
- Collaborative Document Editing: Tools such as *Google Docs*, *Notion*, and *Dropbox Paper* enable multiple users to co-edit documents in real time and track revisions.

Knowledge and Information Management Tools

Problem-solving relies on accurate, well-organized, and easily accessible knowledge. These tools help teams store, retrieve, and synthesize information.

Knowledge Repositories and Wikis:

- Collaborative Knowledge Bases: *Confluence*, *Notion*, and *MediaWiki* enable teams to build structured knowledge bases, ideal for reference materials, FAQs, and internal documentation.

AI-Powered Research Assistants:

- Literature Review and Research Aggregation: *Elicit*, *Consensus.app*, and *Perplexity AI* assist in automating research tasks, retrieving relevant studies, articles, and expert opinions.

Annotation and Collective Sense-Making:

- Social Annotation and Highlighting Tools: *Hypothesis*, *Diigo*, and *Obsidian* allow teams to annotate web pages, PDFs, and research papers, facilitating collective sense-making.

Task and Workflow Management Tools

To keep problem-solving efforts structured, teams need tools to assign tasks, track progress, and manage deadlines.

Task Planning and Agile Workflows:

- Task Boards and Kanban Systems: *Trello*, *Asana*, and *ClickUp* provide drag-and-drop task organization, making workflows transparent and manageable.
- Agile Project Management Tools: *Jira*, *Monday.com*, and *Kanbanize* help teams implement scrum and kanban methodologies, prioritizing tasks dynamically.

Workflow Automation and AI-Augmented Tasking:

- AI-Powered Productivity Boosters: *Airtable*, *Coda*, and *Zapier* integrate automated workflows, predictive task allocation, and data synchronization.

Integrated Collaborative Workspaces

These tools provide all-in-one platforms that include communication and collaboration tools, knowledge and information management tools, and task and workflow management tools. They serve teams that require a central hub for ongoing problem-solving and decision-making efforts.

Online Workspaces for Team Collaboration:

- Project and Document Collaboration: *GroveSite*, *teamspace*, and *Huddle* support news pages, searchable document repositories, threaded discussions, project planning, team directories, and blast emails. Some include permission controls.
- Role-Based Access and Workflow Integration: *SharePoint* and *Igloo* provide structured team spaces with permission controls, workflow automation, and version tracking.

Decision-Making and Knowledge Management Platforms:

- Team-Based Knowledge Repositories: *Notion*, *Confluence*, and *Basecamp* help teams organize knowledge, track meeting decisions, and store research insights.
- Integrated Task and Discussion Tools: *HyperOffice* and *Samepage* combine task assignments, document co-editing, and team messaging for seamless collaboration.

Idea Generation and Creativity Tools

To solve problems effectively, groups need to generate, structure, and refine ideas. These tools help visualize thinking processes, encourage creativity, and manage brainstorming sessions. Note that EBS technology, which I describe in a later section, also falls into this category.

Mind Mapping and Concept Structuring:

- Mind Mapping Tools: Platforms like *MindMeister*, *XMind*, and *Inspiration* help teams organize thoughts through visual diagrams that link concepts and show hierarchical relationships.
- Concept Mapping: Tools like *CmapTools* and *TheBrain* focus on knowledge representation, making connections between complex ideas easier to navigate.

Digital Whiteboarding and Brainstorming:

- Online Whiteboards: *Miro*, *Mural*, and *Jamboard* support real-time sketching, sticky-note organization, and collaborative diagramming. Good for design thinking, root cause analysis, and flowcharting.
- Sticky Note and Idea Management Systems: *Stormboard* and *Lucidspark* provide structured brainstorming workflows, including voting on ideas, clustering suggestions, and prioritizing concepts.

Decision Support and Consensus-Building Tools

Decision-making requires structured frameworks to analyze options, weigh trade-offs, and build consensus. These tools provide structured decision-making methodologies.

Decision Structuring and Multi-criteria Analysis:

- Weighted Decision Matrices: *Xleap*, *Logical Decisions*, *1000minds*, and *TransparentChoice* assist in breaking down complex choices by assigning weights to different criteria, helping teams make rational decisions.

- Pairwise Comparison and Prioritization Tools: *Decision Lens* and *AHP Online System* use methods like the Analytic Hierarchy Process (AHP) to compare choices systematically.

Dialogue Mapping and Deliberative Tools:

- Structured Debate and Logic Tools: *bCisive*, *Rationale*, *Kialo*, and *DebateGraph* provide a visual representation of arguments and counterarguments, improving critical thinking and rational deliberation. I will elaborate on dialogue mapping in the next section.

Crowdsourcing and AI-Augmented Decision-Making Tools

By integrating AI, crowdsourcing, and real-time collective intelligence, these tools enhance group decision-making and forecasting.

Crowdsourcing and Wisdom of the Crowd:

- Mass Collaboration Platforms: *Kaggle* and *Zooniverse* leverage expert and layperson contributions to solve complex problems collectively.

Swarm Intelligence and Real-Time Consensus:

- Adaptive Collective Intelligence: UNANIMOUSAI's *Swarm* combines the power of AI with the swarm intelligence of large human groups to quickly generate optimized insights, forecasts, and assessments.

Scenario Planning and Simulation Tools

In high-stakes decision-making, teams may need to simulate different outcomes before committing to a course of action.

Scenario Analysis and Risk Modeling:

- What-If Simulations: *AnyLogic* and *GoldSim* model complex systems, stress-test decisions, and anticipate unintended consequences.

Serious Games and Role-Playing for Decision Training:

- Simulated Decision-Making Environments: *Mursion* and *Harvard Business Publishing Simulations* provide realistic, interactive simulations for leadership training.

Future Scenario Analysis and Stress Testing:

- Strategic Planning and Foresight Tools: *Synario* takes teams through the process of constructing alternative future scenarios and testing decision resilience.
- Disruptive Trend Analysis: *SenseMaker* and *Futures Platform* help teams anticipate market shifts, social transformations, and emerging risks.

System Dynamics and Causal Loop Modeling Tools

Understanding complex systems requires tools that map interdependencies, feedback loops, and long-term effects to improve strategic decision-making.

Causal Loop Diagrams and Stock-Flow Models:

- System Mapping Tools: *Vensim*, *Stella Architect*, *Insight Maker*, and *MentalModeler* enable teams to visualize reinforcing and balancing feedback loops, model system behaviors, and simulate long-term impacts.
- Dynamic Simulation Platforms: *iThink* and *Powersim* help teams model resource flows, policy interventions, and unintended consequences.

Decision Trees and Probabilistic Decision Modeling Tools

Teams making decisions under uncertainty benefit from structured models that map choices, probabilities, and expected outcomes.

Decision Trees and Bayesian Networks:

- Structured Decision Analysis: *DPL (Decision Programming Language)*, *PrecisionTree*, and *TreeAge Pro* provide intuitive decision trees, risk quantification, and probability-based trade-off analysis.
- Bayesian Network Modeling: *BayesiaLab* and *GeNIe* enable teams to incorporate expert knowledge and data-driven probabilities for scenario evaluation.

Monte Carlo Simulation and Stochastic Modeling Tools

Simulating thousands of potential outcomes helps teams assess risks, variability, and uncertainties in decision-making.

Risk Assessment and Forecasting Tools:

- Probability-Based Risk Simulations: *@Risk*, *Crystal Ball*, and *Simul8* enable teams to conduct Monte Carlo simulations, apply probability distributions, and forecast financial, project, and operational risks.
- Stochastic Process Modeling: *GoldSim* and *Simulink* help teams model probabilistic event sequences, reliability analysis, and uncertainty propagation.

Idea and Innovation Management Tools

Harnessing collective intelligence for ideation, evaluation, and implementation of innovative solutions. These tools facilitate idea generation, refinement, and prioritization within organizations and communities.

Idea Generation and Crowdsourcing:

- *IdeaScale* and *Crowdicity*: Platforms that enable organizations to crowdsource ideas from employees, customers, or the public, fostering diverse input and collaborative innovation.

Idea Evaluation and Prioritization:

- *Brightidea* and *Spigit*: Use AI-driven analytics, voting mechanisms, and scoring models to rank and prioritize ideas based on feasibility, impact, and strategic alignment.
- *Hype Innovation* and *Planbox*: Provide structured workflows and stage-gate processes to track the lifecycle of ideas from inception to execution.

AI-Driven Insight Extraction:

- *InnovationCast* and *Qmarkets*: Leverage AI to identify trends, cluster similar ideas, and generate actionable insights from large volumes of input.

Dialogue Mapping

Dialogue mapping, sometimes called *argument mapping* or *conversation mapping*, involves mapping the elements of a dialogue or conversation. Dialogue mapping is the outgrowth of Issue-Based Information Systems (IBIS), an idea first proposed in 1970 by Horst Rittel, an urban planner and designer. Rittel's idea was to design an information system that supports group problem-solving. He was especially concerned with devising a way to attack ill-defined problems, which he called *wicked problems*, where the number and nature of the problem's elements are poorly understood. The central elements of IBIS are topics, issues positions, and arguments (which I prefer to call reasons), each of which is explained below. It will help to refer to Figure 4.5 as you read through the explanation.

We sometimes use the phrases *topic* of discussion or topic of conversation. Intuitively, we understand the term to mean "what is being talked about," or the "aboutness" of some stretch of dialogue. Lengthy dialogues

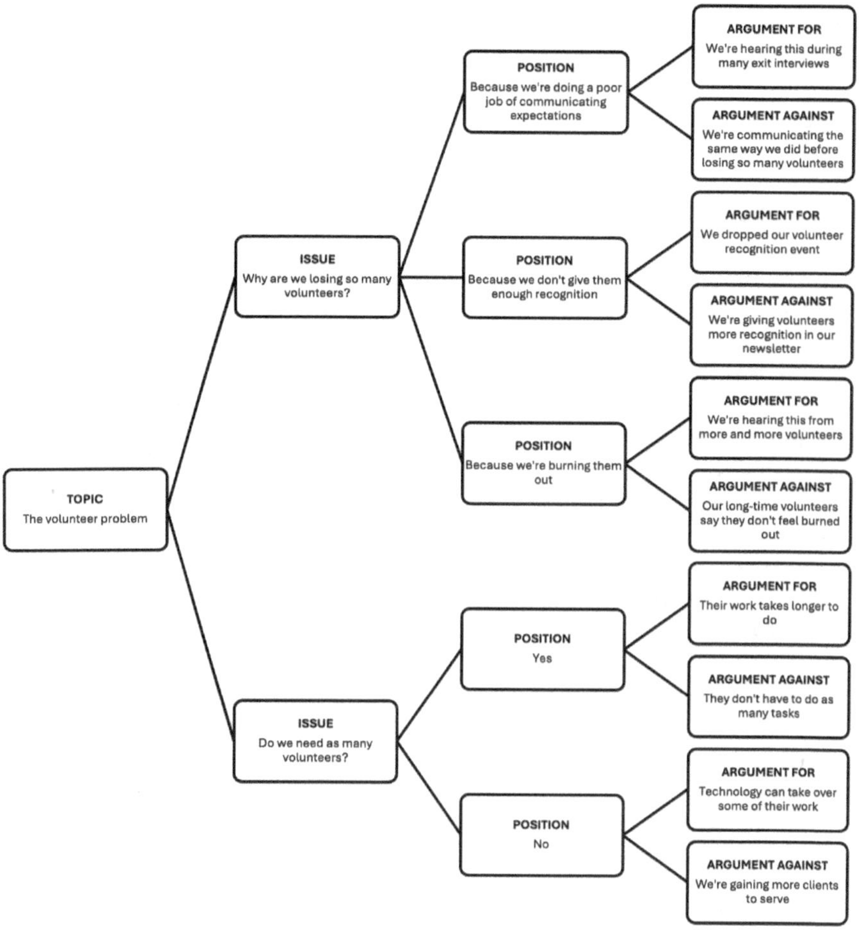

Figure 4.5 A simple dialogue map showing the elements of a problem-solving conversation. The map was created with the diagramming tool Inspiration.

typically have multiple topics and sub-topics. In casual conversation the topics are unplanned and unpredictable. After the fact, you could describe the "aboutness" of a casual conversation in terms of a hierarchical framework of topics and sub-topics, but prior to the conversation you would have no way of knowing what it will be about. This contrasts with a formal, task-oriented dialogue, such as a strategic planning session, in which the topical framework is pre-planned and imposed on the participants. But even formal conversations veer into the unplanned and unpredictable. People introduce new, relevant topics or wander off-topic into irrelevancies, making it difficult for the participants to keep track of what they're talking about. Even harder to track are dialogues having to do with wicked problems, which often start with no more topical structure than a trigger phrase like "the employee turnover problem," "the financing problem," or "the crime problem."

Oftentimes, as people talk about topics, *issues* are brought up and disputed. An issue is a point of controversy that is best stated in the form of a question. One way of classifying issues is to say that there are two types—descriptive and prescriptive. Descriptive issues involve questions about what was, is, or will be the case. In other words, the questions ask for a description of some past, present, or future thing. Examples are: What caused our revenue to decrease last year? Does more advertising always result in an increase in revenue? What will our revenue be next year? Prescriptive issues involve "ought" or "should" questions about the past, present, or future. In other words, the questions ask what should have been prescribed or what should be prescribed, now or in the future. Examples are: Should we have increased our advertising budget last year? Should we maintain the current advertising budget? Should we increase the advertising budget next year?

It's usually the case that people have different *positions* on an issue. More formal terms for position are *assertion*, *claim*, and *conclusion* and less formal are *idea*, *proposal*, and *alternative*. One way of defining the term position is to say that it is a statement that a person wants others to believe. Another way is to say that a position is a descriptive or prescriptive answer to an issue question. A useful metaphor for understanding issues and positions is to imagine an issue as the point at which there is a fork in the road. One person holds to the position that "this road" is the right or best way forward, that is, that his description or prescription is the right one or the best one. Another person takes the position that "that road" is the correct or superior route, and perhaps others conclude that a third or fourth road is the way to go. For example, in response to the question (issue) "Should we maintain the current advertising budget?" one person may hold to the position that it should be decreased, a second that it should remain the same, and a third that it should be increased.

People usually cite one or more *reasons* for or against a position, which is to say, their reasons for supporting the position or opposing it. A reason is an explanation or rationale for why someone should or shouldn't believe a position. Oftentimes, a position and a reason are packaged in the same sentence, as happens when someone says, "I think we should do X because Y." A person may also package reasons against a position, such as when the person says, "I don't think we should do X because Z." In both cases, the combination of the position and reason constitutes an *argument*, which has the general form "I think this for that reason."[22]

There are many different kinds of reasons, some valid and some invalid, some better and some worse, and there are valid and invalid ways of reasoning. I won't get into all that here, other than to say that many reasons are statements that present information (evidence), such as relevant facts, examples, and statistics. For example, a person promoting the position that his company should increase its advertising budget might cite reasons like (a) we increased our advertising budget last year and sales increased substantially (a relevant fact); (b) the Widget Company increased their ad budget and their sales improved significantly (anecdotal evidence); and (c) industry research demonstrates that in 90 percent of the cases, the benefits of advertising outweigh the costs (statistical evidence).

To summarize, dialogues develop around a framework of *topics* and *subtopics*. As people talk about the topics, various *issues* emerge. The issues are typically phrased as questions. People take different *positions* on each of the issues, which is to say, they propose different answers to the questions. They present *reasons* for their position and may also present reasons against another person's position. Whether for or against, common reasons are a relevant fact, anecdotal evidence, or statistical evidence.

The foregoing paragraph paints a nice, tidy picture of dialogue. In practice, nothing could be further from the truth. Real discussions are messy. People jump ahead or back or otherwise hopscotch through the topic, or they digress and stray off on tangents. They may fail to identify the issues or do a poor job of articulating the ones that are identified, most often by presenting the issue as a controversial statement rather than converting it to a question. People frequently state their positions in an ambiguous way, and it isn't always clear which issue the position is connected to. They may also cite poor or invalid reasons for or against a position, if they cite any reasons at all. In group discussions these problems are compounded by the sheer volume of the topics, issues, positions, and reasons that people need to keep track of.

Dialogue mapping is an effective way to track and manage messy, voluminous group discussions. While it's possible to do it on a whiteboard, using a software tool is more effective. You can use a simple diagramming tool, such as *Inspiration*, or you can use a specialized dialogue mapping software, such as *bCisive*. A simple example of a dialogue map is shown in Figure 4.5. In actual practice, the map would contain many more elements and would result in one or more conclusions about the nature of the problem and what to do about it.

Creating a dialogue map has multiple benefits. First, it provides a way for everyone to contribute what they know about the topic (i.e., what they know about the topic's subtopics, issues, positions, and reasons) and to see how their piece of the puzzle relates to the others.[23] Second, over the course of the conversation, it serves as the group memory and eliminates the need for the participants to remember what's been talked about. This is especially useful when the group implements the long chains of inference discussed and diagrammed (using Feynman diagrams) in Chapter 1. Third, it results in a shared understanding of the structure of the problem and the reasoning that produced a solution. Fourth, creating a visual structure of the problem makes it more likely that key elements of the problem will not be overlooked. Or, to put it another way, it results in a more comprehensive understanding of the problem. Fifth, a dialogue map makes it easier to deal with dysfunctional group behaviors. For example, when a person keeps bringing up the same issue (wheel spinning), you can point to where the matter has already been addressed on the map, and when people wander off on tangents, you can ask them to point out where the tangent fits on the map. And sixth, the map provides an organized record of the conversation and a place to begin if the conversation later needs to be extended.

A perceived downside of dialogue mapping is that entering the elements into the software slows the conversation, causing some participants to become impatient. But the added time gives the participants more time to think. And ensuring a comprehensive understanding of a problem by taking more time to think about it and map it makes it more likely you won't have to later spend even more time (and money) on the problem when the first, ill-considered solution fails. As the saying goes, "Patience is bitter, but its fruit is sweet."

Facilitating a dialogue mapping session is like being a translator because it requires that you translate people's natural language into the topic-issue-position-reason language of the map. The hard part is learning to tease these four elements out of everyday speech—for example, converting controversial statements into issues phrased as questions, separating positions and reasons that are packaged in the same sentence, and tracking conversational exchanges that are embedded within other exchanges. An excellent resource for learning how to facilitate a dialogue mapping session is Jeff Conklin's book *Dialogue Mapping: Building Shared Understanding of Wicked Problems*.[24]

I asked ChatGPT how generative AI could be used to augment dialogue mapping.[25] Following is its answer.

Prompt

Read the foregoing text. Then explain how generative AI could be used to augment dialogue mapping.

ChatGPT's Response

Generative AI can significantly augment dialogue mapping by automating and enhancing various aspects of the process, improving efficiency, accuracy, and engagement. Here's how:

1. *Real-time Transcription & Structuring*
   - Natural Language Processing (NLP) for Speech-to-Text: AI can transcribe spoken dialogue in real-time and identify key elements—topics, issues, positions, and reasons—automatically.
   - Semantic Analysis for Structuring: AI can parse conversation data and suggest a structured representation in an Issue-Based Information System (IBIS) format, reducing the cognitive load on the facilitator.
2. *Automated Topic & Issue Detection*
   - AI-powered Topic Modeling: Using techniques like Latent Dirichlet Allocation (LDA) or Transformer-based models (BERT, GPT), AI can identify and categorize topics and subtopics dynamically as they emerge in the discussion.
   - Question Identification: AI can recognize when an issue is being debated and reframe statements into properly structured issue questions (e.g., turning "Our marketing isn't working" into "How can we improve our marketing effectiveness?").
3. *Position Extraction & Reasoning Analysis*
   - Position Differentiation: AI can analyze multiple perspectives on an issue and suggest distinct positions, helping to clarify ambiguities.
   - Reason Validation & Classification: AI can classify reasons based on their type (e.g., factual evidence, anecdotal evidence, statistical reasoning) and assess the validity of arguments based on logical consistency and supporting data.
4. *Visualization & Real-time Updates*
   - Dynamic Dialogue Mapping: AI can update a dialogue map in real time, highlighting relationships between elements (e.g., linking arguments to positions, categorizing issues).

- Interactive Graphs & Summaries: AI can generate visual representations of the dialogue structure, making it easier for participants to follow discussions.

5. *Enhancing Group Memory & Retrieval*
   - Contextual Memory for Discussion Continuity: AI can store and retrieve past dialogue maps, allowing discussions to pick up where they left off.
   - Searchable Knowledge Base: AI can maintain a structured archive of past conversations, making it easier to track the evolution of a problem and revisit previous reasoning.
6. *Detecting Logical Fallacies & Biases*
   - Critical Discourse Analysis: AI can flag logical fallacies (e.g., straw man arguments, false dilemmas) and cognitive biases (e.g., confirmation bias).
   - Sentiment & Pragmatic Analysis: AI can detect emotional tone, sarcasm, and implied meanings, helping facilitators refine and clarify discussions.
7. *Facilitating Large-scale, Distributed Discussions*
   - Automated Summarization & Synthesis: AI can generate concise summaries of long conversations, making it easier for participants to grasp key takeaways.
   - Multimodal Input Support: AI can integrate text, voice, and even video discussions into a unified dialogue mapping framework.
8. *Guiding Participants in Real time*
   - Conversational Prompts & Nudges: AI can provide real-time suggestions, such as rewording an issue more clearly, ensuring all perspectives are considered, or prompting participants to provide evidence for their claims.
   - Tangent Detection & Management: AI can detect when the discussion is straying off-topic and prompt facilitators to steer the conversation back on track.
9. *Integration with Decision-support Systems*
   - Bayesian Reasoning for Probabilistic Inference: AI can help quantify uncertainty in positions and evaluate the likelihood of different outcomes.
   - Simulation & Scenario Planning: AI can generate simulations based on different positions and their consequences, helping decision-makers anticipate potential outcomes.

Conclusion

Generative AI can revolutionize dialogue mapping by automating transcription, structuring conversations, extracting key elements, visualizing relationships, and detecting logical fallacies. By acting as an intelligent co-facilitator, AI can make the process more scalable, efficient, and insightful, especially when dealing with wicked problems that require collective intelligence.

I next asked ChatGPT to evaluate the degree to which generative AI is currently capable of performing the foregoing activities.[26] Following is its summarized response.

Prompt

Evaluate your answer to determine the degree to which the current capabilities of generative AI can support your responses.

ChatGPT's Summary Response

Feature	*Feasibility Today*	*Key Limitation(s)*	*Key AI Improvement Needed*
Enhancing Group Memory & Retrieval	Feasible	Context tracking errors	Improved long-term AI memory
Real-time Transcription & Structuring	Feasible with limitations	Poor discourse segmentation	Better dialogue structuring models
Automated Topic & Issue Detection	Partially feasible	Ambiguity in issue framing	Enhance topic/question disambiguation
Position Extraction & Reasoning Analysis	Partially feasible	Struggles with implicit arguments	Stronger logic-aware NLP
Facilitating Large-scale, Distributed Discussions	Partially feasible	Needs human moderation	Better intent recognition & summarization

Visualization & Real-time Updates	Limited feasibility	No real-time updating	AI-driven live mapping tools
Detecting Logical Fallacies & Biases	Limited feasibility	Struggles with nuanced fallacies	Better critical reasoning models
Guiding Participants in Real-time	Limited feasibility	No adaptive facilitation	AI with real-time conversational steering
Integration with Decision-support Systems	Limited feasibility	No probabilistic reasoning	Bayesian-enhanced dialogue AI

Final Assessment

Generative AI can already enhance some aspects of dialogue mapping, but full automation and real-time facilitation remain limited.

- AI excels at transcription, summarization, and topic detection but struggles with logical reasoning, dynamic visualization, and real-time facilitation.
- Key areas of improvement include pragmatic language understanding, conversational adaptability, and integration with decision-support frameworks.

Conclusion

Today's AI can act as an *assistant* to a dialogue mapper, but it is not yet capable of fully replacing human facilitation in complex discussions. However, as AI advances in discourse processing and real-time interaction, its role in augmenting group deliberation, structuring reasoning, and improving collective intelligence will become increasingly powerful.

Electronic Brainstorming

Electronic brainstorming (EBS) is a group idea-generation technology that emerged from research on group support systems conducted by the information science professor Jay Nunamaker and his colleagues at the University of Arizona. Their primary motivation for developing the technology was to overcome the earlier described process losses of traditional brainstorming meetings—production blocking, cognitive interference, and evaluation apprehension. A meta-analysis of the EBS literature confirms that compared to the traditional face-to-face interacting groups, EBS produces a higher number of ideas and higher-quality ideas.[27] It produces higher-quality ideas by increasing the total number of ideas that are generated, by mitigating the process losses, by improving the ability to reference and build on previous ideas, and by providing voting tools that enable the group to exercise group judgment that is superior to individual judgments. As the Nobel Prize-winning chemist Linus Pauling said, "The best way to have a good idea is to have lots of ideas and throw away the bad ones."[28] In effect, EBS enables a group to generate lots of ideas and vote to throw away the bad ones.

Several commercial EBS systems have been created over the years, one of which is XLeap, the system I use to facilitate meetings. As I said in the introduction, the idea of increasing a group's collective intelligence is what originally sparked my interest in EBS.[29] Now, a quarter-century later, I am even more excited about the possibility of making groups smarter by combining EBS with generative AI. I'll explain why in a later section devoted to that topic, but to do so, I first need you to understand how XLeap and generative AI work.

XLeap supports virtual meetings, both synchronous and asynchronous, as well as face-to-face meetings. In synchronous virtual meetings, users simultaneously log on to both XLeap and a videoconferencing tool, such as Zoom, Microsoft Teams, or Google Meet. The videoconferencing tool provides the video and audio capabilities. XLeap is used to implement the activities described in the rest of this section.

XLeap can be used to support everything from boardroom- to ballroom-size face-to-face meetings. There's almost no limit to the number of participants it can simultaneously support. As a practical matter, however, most face-to-face meetings involve 20 people or less. I have also used it to support 200-person ballroom-size meetings in which one laptop is placed at each roundtable, and one person at the table scribes for the rest of the group. And I've used it to facilitate virtual meetings totaling as many as 60 participants.

The usual setup for a small group, face-to-face meeting is shown in Figure 4.6. Each participant is equipped with a computer. The facilitator is located at the front of the room, where there are two computers. One is used to project the participants' input on the projector screen (which the participants can also view on their own computer screens), and the other is used to operate the EBS system. XLeap's EBS technology supports five major types of activities—presentation, brainstorming, voting, deep dive, and reporting. The first four activities are used to carry out the steps of the process that is being implemented (e.g., a problem-solving process or a

Figure 4.6 A meeting room set up with computers for an electronic brainstorming session.

Source: Co.Innovation Consulting, David Holt Design

strategic planning process). The reporting function produces a report that contains all the participants' input, which typically totals about 30 pages for a one-day workshop.

In an EBS meeting, the participants spend about half of their time typing their comments and submitting their votes. The other half is spent discussing the comments or the vote results. In other words, the participants spend about half the time typing and half the time talking.

Presentation Activity

The presentation activity can be used to present PDF versions of a slideware deck (e.g., a PowerPoint, Keystone, Google Slides deck). The advantages of showing the slides using the presentation activity rather than showing them using, say, PowerPoint are these:

- As shown in the right part of Figure 4.7, XLeap's presentation capability enables the participants to comment on each slide. In Figure 4.7, they are being asked to comment on the floor plan located in the left half of the figure. The prompt request is located at the top of the right part of the screen, the box for inputting the prompt is at the bottom of the screen, and the participants' comments are in the middle of the screen.

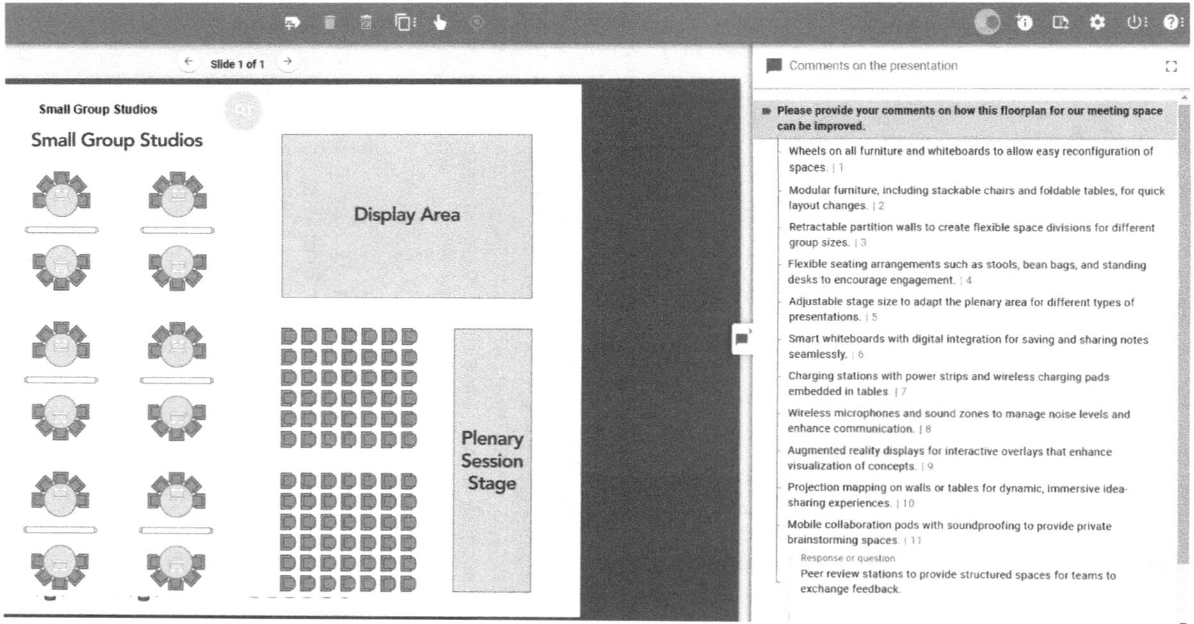

Figure 4.7 Screenshot of the XLeap presentation activity.

Source: Co.Innovation Consulting, XLeap

Participants can be asked to comment on a body of text or on an image, such as a floor plan, photograph, web page, logo, product prototype, or some other kind of image.

- The participants can use "sticky dot" voting to identify the comment(s) they prefer. Or, alternatively, the comments can be sent to one of the voting tools described in the Voting Tools section below. If there are multiple slides (e.g., to show multiple versions of a floor plan), the participants can use sticky dot voting to select the slide (version) they prefer. In this way, XLeap makes it possible to take advantage of the collective judgment of the group.

The most common way to use the presentation activity is to do a "regular" slide presentation that introduces a subsequent brainstorming or voting activity. The introduction might explain where the brainstorming or voting activity fits into the meeting process, or it might provide background information for the brainstorming or voting activity.

Brainstorming Activity

The brainstorming activity screen is shown in Figure 4.8. The screen is divided into three areas. At the top of the screen is the question or instruction for the activity. At the bottom of the screen is a box for entering the participant's response. After typing the response, the participant clicks the POST icon or presses the enter key, which sends the response to the middle of the screen and clears the box for another entry. The response is listed in the middle of the screen along with the other participants' responses in the order they are entered. Following are some of the capabilities and advantages of the brainstorming activity:

- A recent, and extremely useful, addition to XLeap is the integration of ChatGPT and other generative AI platforms into the brainstorming activity. With the addition of this capability, ChatGPT (or another generative AI platform) will respond to the question or instruction along with the other participants. The activity can be set up to give ChatGPT very explicit instructions about how to respond, including the number of responses it is to generate, the level of detail of the responses, and the degree of creativity that it should use to generate the responses.
- Because everyone can enter their responses *simultaneously*, EBS mitigates the two types of process losses called production blocking and cognitive interference that result from sequential conversation. Note that simultaneous entry is also enabled in the presentation, deep dive, and voting activities.
- Simultaneous entry enables the group to capture dozens of ideas in a matter of minutes, which, in a 20-person group, is something that would require as much as an hour to do using the traditional approach

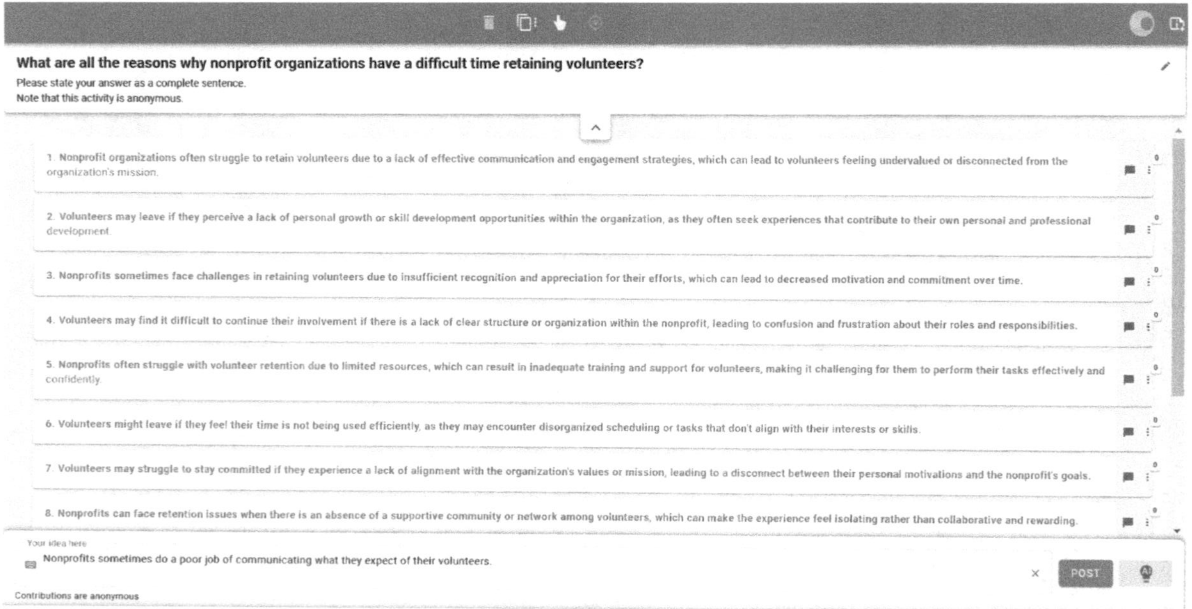

Figure 4.8 Screenshot of the XLeap brainstorming activity.

Source: Co.Innovation Consulting, XLeap

of having each group member voice their responses and capture what they said on a flipchart or whiteboard.

- Once the responses are entered, they can be edited, deleted, merged, and re-ordered, which provides much more flexibility than a flipchart or a whiteboard.
- The participants' responses can be categorized by sorting them into folders (e.g., themes, projects, priorities). The folders can be created before the meeting or on-the-fly. Sorting the responses into the folders makes it easier to identify *gaps* (additional ideas that should be added to each folder), *redundancies* (duplicate ideas in each folder), and *synergies* (ways the ideas in a folder can be combined to enhance one another).
- A brainstorming activity can be set up to enable *attributed entry*, where each participant's name or team name is attached to their responses. Or, the activity can be set up for *anonymous entry*, which surmounts the process loss known as evaluation apprehension. It's also possible to use the anonymous entry feature in the presentation, deep dive, and voting activities.
- Brainstorming activities can also be set up to implement the nominal group technique, which eliminates the earlier described anchoring effect.
- Information can be imported into the brainstorming activity, and the responses can be exported out of the activity for use elsewhere.
- The participants can comment on each other's responses and on another's comment on a response, and on another's comment on a comment, and so on, which enables a multi-level hierarchical threaded discussion.
- The responses, or a selection of them, can be copied and pasted into a follow-on brainstorming activity.
- The group can use sticky dot voting to select one or more responses. Or the responses, or a selection of them, can be copied into a separate voting activity. Alternatively, the participants can use sticky dot voting to select one or more of the folders, or the folders can be copied into a separate voting activity.

As you consider the capabilities of the brainstorming activity, remember that one reason that groups can be smarter than their smartest member is that the group members collectively contribute the "pieces of the puzzle" and that they use *group reasoning* to fit the pieces together. And next, as you consider the capabilities of the voting activity, remember that the other reason groups are smarter than their smartest member is the *group judgment* that is obtained by using voting to aggregate their judgments.

Voting Activity

XLeap supports sticky dot voting within the presentation, brainstorming, and deep dive activities. The other voting tools are implemented in voting activities that are set up separate from these three activities. In all cases, the participants are voting to select one or more of the alternatives or to rank order them. Either the alternatives were created in a previous brainstorming activity and copied and pasted into the voting activity, or they were imported to the voting activity from elsewhere. XLeap supports the following kinds of voting. The benefits of each type of voting and the circumstances in which they apply were described in Chapter 3.

- With *budget allocation voting* (termed *allocating points* in Chapter 3) the voters allocate a specified number of votes (say, 100) to the alternatives.
- *Multiple selection voting* involves selecting one or more alternatives. The tool can be set up to specify the number of alternatives that a participant can choose. A screen shot of the multiple selection voting activity is shown in Figure 4.9.
- *Estimate voting* is used to estimate a number for each of the items on the list. Examples include using it to estimate the cost of alternative ways of doing something, the cost of each part of a product, or the time required to complete each step of a process.
- With the *rank order voting* tool, the voters drag and drop the alternatives into a high-to-low or low-to-high order according to a specified criterion, such as importance, feasibility, or impact.
- In *Likert scale voting*, the voters rate each alternative on a scale, such as a 1 to 5 scale, 1 to 10 scale, or some other scale, including minus to plus scales, such as a –5 to +5 scale.
- In *multi-criteria voting*, each alternative is rated on a Likert scale according to two or more criteria. For example, a set of job candidates might be rated on technical skills, experience, and education. Optionally, a weight can be assigned to each of the criteria to reflect their relative importance. For example, experience might be deemed twice as important as technical skills and education.

Two other features of the voting activity are worth mentioning. First, the voting tools calculate the standard deviation for the vote result for each alternative so that the group can identify the degree of agreement (or disagreement) among the members with respect to each alternative. Second, you have the option to let the voters abstain from voting for an alternative, which enables voters to opt out when they don't believe they have sufficient knowledge to make an informed judgment.

Deep Dive Activity

The deep dive activity is like the brainstorming activity in the sense that it is used to capture the participants' responses. But instead of devoting the entire activity to a single question as is done in the brainstorming activity, the participants answer (dive into) multiple questions. The activity can be set up to allow them to proceed from one question to the next at their own pace, or it can be set up so that the facilitator pulls the participants into each of the questions. A screen shot of the deep dive activity is shown in Figure 4.10.

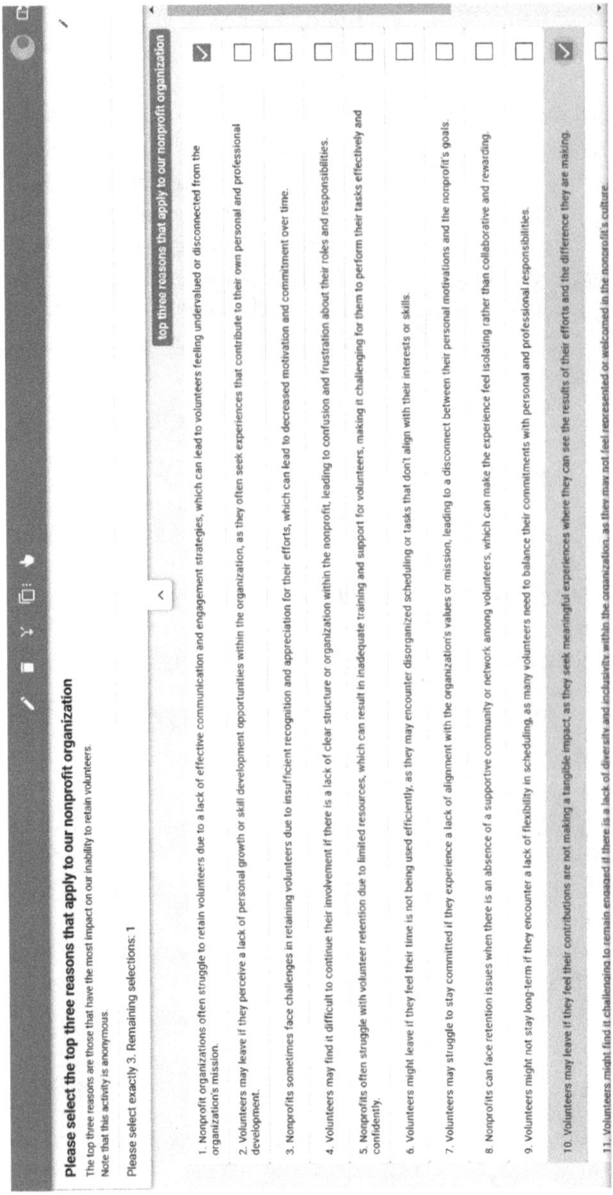

Figure 4.9 Screenshot of the XLeap multiple selection voting activity.

Source: Co.Innovation Consulting, XLeap

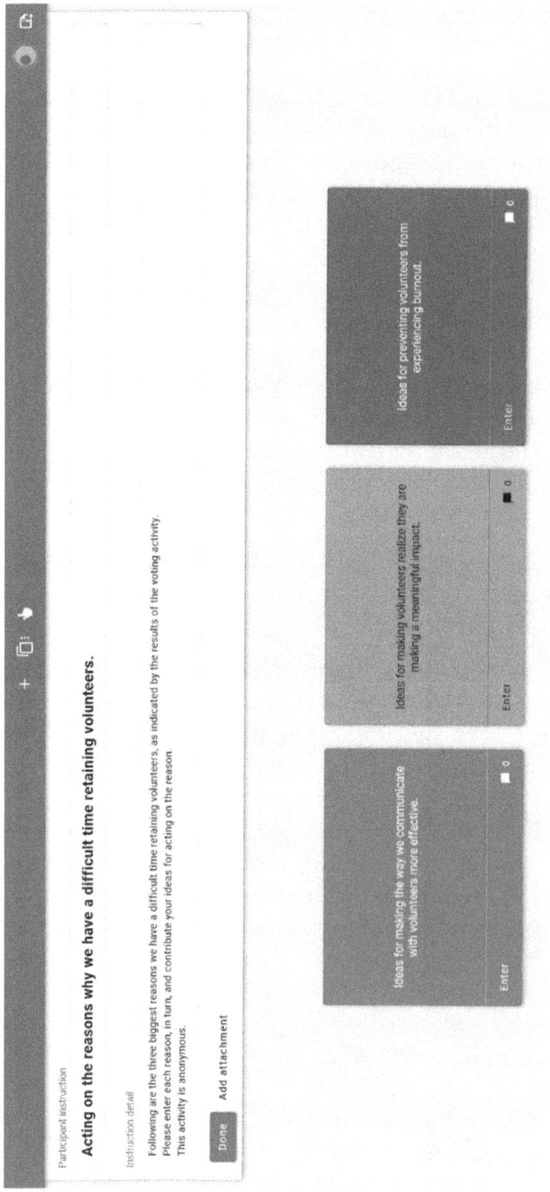

Figure 4.10 Screenshot of the XLeap deep dive activity.

Source: Co.Innovation Consulting, XLeap

Reporting

XLeap enables you to immediately create a customized report that contains the users' input for all the presentation, brainstorming, voting, and deep dive activities or, optionally, just a selection of the activities. The report is downloaded as a .docx file. A typical one-day workshop generates on the order of a 30-page report. As I explain in the following section on generative AI, relative to the usual ways of capturing meeting input, such as flipcharts, this constitutes an enormous amount of data for generative AI to query for useful insights.

Generative AI

I explained in the Chapter 1 that generative AI can be used for a variety of purposes, including creating content (text, images, music, video, and computer code); summarizing documents; rewriting documents; analyzing data; exploring hypothetical scenarios; explaining concepts; translating from one language to another; translating text to speech and speech to text; identifying trends or anomalies; forecasting, aggregating, and presenting knowledge; answering questions; generating ideas; and proposing solutions.

Prompt Engineering

I also explained in Chapter 1 that *prompt engineering* is the technical term for the art and science of crafting effective questions and instructions (*prompts*) for generative AI to respond to and that crafting well-thought-out prompts ensures relevant outputs (responses aligned with your goals), creative exploration (novel ideas, solutions, and insights), and efficiency (reduces the need for iterative corrections). Two keys to effective prompt engineering are to be as specific as possible about what you're after and to provide as much context (background information) as you can. You can provide the context in the prompt itself or by uploading one or more documents that contain the background information. Beyond these two keys, there's enough to prompt engineering to fill a book, two of which are cited in this end note.[30] A particularly practical resource is the free weekly newsletter *Almost Timely News*, written by the AI consultant Christopher S. Penn.[31] His RAPPEL framework for crafting a prompt is especially useful[32]:

- *Role*: Tell the model what role you want it to play.
- *Action*: Tell the model what you want it to do.
- *Prime*: Ask the model what it knows about the topic.
- *Prompt*: Write the prompt for the task.
- *Evaluate*: Evaluate the model's response.
- *Learn*: Ask the model to encode the process.

I asked ChatGPT (What better source?) to explain how to craft a prompt to obtain the best possible response from it.[33] Here is what it had to say:

Prompt

Generate a detailed explanation of the things it is important for a user to know to obtain good responses to prompts in ChatGPT.

ChatGPT's Response

How to Obtain Good Responses from ChatGPT: A Detailed Guide

To maximize the effectiveness of ChatGPT and receive high-quality responses, users should understand key principles related to prompt engineering, context-building, and conversational dynamics. Below is a detailed explanation of what's important to consider when crafting prompts.

1. Clarity and Specificity
The more specific your prompt, the better ChatGPT can tailor its response. Ambiguous or vague questions often lead to generic answers.
Best Practices:

- Clearly state what information you're seeking.
- Define terms or concepts if they might be interpreted in multiple ways.
- If you need a structured answer (e.g., bullet points, tables, numbered lists), request it explicitly.

Examples:

- Don't: *Tell me about AI.*
- Do: *Can you explain the key differences between symbolic AI and deep learning in a structured list?*

2. Provide Context
ChatGPT benefits from context to give relevant and precise answers. If you are discussing a topic across multiple turns, consider reminding the model of key points.
Best Practices:

- If the topic is complex, provide background information.
- If you're referencing a previous discussion, summarize key points.
- Mention specific constraints (e.g., "Keep it under 200 words" or "Focus on applications in healthcare").

Examples:

- Don't: *What's the best way to solve this?*
- Do: *Given that I'm working on a groupware system for collective intelligence and want to improve knowledge sharing, what are the best strategies for enhancing user collaboration?*

3. Iterative Refinement
Good responses often emerge through iteration. Start with an initial query, analyze the response, and refine your prompt for more precision.
Best Practices:

- Ask follow-up questions for more depth or clarity.
- If a response is off-track, clarify your intent.
- Use phrases like:
  - "Can you explain this from a different angle?"
  - "Can you provide more examples?"
  - "How would this apply to [specific scenario]?"

Example:

- First query: "Explain distributed cognition."
- *Refinement:* "Can you explain distributed cognition with examples from organizational teamwork?"
- Further refinement: "Now, how does distributed cognition relate to embodied cognition in collaborative AI systems?"

4. Define Constraints and Format Preferences
If you have specific requirements regarding tone, length, complexity, or format, state them clearly.
Best Practices:

- Specify desired depth (e.g., "Explain in layman's terms" vs. "Provide a technical explanation").
- Define length (e.g., "Summarize in two paragraphs" or "Provide a one-page essay").
- Request structured output (e.g., "Give me a table comparing X and Y").

Examples:

- Don't: *Tell me about Bayesian reasoning.*
- Do: *Give me a 3-paragraph explanation of Bayesian reasoning, starting with an intuitive example before explaining the formula and applications.*

5. Use Role-Playing for Expert-Level Responses
If you want a response tailored to a particular perspective or domain, instruct the model to assume a role.
Best Practices:

- Ask ChatGPT to respond as if it were an expert in a particular field.
- Use persona-based prompts like:
  - "Explain like you're a professor in cognitive science."
  - "Act as a systems engineer designing AI-assisted workflows."
  - "You are a legal expert advising on AI regulation—what's your perspective?"

Example:

- Don't: *How does collective intelligence work?*
- Do: *You are an expert in collective intelligence. Explain its key mechanisms with references to network effects, distributed cognition, and emergent decision-making.*

6. Leverage Step-by-Step Reasoning
If your question involves complex reasoning, asking for a step-by-step breakdown improves clarity and depth.
Best Practices:

- Request logical progression in explanations.
- Use prompts like:
  - "Walk me through this step by step."
  - "Explain the reasoning behind each step."

Examples:

- Don't: *How does a neural network work?*
- Do: *Explain how a neural network processes an image, step by step, from input to classification.*

7. Consider Bias and Alternative Perspectives
AI models are trained on diverse datasets but still reflect certain biases. Encouraging diverse viewpoints can lead to more balanced insights.
Best Practices:

- Ask for counterarguments or alternative perspectives.
- Frame questions to avoid confirmation bias (e.g., instead of "Why is X bad?", ask "What are the pros and cons of X?").

- Use comparative prompts (e.g., "Compare Western and Eastern approaches to problem-solving in AI ethics").

Examples:

- Don't: *Why is AI always biased?*
- Do: *What are the main sources of bias in AI, and how can they be mitigated?*

8. Use Delimiters to Separate Complex Queries
If asking multi-part questions, using clear separators improves response quality.
Best Practices:

- Use bullets, brackets, or quotes to delineate different parts.
- Avoid asking too many things at once; break the query into multiple steps.

Example:
Don't: How does deep learning work and what are its advantages and disadvantages? Also, can you compare it with symbolic AI?
Do:

1. *Explain how deep learning works in simple terms.*
2. *List its advantages and disadvantages.*
3. *Compare it with symbolic AI in terms of interpretability and generalization.*

9. Provide Examples for Clarification
If discussing abstract concepts, examples help ground the explanation.
Best Practices:

- Request real-world applications or analogies.
- Provide an example and ask for an assessment.

Examples:

- Don't: *What is frame semantics?*
- Do: *Can you explain frame semantics using an example from political discourse?*

10. Maintain Conversational Flow
ChatGPT can track context within a session, but if the conversation drifts, briefly recap previous points to keep responses on target.

Best Practices:

- If switching topics, state it clearly (e.g., "New topic:. . .").
- If continuing a discussion, reference previous key points.

Example:
User: "Explain Bayesian inference."
ChatGPT: *[Gives a response]*
User: "How does this apply to reinforcement learning?" *(Good continuation)*
User: "Now explain neural networks." *(Switching topics—better to introduce explicitly)*

Final Thoughts

By following these principles, users can significantly improve the quality and relevance of ChatGPT's responses. The key takeaways are:

1. Be clear and specific in your queries.
2. Provide context when necessary.
3. Use iteration to refine responses.
4. Define constraints and formatting preferences.
5. Utilize role-playing for expert-level answers.
6. Request step-by-step explanations for clarity.
7. Encourage alternative perspectives.
8. Use delimiters for complex prompts.
9. Provide examples to clarify abstract concepts.
10. Maintain conversational flow to build on previous responses.

Would you like any adjustments to this guide, such as adding more examples or focusing on a particular aspect?

Four ways of crafting more sophisticated prompts are to employ *universal semantic relationships*, *semantic pointer theory* (SPT), *cognitive linguistics theory*, and the *subject-predicate core of language*, all of which were explained in Chapter 1.

In Chapter 1, I asked ChatGPT to explain the value of instructing it to use *universal semantic relationships* in a prompt. Here I also ask it to give an example and explain how to phrase the prompt.[34]

Prompt

Read the foregoing text pertaining to universal semantic relationships. Then tell me if instructing a generative AI model to consider the relationships when responding to a prompt would cause it to generate a better response and, if so, why. Provide an example that pertains to a social problem. Then tell me how to write a prompt that contains an instruction for you to consider universal semantic relationships.

ChatGPT's Response

Evaluating Whether Considering Universal Semantic Relationships Improves Generative AI Responses

Yes, instructing a generative AI model to consider universal semantic relationships when responding to a prompt would likely lead to a better response. Here's why:

1. Richer Contextual Understanding—The meaning of a concept is not isolated; it emerges from its relationships with other concepts. By incorporating these relationships, the AI can generate responses that are more nuanced and interconnected.
2. Enhanced Coherence and Depth—Responses that explicitly integrate multiple semantic relationships (e.g., function, cause-effect, sequence) offer a more structured and thorough explanation rather than a flat, one-dimensional definition.
3. Greater Relevance to User Intent—Different prompts require different types of relationships to be emphasized. For example, if a user asks about a tool, its function and means-end relationships are likely more relevant than its sequence relationship. If the user asks about a historical event, cause-effect and sequence relationships are crucial.
4. Improved Reasoning and Explainability—Semantic relationships help structure logical reasoning, making AI responses easier to follow and understand.

Example Prompt Incorporating Universal Semantic Relationships
Prompt:
"Develop a strategy to reduce food insecurity in urban communities by considering its universal semantic relationships."

AI-Generated Response:

Food insecurity in urban communities is a pressing issue that affects public health, economic stability, and social equity. By analyzing this problem through universal semantic relationships, we can design a structured and effective strategy to address it.

- Strict Inclusion: Food insecurity is a kind of economic and social hardship.
- Cause-Effect: Food insecurity is caused by low income, high living costs, limited access to grocery stores, and systemic inequalities. In turn, it leads to malnutrition, poor health outcomes, and lower academic or workplace performance.
- Rationale: Addressing food insecurity improves public health, reduces healthcare costs, and strengthens communities.
- Location for Action: Solutions should be implemented in food banks, urban farms, schools, and community centers.
- Function: Community food programs, urban agriculture initiatives, and policy reforms function as mechanisms to reduce food insecurity.
- Means-End: Increasing access to affordable fresh produce, expanding food assistance programs, and supporting local food production are ways to mitigate food insecurity.
- Sequence: A successful strategy follows these stages: (1) identifying food deserts, (2) establishing community-based solutions such as food co-ops and urban farms, (3) integrating government assistance programs, and (4) implementing long-term policy changes to ensure food security.
- Attribution: Effective food security programs should be sustainable, community-driven, and accessible to all income levels.

By structuring solutions through universal semantic relationships, we can ensure a comprehensive and systemic approach that tackles both the causes and consequences of food insecurity in urban communities.

Writing a prompt that instructs me to consider universal semantic relationships

To write a prompt that explicitly instructs me (or a generative AI model) to consider universal semantic relationships, follow these steps:

1. Structure of the Prompt

A well-structured prompt should include:

- The topic or problem you want analyzed.
- The instruction to use universal semantic relationships in the response.
- Optional: Emphasize specific relationships that are most relevant to your query.

2. Example Template
"Analyze [TOPIC] by explicitly considering universal semantic relationships, such as strict inclusion, cause-effect, function, means-end, rationale, sequence, location for action, and attribution. Provide a response that integrates these relationships to ensure a comprehensive and well-structured explanation."

3. Example Prompts
General Inquiry Prompt:
"Explain the impact of climate change by explicitly considering universal semantic relationships, including strict inclusion, cause-effect, function, means-end, sequence, and attribution. Provide a response that integrates these relationships for a thorough and structured explanation."
Problem-Solving Prompt:
"Develop a strategy to reduce income inequality by explicitly considering universal semantic relationships. Address cause-effect, means-end, function, sequence, and location for action to ensure a structured and actionable response."
Comparative Analysis Prompt:
"Compare and contrast capitalism and socialism by applying universal semantic relationships, such as cause-effect, function, means-end, rationale, and sequence. Structure the response to highlight key differences and similarities systematically."

4. Tips for Writing a Strong Prompt

- Be specific about the topic.
- Mention "universal semantic relationships" explicitly.
- List the key relationships you want to emphasize (if necessary).
- Specify the desired structure or depth of the response.

In Chapter 1, I also asked ChatGPT to explain the value of instructing it to use the concept of *semantic pointers* when responding to a prompt. Here, I asked it to explain how to phrase the prompt.[35] It responded in the following way:

Prompt

Tell me this. What is the value of instructing a generative AI tool like ChatGPT to employ the concept of semantic pointers when responding to a prompt? How would you suggest that the prompt be phrased?

ChatGPT's Response

Instructing a generative AI tool like ChatGPT to employ the concept of semantic pointers enhances its ability to provide responses that are not only contextually relevant but also richly associative and multi-dimensional. Semantic pointers, as compressed bundles of neural activations pointing to deeper layers of meaning, allow the AI to:

- Capture Contextual Richness: The AI can draw on a broad network of associations without overwhelming the response with unnecessary details. This allows for nuanced answers that are tailored to the specific needs of the user.
- Facilitate Deeper Exploration: By unpacking relevant associations only when necessary, the AI can guide the conversation into progressively deeper levels of meaning without losing focus.
- Adapt Dynamically: It enables the AI to handle ambiguous or open-ended prompts by activating the most relevant high-level associations first and refining them based on user feedback.
- Enhance Cognitive Diversity: When used in group settings, the AI's ability to retrieve and connect diverse associations mirrors the unbundling process in human cognition, enriching the discussion with fresh perspectives.

How to Phrase the Prompt: To leverage the concept of semantic pointers, the prompt should:

- Encourage the AI to focus on central, high-level concepts initially.
- Specify the need for associative links, contextual relevance, or unpacking of ideas in stages.

- Include instructions for iterative clarification or elaboration.

Example Prompt: "Using the concept of semantic pointers, provide a high-level explanation of [topic]. Include key associative concepts and connections relevant to the topic, and be prepared to unpack any of these associations in greater detail based on follow-up questions or clarification requests."

Applied Example: "Using semantic pointers, explain how urban design influences mental health. Begin with the core connections and key associations, such as stress reduction and social interaction, and be ready to elaborate on specific aspects, like green spaces or walkability, as needed." This phrasing directs the AI to work in layers, starting with core ideas and expanding selectively, ensuring responses are both concise and capable of depth.

I asked ChatGPT in Chapter 1 to explain the value of instructing it to use *cognitive linguistics* when responding to a prompt. Here, in addition, I asked it to explain how to phrase the prompt.[36] Following is how it responded:

Prompt

Tell me this. What is the value of instructing a generative AI tool like ChatGPT to employ the concept of cognitive linguistics when responding to a prompt? How would you suggest that the prompt be phrased?

ChatGPT's Response

Cognitive linguistics theory provides a rich framework for meaning construction, emphasizing how language reflects embodied experience, conceptual structures, and usage-based learning. Instructing ChatGPT to apply cognitive linguistics concepts enhances its ability to generate responses that are:

- Conceptually Grounded: AI explanations align with human cognitive patterns, making them more intuitive and natural.
- Contextually Adaptive: AI can tailor language use based on frame semantics, metaphorical mappings, and discourse structures.
- Semantically Coherent: ChatGPT can preserve meaning across different expressions through mental spaces and conceptual blending.
- Dynamic and Flexible: It can interpret figurative language, reconstruct implied meanings, and adjust responses to fit pragmatic context.
- More Humanlike in Communication: Using embodied cognition and radial category structures, AI-generated text better reflects how humans conceptualize and express ideas.

Key Cognitive Linguistics Concepts and Their AI Benefits

1. *Frame Semantics*
    - What It Does: Explains meaning in terms of structured mental schemas (frames).
    - AI Benefit: Ensures responses activate the appropriate conceptual frame for a query, preventing misinterpretations.
    - Example:
        - Instead of defining "investment" abstractly, ChatGPT would activate the economic frame, linking it to related ideas like "risk," "return," and "market behavior."
2. *Conceptual Metaphor Theory*
    - What It Does: Shows that abstract thought is structured through metaphorical mappings from embodied experience.
    - AI Benefit: Enables AI to interpret figurative language correctly and generate metaphorical explanations that resonate with human cognition.
    - Example:
        - Prompt: "Explain neural networks using metaphor."
        - AI Response: "A neural network is like a team of experts, where each member specializes in a different aspect of a problem, and together they refine the answer."

3. *Mental Spaces and Conceptual Blending*
    - What It Does: Describes how the mind integrates separate domains to create meaning dynamically.
    - AI Benefit: Enables AI to synthesize novel ideas, making creative problem-solving more effective.
    - Example:
        - Prompt: "Blend the concept of blockchain with biological evolution."
        - AI Response: "Like genetic inheritance, blockchain records a 'lineage' of transactions, ensuring each block is built upon a verified history, much like DNA mutations build upon previous adaptations."
4. *Embodied Cognition*
    - What It Does: Suggests meaning arises from bodily interaction with the world.
    - AI Benefit: AI can generate more grounded, sensorimotor-based explanations that align with human experiences.
    - Example:
        - Instead of just explaining "balance" as an abstract idea, AI might link it to physical equilibrium, helping users grasp concepts through lived experience.
5. *Radial Categories and Prototype Theory*
    - What It Does: Argues that word meanings form networks of related senses rather than rigid definitions.
    - AI Benefit: Helps AI handle polysemy (multiple meanings) more flexibly.
    - Example:
        - The word "game" can mean "a sport," "a video game," or "a strategic situation." AI using prototype theory would rank meanings based on context.

How to Phrase a Prompt to Instruct ChatGPT to Use Cognitive Linguistics

To take advantage of cognitive linguistics principles, phrase your prompt as follows:

1. *Request a Frame-Based Explanation*
   - "Explain the concept of [X] using frame semantics, highlighting key roles and relationships."
   - "Activate the [finance/science/legal] frame when explaining [X]."
2. *Ask for Metaphor-Based Responses*
   - "Use conceptual metaphor theory to explain [X] in an intuitive way."
   - "Frame [X] using an embodied metaphor."
3. *Encourage Conceptual Blending*
   - "Blend [Concept A] with [Concept B] using conceptual integration networks."
   - "Describe how two seemingly unrelated concepts can be linked through conceptual blending."
4. *Use Embodied Cognition for Sensory-Based Understanding*
   - "Explain [X] using embodied cognition principles—how does it connect to physical experience?"
   - "Generate an explanation that makes [abstract concept] more grounded in perception and action."
5. *Handle Meaning Flexibly Using Prototype Theory*
   - "Describe how [X] is a radial category, identifying its core prototype and peripheral meanings."
   - "Explain why certain words have multiple meanings based on prototype theory."

Example Applications of Three of the Principles

Frame Semantics (Business)—"Market Ecosystem"

- Topic: Understanding Competitive Strategy in Platform-Based Markets
- Prompt: "Use Frame Semantics to explain how tech giants like Apple and Amazon dominate their markets."
- Response: "Tech giants operate within a *market ecosystem*, where different companies take on roles similar to those in a biological system. Apple and Amazon act as *keystone species*, shaping the environment for smaller companies. Disruptive startups are

like *predators*, challenging incumbents, while app developers and service providers function as *symbionts*, relying on platform ecosystems to survive. Viewing markets through this ecological frame helps explain why a dominant platform's health affects the entire industry—just as the disappearance of a keystone species would disrupt an entire food chain."

Conceptual Metaphor Theory (Social Problems)—"The War on Misinformation"

- Topic: Understanding the Fight Against Misinformation
- Prompt: "Use Conceptual Metaphor Theory to explain misinformation as a social problem."
- Response: "Misinformation spreads like a *war*, where truth and falsehood engage in constant battle. Fact-checkers and media literacy educators act as *defensive forces*, building resistance against misinformation attacks. Social media platforms function as *battlefields*, where algorithms can either strengthen defenses or inadvertently supply *weapons* to disinformation campaigns. This war metaphor shapes how governments and tech companies approach the problem—often prioritizing *defensive strategies* like censorship and content moderation over more diplomatic approaches, such as fostering critical thinking and resilience in the public."

Mental Spaces & Conceptual Blending (Science)—"Quantum Computing as Parallel Universes"

- Topic: Making Quantum Computing Intuitive for Non-Experts
- Prompt: "Use Mental Spaces & Conceptual Blending to explain how quantum computing works."
- Response: "Quantum computing is often understood through a blend of two conceptual spaces: *classical computing* (where bits are 0s and 1s) and the *many-worlds interpretation of quantum mechanics* (where particles exist in multiple states across parallel universes). In this blended model, qubits are like *simultaneous explorers* in different worlds, testing multiple possibilities at once. When a quantum computer processes information, it's as if it's computing across *parallel universes* and only, revealing the correct answer when measured. This conceptual blend helps people grasp the power of quantum superposition and why quantum computers can solve certain problems exponentially faster than classical ones."

I next asked ChatGPT to identify *other linguistic and cognitive theories* that could be integrated into prompts to increase the quality of generative AI's responses.[37] Here is its response:

Prompt

In other prompts, I asked you to explain the value of instructing generative AI to consider semantic pointer theory and cognitive linguistic theory when generating a response to a prompt. Are there other linguistic or cognitive theories that will improve generative AI's responses? Include an example of the way each of the theories might be used in a prompt that pertains to identifying the causes of an undesired state or ways to act on a cause to transform it into the cause of a desired state.

ChatGPT's Response

Yes! There are several additional linguistic and cognitive theories that can enhance generative AI's responses, particularly in ways that complement Semantic Pointer Theory (SPT) and Cognitive Linguistics. Below, I outline some valuable theories and frameworks that would further improve generative AI's reasoning, coherence, and contextual sensitivity:

1. Distributed Cognition (DCog)

- How to integrate into a prompt: Explicitly ask the AI to consider multiple agents, tools, and environments as part of the causal system rather than treating the problem as isolated to one individual or factor.
- Example Prompt: "Our team struggles with poor communication, leading to missed deadlines. Instead of treating this as an individual issue, analyze how knowledge, tools, workflows, and team interactions distribute responsibility. How can we redesign these elements to turn communication failures into communication strengths?"
- Why this improves AI's response: AI will look at systemic interactions rather than just suggesting individual behavioral fixes (e.g., "be more clear" vs. "introduce shared dashboards for asynchronous updates").

2. *Predictive Processing & Active Inference*

- How to integrate into a prompt: Ask the AI to analyze mismatched expectations and suggest ways to realign mental models of different stakeholders.
- Example Prompt: "Customer complaints about our product's usability are rising. Instead of just listing issues, analyze how users' expectations mismatch with how the product actually works. How can we reshape their predictive models to improve their experience and satisfaction?"
- Why this improves AI's response: AI will generate responses that align marketing, onboarding, and interface design with user expectations rather than just fixing isolated usability issues.

3. *Polyvagal Theory (for Social and Emotional AI)*

- How to integrate into a prompt: Ask the AI to analyze emotional and physiological states contributing to the problem and suggest interventions that target psychological safety and engagement.
- Example Prompt: "Our workplace has high stress levels, leading to low productivity. Instead of generic advice, analyze how workplace structures activate stress or calm responses in employees. How can we shift our organizational dynamics to promote psychological safety and engagement?"
- Why this improves AI's response: AI will focus on stress regulation mechanisms (e.g., workplace rhythm, social trust, recovery periods) rather than just saying, "Try mindfulness."

4. *Conceptual Metaphor Theory (CMT)*

- How to integrate into a prompt: Ask the AI to analyze how existing metaphors frame the problem and suggest metaphorical re-framing to shift thinking toward solutions.
- Example Prompt: "Our education system is stuck and failing to innovate. Instead of a literal analysis, examine the dominant metaphors people use (e.g., 'education as a factory'). How do these metaphors shape policy decisions, and what alternative metaphors (e.g., 'education as a garden') could inspire a shift toward a better system?"
- Why this improves AI's response: AI will go beyond technical fixes and suggest deeper cognitive shifts that influence how people perceive and approach the problem.

5. *FrameNet & Embodied Construction Grammar (ECG)*

- How to integrate into a prompt: Ask the AI to identify conflicting conceptual frames that shape the issue and recommend ways to reframe the problem for better outcomes.
- Example Prompt: "Our city struggles with traffic congestion. Instead of just listing solutions, analyze how different stakeholders frame the issue (e.g., drivers see it as 'lack of roads,' environmentalists see it as 'too many cars'). How can we reframe transportation as an accessibility problem to align interests and drive effective change?"
- Why this improves AI's response: AI will diagnose framing conflicts and offer solutions that bridge perspectives, making policy recommendations more actionable.

6. *Radical Embodied Cognitive Science*

- How to integrate into a prompt: Ask the AI to incorporate sensory-motor experiences into its analysis rather than treating the issue as an abstract cognitive problem.
- Example Prompt: "Students struggle to understand physics concepts like inertia and force. Instead of a purely theoretical explanation, suggest ways to ground learning in sensory-motor experiences. How can students physically interact with the concepts to improve comprehension?"
- Why this improves AI's response: AI will generate more experiential and hands-on solutions, such as real-world analogies or interactive learning approaches.

7. *Enactivism*

- How to integrate into a prompt: Ask the AI to consider learning and change as an interactive, participatory process rather than a one-way transfer of information.
- Example Prompt: "People in my community are disengaged from local politics. Instead of just listing reasons for disengagement, analyze how the lack of interactive civic participation reinforces the problem. What action-based strategies can re-engage residents through lived experiences rather than just information?"
- Why this improves AI's response: AI will prioritize engagement strategies like community-based events, participatory

budgeting, or gamification rather than just saying, "Provide more information."

8. *Socio-Cultural Theory (Vygotsky)*

- How to integrate into a prompt: Ask the AI to consider social and cultural influences on problem-solving and suggest collaborative solutions rather than isolated individual actions.
- Example Prompt: "Our organization's mentorship program isn't working. Instead of just suggesting improvements, analyze how social and cultural factors influence mentoring effectiveness. How can we redesign the program to align with collective learning and scaffolding principles?"
- Why this improves AI's response: AI will suggest mentor-mentee learning dynamics, peer collaboration, and culturally relevant mentorship models instead of generic advice.

9. *Relevance Theory (RT)*

- How to integrate into a prompt: Ask the AI to prioritize the most relevant causes and interventions instead of listing every possible factor.
- Example Prompt: "Our meetings are too long and unproductive. Instead of just listing general meeting improvements, analyze what information is currently irrelevant or redundant. How can we streamline discussions to focus only on maximally relevant content?"
- Why this improves AI's response: AI will cut out unnecessary details and focus on maximally useful meeting structures.

10. *Connectionist Models & Neural Syntax*

- How to integrate into a prompt: Ask the AI to detect communication breakdown patterns rather than treating misunderstandings as random.
- Example Prompt: "Our team members often misinterpret each other's emails, leading to conflicts. Instead of generic communication tips, analyze linguistic patterns that cause ambiguity. How can we restructure our messages to improve clarity?"
- Why this improves AI's response: AI will suggest sentence restructuring, linguistic clarity techniques, and even AI-assisted tone analysis rather than just recommending "better communication."

Final Takeaway

By explicitly embedding cognitive and linguistic theories into the prompt, we can shape how AI interprets problems and guide it toward deeper, more insightful responses. This structured approach ensures that AI not only identifies root causes but also suggests transformative solutions that are context-aware, systemic, and actionable.

Finally, I asked ChatGPT to create prompt templates that incorporate the *subject-predicate core of language* explained in Chapter 1.[38] Here is how it responded:

Prompt

What are some optimized prompt templates that leverage the subject-predicate core of language?

ChatGPT's Response

Here are some optimized prompt templates that leverage the subject-predicate core of language to improve generative AI responses. Each template ensures clarity, structure, and precise inference, making them useful for AI-assisted research, analysis, and content generation.

1. Explanatory Prompts
(Use these when seeking clear, structured explanations.)

- How does [subject] (subject) [predicate] (predicate) using [specific method/concept]?
  - Example: *How does generative AI (subject) simulate (predicate) human-like creativity using transformer models?*
- What are the key principles that allow [subject] to [predicate]?
  - Example: *What are the key principles that allow neural networks (subject) to learn (predicate) from data?*

- Explain how [subject] interacts with [another subject] in the process of [predicate].
  - Example: *Explain how cognitive biases (subject) interact with machine learning models (another subject) in the process of decision-making (predicate).*

2. *Comparative & Contrastive Prompts*
(Use these for differentiation and nuanced understanding.)

- What are the differences and similarities between how [subject] and [another subject] [predicate]?
  - Example: *What are the differences and similarities between how humans (subject) and AI (another subject) process (predicate) language?*
- How does [subject] [predicate] differently from [another subject]?
  - Example: *How does generative AI (subject) produce (predicate) creative outputs differently from human artists (another subject)?*
- What are the advantages and limitations of [subject] in [predicate]?
  - Example: *What are the advantages and limitations of Bayesian reasoning (subject) in AI decision-making (predicate)?*

3. *Predictive & Future-Oriented Prompts*
(Use these for AI-driven forecasting and speculation.)

- How is [subject] expected to [predicate] in the next [timeframe]?
  - Example: *How is AI governance (subject) expected to evolve (predicate) in the next decade?*
- What emerging trends suggest that [subject] will [predicate] in the near future?
  - Example: *What emerging trends suggest that collective intelligence systems (subject) will reshape (predicate) decision-making in organizations?*
- What factors will most influence how [subject] [predicate] over time?
  - Example: *What factors will most influence how generative AI (subject) integrates (predicate) into scientific discovery?*

4. Problem-Solving & Diagnostic Prompts
(Use these for identifying and addressing challenges.)

- Why does [subject] struggle with [predicate], and what solutions exist?
  - Example: *Why does AI (subject) struggle with (predicate) common sense reasoning, and what solutions exist?*
- What are the most effective strategies for improving how [subject] [predicate]?
  - Example: *What are the most effective strategies for improving how AI systems (subject) align (predicate) with human values?*
- What are the key obstacles preventing [subject] from [predicate]?
  - Example: *What are the key obstacles preventing decentralized AI (subject) from achieving (predicate) widespread adoption?*

5. Systems & Interconnectivity Prompts
(Use these for exploring complex relationships and feedback loops.)

- How does [subject] influence [another subject] in the context of [predicate]?
  - Example: *How does cognitive load (subject) influence group decision-making (another subject) in the context of online collaboration (predicate)?*
- What role does [subject] play in enabling [another subject] to [predicate]?
  - Example: *What role does distributed intelligence (subject) play in enabling organizations (another subject) to optimize (predicate) real-time decision-making?*
- How do multiple factors interact to shape how [subject] [predicate]?
  - Example: *How do cultural norms, technology, and governance interact to shape how AI ethics (subject) evolves (predicate) globally?*

6. Narrative & Case-Based Prompts
(Use these when seeking AI-generated case studies, examples, or storytelling approaches.)

- Can you provide a case study where [subject] successfully [predicate]?

    - Example: *Can you provide a case study where swarm intelligence (subject) successfully optimized (predicate) large-scale problem-solving?*

- Describe a hypothetical scenario in which [subject] must [predicate] under challenging conditions.
    - Example: *Describe a hypothetical scenario in which a decentralized AI network (subject) must coordinate (predicate) disaster relief efforts under uncertain conditions.*
- What historical examples illustrate how [subject] has [predicate]?
    - Example: *What historical examples illustrate how collective intelligence (subject) has driven (predicate) scientific breakthroughs?*

Final Thoughts

These prompt templates work better than general, unstructured questions because they:

1. Anchor the AI's response in a clear conceptual framework.
2. Reduce vagueness by specifying relationships between concepts.
3. Leverage cognitive structures (e.g., Frame Semantics, Bayesian Reasoning) to improve AI retrieval.
4. Encourage depth and specificity, leading to more insightful answers.

Would you like custom-tailored prompts for a particular area of your research?

What Questions to Ask

Prompt engineering, as I said earlier, addresses *how* to ask generative AI for answers, but it doesn't say *what* to ask. Knowing what questions to ask generative AI is even more important than knowing how to ask them because good questions reveal useful insights. Consider, for example, the problem-solving process diagrammed in Figures 1.1 and 3.6. In the course of solving a problem, you should ask generative AI (and your group) variations of the following questions[39]:

1. *What are all the possible causes of the undesired effect?*
    - At the same time, ask your group to brainstorm the possible causes.
    - If your group's knowledge of the causes is insufficient, you'll have to conduct research to determine possible causes.

- For complex problems, answering this question might require a multi-layered root cause analysis or it might require using one of the above-described diagramming tools to map a causal system in which there are feedback loops.
- Another way to ask this is to say, "What are all the reasons why the undesired effect/state is happening?" (Or happened or might happen.)
- Even more sophisticated is to integrate the foregoing cognitive and linguistic theories into the prompt.
- Once all the possible causes are identified, you may have to perform research to validate or invalidate them, or you can vote to select and prioritize causes.

2. *The undesired effect is ___ and the desired effect is ___. One cause of the undesired effect is X. What are all the ways we can act on X to transform it into a cause of the desired effect?*

   - Each of the ways is a possible solution.
   - Ask this for each of the causes.
   - Remember, asking "What are all the ways . . .?" is better than asking "How can we . . .?"
   - Your group should also brainstorm ways to act on the causes.
   - Here, again, you might want to integrate the foregoing cognitive and linguistic theories into the prompt.

3. *In what ways can we combine three [or some other number] of the solutions to create a solution that is superior to any one of the solutions alone?*

   - When you have a long list of solutions, this is a very useful question to ask, as it is a good way to discover solutions possessing emergent properties that make them superior to lone solutions.
   - Generative AI is amazingly good at identifying combinations with useful emergent properties that humans are unlikely to identify.
   - You should ask this question multiple times to create different combinations of solutions.

4. *Considering these criteria (list the criteria), which of these solutions is best?*

   - The group should develop the list of criteria. You can also ask generative AI to generate a list of criteria to consider.
   - This is where you can use XLeap's multicriteria voting tool to obtain your group's judgment on the matter.

Following is an example in which I asked ChatGPT variations of the first three questions.[40] Bear in mind that in actual practice, both ChatGPT and the problem-solving group would be responding to these questions. Also note that this is a good example of how humans can do things that generative AI cannot. Recall I said earlier that generative AI has never seen, heard, felt, tasted, or touched what you have, which means that it doesn't know the specifics of your particular problem. In the following case, the human managers of the nonprofit organization, not generative AI, know that poor communication (item #2) is a problem in their organization, which causes them to enter the second prompt.

1st Prompt

List 20 reasons why nonprofit organizations have a difficult time retaining volunteers.

ChatGPT's Response

Nonprofit organizations often struggle to retain volunteers due to a variety of structural, psychological, and organizational challenges. Here are 20 key reasons:
Organizational and Structural Challenges

1. Lack of Clear Roles—Volunteers may feel lost or unproductive if tasks are vague or poorly defined.
2. Poor Communication—Infrequent or unclear communication can lead to disengagement and confusion.
3. Inefficient Leadership—Ineffective volunteer coordination and leadership can result in frustration and low motivation.
4. Lack of Training and Support—Volunteers may feel unprepared or undervalued if they are not properly onboarded.
5. Burnout from Overwork—Some organizations over-rely on dedicated volunteers, leading to exhaustion and dropout.
6. Insufficient Recognition—Volunteers who feel unappreciated or unseen are less likely to stay engaged.
7. Bureaucratic Frustration—Excessive paperwork or rigid rules can discourage volunteers from continuing.
8. Mission-Drift or Ethical Concerns—Volunteers may disengage if they perceive the organization's goals as misaligned with their values.
9. Unclear Impact—If volunteers do not see tangible results from their efforts, they may lose motivation.
10. Unpleasant Work Environment—Toxic culture, cliques, or interpersonal conflicts can drive people away.
    Psychological and Social Factors
11. Lack of Personal Growth—Volunteers may leave if they do not feel they are learning or growing from the experience.

12. Limited Social Connection—If volunteers do not form friendships or feel a sense of belonging, they may not stay.
13. Competing Priorities—Work, family, or personal commitments often take precedence over volunteering.
14. Mismatch of Skills and Interests—If a volunteer's talents are not utilized effectively, they may seek opportunities elsewhere.
15. Emotional Toll—Working with difficult social issues (e.g., poverty, illness, crisis response) can be emotionally draining.
16. Short-Term Commitment Culture—Many people prefer short-term volunteering rather than ongoing involvement.
17. Generational Differences—Younger volunteers may seek dynamic, flexible engagement, while older volunteers may value stability and tradition.
18. Perception of Inefficiency—Volunteers may leave if they feel the organization is disorganized or ineffective in achieving its goals.
19. Lack of Autonomy—Volunteers who feel micromanaged or not trusted may disengage.
20. Social and Economic Barriers—Transportation, financial constraints, or lack of accessibility can prevent continued participation.

Would you like insights on solutions to these challenges as well?

2nd Prompt

Yes. Consider item #2. List 20 ways for a nonprofit organization to communicate with its volunteers in a way that will enable it to retain them.

ChatGPT's Response

To improve volunteer retention through effective communication, nonprofit organizations can adopt the following 20 strategies:

Establish Clear and Consistent Communication Channels

1. Dedicated Volunteer Newsletter—Send a monthly or biweekly email newsletter with updates, success stories, and upcoming opportunities.
2. Volunteer Portal or App—Provide a digital platform where volunteers can access schedules, training materials, and organization news.

3. Text Message Updates—Use SMS or messaging apps (e.g., WhatsApp, Slack, or GroupMe) to send reminders and urgent updates.
4. Regular Virtual or In-Person Meetings—Schedule check-ins with volunteers to discuss challenges, provide updates, and gather feedback.
5. Personalized Emails—Address volunteers by name and reference their contributions in email communications to build rapport.

Foster Two-Way Communication and Engagement

6. Open-Door Policy—Encourage volunteers to ask questions, share concerns, and provide feedback without fear of dismissal.
7. Surveys and Feedback Forms—Regularly ask for volunteer input through surveys and implement meaningful changes based on responses.
8. Suggestion Box (Digital or Physical)—Provide an anonymous way for volunteers to share ideas and concerns.
9. Volunteer Representatives or Committees—Appoint experienced volunteers as liaisons to represent others and relay feedback to leadership.
10. Exit Interviews—Conduct informal interviews when volunteers leave to understand their reasons and improve retention strategies.

Keep Volunteers Informed and Inspired

11. Impact Reports—Regularly share statistics, testimonials, and case studies showing how volunteer contributions make a difference.
12. Storytelling Through Social Media—Highlight volunteers and their work through blog posts, videos, and testimonials.
13. Behind-the-Scenes Access—Give volunteers insider insights into how decisions are made and how their work fits into the bigger picture.
14. Recognition Announcements—Publicly acknowledge volunteers' efforts in emails, newsletters, and meetings.
15. Consistent Branding and Messaging—Use a unified voice and tone to reinforce the organization's mission and culture.

Provide Flexibility and Adaptability

16. Customizable Volunteer Schedules—Allow volunteers to sign up for shifts that fit their availability.

17. Clear and Concise Instructions—Avoid overwhelming volunteers with unnecessary details; focus on the essentials.
18. Responsive Communication—Ensure staff promptly respond to volunteer inquiries and concerns.
19. Emergency and Crisis Communication Plan—Keep volunteers informed about unexpected changes, safety protocols, or urgent needs.
20. Personalized Check-Ins—Have staff or senior volunteers reach out to individuals periodically to ensure they feel supported and engaged.

Would you like deeper insights on any of these strategies, or do you need a communication plan template?

3rd Prompt

Combine 3 of the foregoing solutions to create a solution that is superior to any one of the solutions alone.

ChatGPT's Response

A superior solution can be created by combining Personalized Check-Ins (#20), Impact Reports (#11), and Regular Virtual or In-Person Meetings (#4) into an integrated "Volunteer Engagement Cycle."

The Volunteer Engagement Cycle

This approach ensures ongoing personal connection, meaningful impact reinforcement, and structured feedback loops, which collectively enhance volunteer retention.

How It Works:

1. Regular Personalized Check-Ins (One-on-One Connection)
   - Assign a staff member or experienced volunteer mentor to periodically check in with individual volunteers.
   - These check-ins (via phone, email, or casual in-person chats) address concerns, celebrate progress, and offer tailored support.

- Volunteers feel valued and heard, reducing disengagement.

2. Impact Reporting (Motivation & Reinforcement)
   - Share concrete success stories and data with volunteers via email, newsletters, or quick updates in check-ins.
   - Highlight the direct impact of their contributions (e.g., "Your efforts last month helped provide meals to 500 families.").
   - Creates a sense of purpose and strengthens emotional investment.
3. Regular Virtual or In-Person Meetings (Community & Feedback Loop)
   - Hold structured but engaging meetings where volunteers can share their experiences, challenges, and ideas.
   - Use these meetings to discuss the impact reports, reinforcing their contributions.
   - Gather feedback to refine roles, improve efficiency, and enhance the volunteer experience.

Why This Combination is More Effective Than Any One Solution Alone:

- Check-ins build personal connections, preventing volunteers from feeling like just another cog in the machine.
- Impact reports provide tangible motivation, ensuring volunteers see the real-world effects of their work.
- Meetings create a feedback loop and a sense of community, making volunteers feel like part of something bigger.

Would you like this formatted into a communication strategy document?

The foregoing series of three prompts is just one example of the questions that generative AI might be asked to answer. I asked ChatGPT for more examples.[41] Here is its response:

Prompt

I entered a series of prompts in the foregoing conversation. Describe three examples of a series of prompts that a group might enter, such as, for example, the series of prompts a team of scientists might ask to understand the what and why of some phenomenon.

ChatGPT's Response

Here are three examples of series of prompts that different groups might enter to systematically investigate a phenomenon or solve a problem. Each example follows a structured inquiry process, similar to how your prompts progressively explored volunteer retention.

1. *Scientific Research Team Investigating Climate Change Impact on a Local Ecosystem*

   A team of environmental scientists is studying how climate change affects biodiversity in a specific region. Their inquiry follows these phases:

   Phase 1: Understanding the What (Observation & Data Collection)

   1. *What observable changes in biodiversity have been recorded in this ecosystem over the past 50 years?*
   2. *What specific species have experienced population declines or increases?*
   3. *How have temperature and precipitation patterns changed over time in this region?*
   4. *What other environmental variables (e.g., pollution, deforestation) might also be affecting biodiversity?*

   Phase 2: Investigating the Why (Causal Analysis & Hypothesis Testing)

   5. *How do temperature fluctuations correlate with species population changes?*
   6. *What role does habitat fragmentation play in the observed changes?*
   7. *Are there direct links between climate-driven shifts and species migration patterns?*

8. *What models best predict future biodiversity shifts based on current trends?*

Phase 3: Developing Solutions (Application & Mitigation Strategies)

9. *What conservation strategies have been successful in mitigating climate-related biodiversity loss?*
10. *How can community-based conservation efforts help maintain ecosystem balance?*
11. *What policy recommendations could be made based on this research?*
12. *How can technology (e.g., AI, remote sensing) help monitor future changes more effectively?*

2. *Business Innovation Team Exploring AI Integration in Customer Service*

A corporate team is exploring how artificial intelligence can enhance customer service operations. They follow a systematic inquiry to assess feasibility and implementation.

Phase 1: Understanding the Current State (Problem Definition)

1. *What are the most common pain points in our current customer service operations?*
2. *What feedback have customers provided about their experiences with our support system?*
3. *How does our current customer service compare to industry benchmarks?*
4. *What are the current costs and efficiency levels of our support team?*

Phase 2: Evaluating AI Solutions (Feasibility & Risks)

5. *What types of AI technologies (e.g., chatbots, sentiment analysis, voice assistants) could address these pain points?*
6. *How do AI-driven customer service models impact customer satisfaction in other industries?*
7. *What are the potential risks of AI adoption, such as loss of personalization or customer frustration?*
8. *What ethical concerns (e.g., bias in AI responses, data privacy) should we consider?*

Phase 3: Implementation Strategy (Designing an AI-Integrated System)

9. *What hybrid model (human + AI) would work best for our business?*

10. *How should AI be trained to align with our brand's communication style?*
11. *How will we measure success and continuously refine the AI's performance?*
12. *What employee training and transition strategies will be needed to integrate AI smoothly?*

3. Policy Think Tank Analyzing the Decline in Civic Engagement
A group of political scientists and social researchers is investigating why voter participation and civic engagement have declined in a particular country.

Phase 1: Identifying the Symptoms and Scope of the Problem

1. *What are the recent trends in voter turnout in different demographics?*
2. *How has participation in community organizations changed over the past few decades?*
3. *Are there specific regions or populations experiencing the sharpest declines in civic engagement?*
4. *What forms of engagement (e.g., protests, volunteering, voting) have been most affected?*

Phase 2: Understanding the Causes

5. *What societal and economic factors correlate with declining civic participation?*
6. *How have digital media and social networks changed public engagement in governance?*
7. *What role does political distrust or disillusionment play in voter disengagement?*
8. *How do educational levels impact civic participation rates?*

Phase 3: Formulating Solutions and Policy Recommendations

9. *What initiatives have successfully increased voter participation in other regions?*
10. *How can technology be used to make civic engagement more accessible and appealing?*
11. *What policy changes (e.g., election reforms, civic education programs) could reverse the decline?*
12. *What partnerships between government and community organizations could enhance engagement?*

Key Takeaway:

Each of these series of prompts follows a structured inquiry that moves from identifying the problem (What?), to analyzing causes (Why?), and then to developing solutions (How?). This iterative approach mirrors how groups—scientists, business teams, and policy analysts—investigate and address complex issues.

Would you like me to refine or extend one of these examples for a particular context?

Asking Ingenious Questions

Recall my earlier discussion of Einstein's search for the "right question" and Nielsen's quest for "ingenious questions." Is there some sure-fire formula for generating ingenious questions? No. But I do have an idea for increasing the chances of devising one, which is to turn the usual approach to brainstorming on its head. Rather than a cognitively diverse group brainstorming answers to a question, have them brainstorm questions to answer. One way to do this is to have the group and AI work together by iterating back and forth like this: First have the group brainstorm the questions, then have AI comment on the questions, then have the group use the comments to stimulate ideas for better questions, then repeat the process until an ingenious question emerges. Remember that ingenious, like beauty, lies in the eyes of the beholder.

I asked ChatGPT to generate an example of this process.[42] Its response is set forth below:

Prompt

Read the foregoing text. Then generate an example of the process described in the text.

ChatGPT's Response

Applying AI-Augmented Brainstorming to Identify an Ingenious Product for the Elderly.

Objective: Using AI-human collaboration, we will identify a truly ingenious question—one that humans alone would be unlikely to generate—for entrepreneurs seeking to design an innovative product for the elderly.

Step 1: Initial Brainstorming of Questions by the Entrepreneurs

A diverse team of entrepreneurs (product designers, healthcare specialists, gerontologists, and technologists) brainstorms initial questions about potential products for the elderly.

1. *What are the most common frustrations elderly people face in daily life?*
2. *How can we make aging more comfortable and less stressful?*
3. *What are the biggest barriers preventing seniors from using technology?*
4. *How can we help seniors feel more connected to younger generations?*
5. *What role can AI play in improving the quality of life for elderly individuals?*

Step 2: AI Comments on the Questions

AI evaluates the assumptions and limitations in these questions and suggests areas for deeper inquiry.

- AI Comment on Q1 (Daily Frustrations): *This assumes that addressing frustrations is the best approach. What if we looked at unseen potential rather than problems?*
- AI Comment on Q2 (Comfort & Stress): *Comfort is important, but does reducing stress lead to a richer life? What if the goal was to create meaningful challenges instead?*
- AI Comment on Q3 (Tech Barriers): *This assumes that seniors are struggling with tech, rather than tech failing to align with senior cognition and behavior. Could we design tech that adapts to them rather than the other way around?*
- AI Comment on Q4 (Intergenerational Connection): *Why frame this as seniors needing connection? What if younger generations are the ones in need of wisdom, and we created a platform that rebalances knowledge flow?*

- AI Comment on Q5 (AI & Aging): *Most AI is designed to compensate for aging—what if we used AI to augment aging-specific advantages instead?*

Step 3: Entrepreneurs Use AI Feedback to Refine Questions

Using AI's critique, the group refines and reframes their questions for deeper insights.

1. *What hidden abilities do elderly people develop that remain untapped?*
2. *How can we design challenges that make aging more stimulating rather than just comfortable?*
3. *Instead of making tech more accessible, how can we make tech intuitively align with the cognitive strengths of aging minds?*
4. *How can we create a system where younger generations actively seek out wisdom from the elderly?*
5. *How can AI amplify the cognitive, social, and emotional strengths that develop with age rather than compensating for decline?*

Step 4: AI Provides Further Refinement

AI detects deeper patterns and suggests even more innovative angles.

- AI Comment on Q1 (Hidden Abilities): *This is promising! What if, instead of looking at untapped abilities, we asked: What abilities emerge only through long-term cognitive accumulation?*
- AI Comment on Q2 (Meaningful Challenges): *The assumption is that challenges should be engaging. But what if we asked: What challenges could only an aging mind uniquely solve better than a younger one?*
- AI Comment on Q3 (Tech Adaptation): *What if the real issue isn't adapting tech, but making aging itself feel more like an advanced interface with the world?*
- AI Comment on Q4 (Reversing Intergenerational Knowledge Flow): *What if we designed a system where younger generations were forced to compete for elder wisdom rather than just receiving it?*
- AI Comment on Q5 (AI & Aging Advantages): *Instead of making AI a "helper," what if we asked: How can AI enable elderly individuals to think in ways no human—young or old—ever has before?*

Step 5: The Group Iterates Again and Generates a Truly Ingenious Question

Using AI's comments, the entrepreneurs move beyond conventional thinking and arrive at a novel, unexpected question—one that humans alone would be unlikely to generate:

> *"How can we design a product that turns aging into an advanced cognitive operating system—one that unlocks new forms of intelligence that younger minds can't access?"*

Why this question is ingenious:

- It breaks away from the assumption that aging is cognitive decline and instead treats it as a gateway to unique intelligence.
- It frames aging as an advanced state of being, not a problem to fix.
- It implies that older individuals may have access to patterns of thinking that younger minds literally can't reach—suggesting new product opportunities in AI, neuroscience, and cognitive augmentation.

Step 6: Using the Ingenious Question to Generate a Truly Unique Product

Now that we have an ingenious question, the entrepreneurs can brainstorm revolutionary product ideas based on this radical reframe of aging.

1. "Neural Alchemy: An AI-Powered Thought Amplifier for Aging Minds"
    - A cognitive tool that maps, synthesizes, and externalizes the unique thought structures that only emerge in later life.
    - Helps elders distill and articulate complex insights with unprecedented clarity, making their minds a unique, invaluable asset.
2. "ElderVision: A Perception-Based Reality Filter"
    - A wearable or AR interface that amplifies perception shifts that come with aging, allowing elders to see patterns and meaning in ways that younger minds cannot.
    - Example: Turning abstract memories into interactive thought landscapes or letting elderly users "filter" reality to recognize deeper connections between events.

3. "The Grandmaster Protocol: Unlocking Elders as High-Order Thinkers"
   - A gamified system where only elders—due to their life experience—can access and solve highly complex, multi-layered challenges.
   - Uses aging as an asset in pattern recognition, wisdom aggregation, and nonlinear problem-solving.

Final Takeaway

By iterating between human creativity and AI insights, the group escaped the gravity of conventional thinking and landed on a question that redefines aging itself. Rather than asking, "How do we help elderly people?", we arrived at: "How can we make aging an advanced cognitive operating system?" This shifts aging from a limitation to an upgrade—a perspective shift that humans alone might never have generated.

Edward Chang, an adjunct professor of computer science at Stanford University, describes another way of identifying ingenious questions in his book *LLM Collaborative Intelligence: The Path to Artificial General Intelligence*. He first emphasizes the fact that LLMs are *polydisciplinary*, meaning they have "simultaneous comprehension of all fields of study, sans the typical boundaries that segregate disciplines."[43] Let that sink in. First consider that there are thousands of fields of study,[44] then consider that the LLM's comprehension was created by reading tens of billions of documents. Chang goes on to explain, "Engaging with an LLM is comparable to a scenario where a 10-year-old boy joins a scholarly discussion with a group of Nobel Laureates. . . . In this analogy, expecting the 10-year-old boy, or anyone with limited expertise, to pose profound questions that elicit insightful answers is unrealistic."[45] For Chang, *profound questions* are questions that reveal *unknown unknowns*.[46] He then proposes, "If we could utilize ChatGPT to access 'unknown unknowns'—insights and knowledge we are not even aware we lack—our evolution could greatly accelerate. The challenge lies in *formulating the right questions*" (italics mine).[47] A much-simplified summary of his book-length explanation of his method for formulating the questions and the "SocraSynth" GPT he has created to implement the method is to have a human moderate a dialogue between two LLMs. The two LLMs might be ChatGPT and Gemini, for example. Or they might be two roles played by ChatGPT—say, GPT-A and GPT-B. The dialogue proceeds as follows (assuming the two LLMs in the dialogue are GPT-A and GPT-B):

- The moderator first introduces a topic.
- GPT-A is instructed to pose a set of questions about the topic.
- GPT-B is instructed to answer GPT-A's questions, then pose questions stimulated by its answers.
- GPT-A is instructed to answer GPT-B's questions, then pose questions stimulated by its answers.
- GPT-B is instructed to answer GPT-A's questions, then pose questions stimulated by its answers.
- And so on.

Aside from giving the instructions, the moderator's role is to keep the dialogue from going off the track (off topic) and to instruct the GPTs to dig deeper into some of the questions. I would only add that a multi-disciplinary group is likely to do a better job of playing the moderator than a single person.

I asked ChatGPT to generate an example of Chang's method.[48] Here is what it produced:

Prompt

Read the foregoing text. Then create a hypothetical conversation between GPT-A and GPT-B pertaining to a business topic.

ChatGPT's Response

Moderator: Today's topic is the future of remote work. GPT-A, please begin by posing a set of questions.

Round 1: Initial Questions from GPT-A

GPT-A:

1. How has remote work evolved over the past decade, and what key technological advancements have enabled its expansion?
2. What are the economic implications of widespread remote work for businesses, employees, and local economies?

3. How does remote work impact organizational culture, collaboration, and team cohesion?
4. What industries are best suited for remote work, and which ones face significant challenges in its implementation?
5. How will AI and automation influence the future of remote work?

GPT-B, please respond and then pose new questions stimulated by your responses.

Round 2: GPT-B's Responses and Follow-Up Questions

GPT-B:

1. *Evolution and Technology*: Remote work has evolved from a niche practice to a mainstream model, primarily driven by high-speed internet, cloud computing, and collaboration tools like Slack, Zoom, and Microsoft Teams. The pandemic accelerated this shift, normalizing hybrid work structures.
2. *Economic Implications*: Remote work has reduced operational costs for businesses (e.g., real estate expenses) while offering employees location flexibility. However, it has also disrupted local economies that relied on office-centric activities, such as urban commercial real estate and service industries.
3. *Organizational Culture & Collaboration*: While remote work enhances flexibility, it can weaken informal collaboration and serendipitous interactions that foster innovation. Companies have attempted to mitigate this through virtual engagement strategies and hybrid models.
4. *Industries Best Suited*: Tech, finance, and knowledge-based industries adapt well to remote work. Meanwhile, sectors like healthcare, manufacturing, and logistics face inherent challenges due to physical presence requirements.
5. *AI & Automation's Role*: AI will likely streamline remote workflows through virtual assistants, automated project management, and smart scheduling. Additionally, AI-driven virtual environments may enhance remote collaboration, reducing the gap between in-office and remote work experiences.

Follow-up questions stimulated by these responses:

1. How will cities and urban planners adapt to the economic shifts caused by the decline in office-based work?

2. What psychological effects does prolonged remote work have on employees, and how can companies address issues like isolation and burnout?
3. Will emerging technologies like the metaverse provide a viable alternative to traditional office environments?
4. How will remote work affect diversity, equity, and inclusion (DEI) initiatives in the workplace?
5. What role will decentralized autonomous organizations (DAOs) play in the evolution of remote work structures?

GPT-A, please respond and generate new questions based on your responses.

Round 3: GPT-A's Responses and New Questions

GPT-A:

1. *Urban Planning Adaptations*: Cities may repurpose office spaces into mixed-use developments, integrating residential, co-working, and community spaces. Additionally, local governments may introduce incentives to attract remote workers to less populated regions.
2. *Psychological Effects & Solutions*: Prolonged remote work can lead to social isolation, blurred work-life boundaries, and decreased engagement. Solutions include structured virtual team interactions, remote-friendly leadership training, and AI-driven well-being monitoring tools.
3. *Metaverse as an Office Alternative*: While the metaverse has potential, its current technological and adoption limitations hinder full-scale implementation. Future iterations with improved VR interfaces and haptic feedback may create more immersive remote workspaces.
4. *Impact on DEI Initiatives*: Remote work can both enhance and hinder DEI efforts. It allows companies to hire diverse talent globally, but can also exacerbate digital divides and inequities in career advancement due to reduced in-person networking.
5. *DAOs & Remote Work*: DAOs could redefine remote work by enabling decentralized decision-making and compensation structures. These autonomous organizations, powered by blockchain, may eliminate traditional hierarchies, allowing for more fluid and flexible work arrangements.

New Questions Based on These Responses:

1. What regulatory and tax implications arise from a globally distributed workforce?
2. How can businesses balance employee autonomy with the need for accountability in remote settings?
3. Will AI-driven hiring and performance evaluation systems introduce new biases in remote work environments?
4. How should leadership styles evolve to manage fully remote or hybrid teams effectively?
5. What are the long-term economic consequences if remote work remains the dominant mode of employment?

GPT-B, please continue the discussion.

Moderator's Reflection:

This iterative dialogue highlights unknown unknowns by progressively uncovering deeper layers of the topic. The process not only refines surface-level inquiries but also fosters novel connections—such as linking urban planning with remote work policies or exploring DAOs as a governance model for remote teams.

Round 4: GPT-B's Responses and New Questions

GPT-B:

1. *Regulatory & Tax Implications*: A globally distributed workforce presents challenges in taxation, employment law, and compliance. Countries may impose stricter regulations on remote work visas, while businesses will need to navigate tax treaties, permanent establishment risks, and jurisdictional labor laws.
2. *Balancing Autonomy and Accountability*: Companies must implement clear performance metrics, regular check-ins, and outcome-based evaluations rather than time-tracking methods. AI-driven productivity tools may help, but businesses should balance surveillance with trust to maintain morale.
3. *AI-Driven Hiring & Performance Biases*: AI systems trained on biased data could exacerbate inequalities in hiring and promotions. Companies should emphasize ethical AI practices, continuous auditing, and hybrid decision-making (human + AI) to minimize discriminatory outcomes.

4. *Evolving Leadership Styles*: Remote work demands a shift from traditional hierarchical management to servant leadership, emphasizing empathy, adaptability, and transparent communication. Effective leaders will leverage asynchronous collaboration tools, prioritize results over presence, and foster virtual community-building.
5. *Long-Term Economic Consequences*: If remote work remains dominant, it may lead to decentralization of economic hubs, reducing wage disparities across regions. However, potential downsides include weakened local economies in business districts, shifts in commercial real estate demand, and challenges in workforce cohesion over the long run.

New Questions Based on These Responses:

1. How will national governments adapt labor laws to accommodate cross-border remote work?
2. Could a rise in fully remote businesses lead to a new form of "digital nomad economies" where entire cities cater to location-independent professionals?
3. How will AI-driven collaboration tools redefine corporate hierarchies in remote-first organizations?
4. What are the potential risks of digital surveillance in remote work environments, and how can privacy be safeguarded?
5. If remote work becomes the norm, what new skill sets will be essential for career growth in the future?

GPT-A, your responses?

Round 5: GPT-A's Responses and New Questions

GPT-A:

1. *Government Adaptations to Cross-Border Remote Work*: Some governments have already introduced digital nomad visas, but global labor laws remain fragmented. Future regulations may standardize cross-border taxation, healthcare access, and remote work rights to prevent loopholes and ensure fair labor practices.
2. *Rise of Digital Nomad Economies*: Cities like Bali, Lisbon, and Mexico City have seen an influx of remote workers, leading to economic booms in co-working spaces, short-term rentals, and

digital-friendly infrastructure. However, this trend also raises concerns about gentrification, cost-of-living inflation, and social integration challenges.

3. *AI-Driven Collaboration & Corporate Hierarchies*: AI-powered collaboration tools (e.g., AI project managers, virtual assistants, smart meeting summaries) could reduce middle management layers and shift organizations toward flatter structures with more self-managed teams.
4. *Digital Surveillance & Privacy Risks*: Employers may increasingly use AI-powered monitoring software to track productivity, keystrokes, and online activity. While this could enhance performance insights, it raises ethical concerns about employee autonomy, psychological stress, and potential misuse. Companies should adopt privacy-first policies and transparency in remote monitoring practices.
5. *Essential Skill Sets for Future Careers*: Asynchronous communication, self-management, digital literacy, and adaptability will be crucial. Additionally, expertise in AI-driven collaboration tools, cross-cultural communication, and emotional intelligence will differentiate professionals in a remote-first job market.

New Questions Based on These Responses:

1. How will remote work impact professional networking and mentorship opportunities for early-career employees?
2. Could decentralized work models like DAOs fully replace traditional corporate structures in the long run?
3. What impact will the shift to remote work have on the educational system, particularly in terms of preparing students for new career paths?
4. How can remote work environments ensure inclusivity for employees with disabilities?
5. Will new work models redefine what it means to be an "employee" versus an "independent contractor"?

GPT-B, your turn.

Moderator's Reflection:

This conversation continues to uncover deeper unknown unknowns, revealing intersections between remote work, global labor laws, AI-driven management, digital economies, and workforce psychology. Would you like the discussion to explore a particular direction further, or continue iterating broadly?

I'll finish this section by asking you to consider the potential of a group of smart people (e.g., a group of scientists, businesspersons, policy analysts, or a multi-disciplinary group) brainstorming questions to answer (or topics to consider), or moderating a dialogue between two LLMs, or using a combination of both methods. I think their potential to identify ingenious questions would be extraordinary.

Combining Generative AI and Electronic Brainstorming

I asked ChatGPT to explain how generative AI and electronic brainstorming could be combined to help a small group carry out the problem-solving process, as I've defined it.[49] (Note that I used "How can . . .?" rather than "What are all the ways . . .?" because I was only wanting one answer.) Here is what it had to say:

Prompt

How can generative AI and electronic brainstorming be combined to help a small group carry out the problem-solving process?

ChatGPT's Response

Combining Generative AI and Electronic Brainstorming for Problem-Solving

Electronic brainstorming (EBS) platforms like XLeap can integrate generative AI (e.g., ChatGPT) to enhance the problem-solving process by increasing creativity, mitigating cognitive biases, and accelerating analysis. Below is how the combination can assist at each step of the problem-solving process.

Step 1: Describe the Undesired Effect (Undesired State)

The group needs to clearly define and articulate the problem they are trying to solve.

How Generative AI + EBS Enhances This Step

1. AI-Generated Problem Descriptions
   - AI can rephrase and refine problem statements based on participant input.

- AI can help frame the problem using different models, such as "What is happening vs. what should be happening?"
- Example: If participants describe an undesired state as "Low customer retention," AI can suggest refining it to:
  - "Customer churn rate has increased by 15% over the last 6 months."
  - "Customers cite dissatisfaction with post-purchase service."

2. AI-Enhanced Comparative Analysis
   - AI can analyze similar problems from industry case studies or past workshop reports to contextualize the issue.
   - Example: If the undesired state is low employee engagement, AI can provide benchmarks from studies on what ideal engagement levels look like.
3. EBS for Structured Input Collection
   - Participants use XLeap's brainstorming activity to describe the problem in their own words.
   - AI can cluster and categorize these inputs into themes.
   - Participants then use voting tools to prioritize the most accurate descriptions.

Step 2: Identify the Causes of the Undesired Effect/State

The group identifies why the problem is occurring.
How Generative AI + EBS Enhances This Step

1. AI-Supported Root Cause Analysis
   - AI can assist in generating root cause hypotheses based on the problem description.
   - AI can apply frameworks like:
     - MECE (Mutually Exclusive, Collectively Exhaustive)—AI helps ensure that identified causes don't overlap (mutually exclusive) and that all relevant causes are considered without gaps (collectively exhaustive).
     - 5 Whys Analysis (e.g., "Why are customers leaving?" → "Why is customer service slow?" → "Why is there high turnover in support teams?")

- Fishbone Diagrams (AI suggests multiple cause categories: process issues, people issues, technology issues, etc.)

2. EBS for Collaborative Cause Identification

- Participants enter potential causes in XLeap's brainstorming activity.
- AI categorizes inputs into direct vs. indirect causes or internal vs. external causes.
- Participants use voting tools to prioritize the most critical causes.

3. AI-Powered Pattern Recognition

- AI can analyze historical data (if available) or previous brainstorming results to suggest patterns in the causes.
- Example: If low employee retention is the problem, AI can highlight common themes across previous employee surveys.

Step 3: Transform Causes into Causes of the Desired Effect

For each cause, the group identifies actions that would reverse or mitigate it, selects the best option, and evaluates its 1st- to 4th-order consequences.

How Generative AI + EBS Enhances This Step

1. AI-Supported Alternative Generation

- AI can generate multiple intervention strategies based on best practices.
- Example: If "inefficient customer onboarding" is identified as a cause, AI might suggest:
    - "Automate customer onboarding with a chatbot."
    - "Personalize onboarding emails based on customer behavior."
    - "Implement a dedicated onboarding success team."

2. EBS for Refining & Selecting Alternatives

- Participants use brainstorming activities to add their own solutions.
- AI clusters and categorizes responses into themes (e.g., tech-driven vs. human-driven solutions).
- Participants vote on the best alternatives.

3. AI-Powered Consequence Analysis (1st to 4th Order Effects)
   - AI can simulate the downstream effects of each alternative:
     - 1st Order: Direct result (e.g., chatbot automation reduces onboarding time).
     - 2nd Order: Secondary effect (e.g., reduced human support might increase complexity for certain customers).
     - 3rd Order: Systemic impact (e.g., lower need for onboarding specialists could shift job roles).
     - 4th Order: Long-term strategic effect (e.g., enhanced automation culture in company).
4. Multi-Criteria Decision Making (AI + EBS Voting)
   - AI can apply decision matrices (e.g., weighing cost, feasibility, and impact of each alternative).
   - Participants use Likert-scale or multi-criteria voting to finalize the best approach.

Step 4: Follow-Up on the Results to Identify Other Useful Insights

After the workshop, the group evaluates the problem-solving effort's success and identifies additional insights.

How Generative AI + EBS Enhances This Step

1. AI-Supported Post-Workshop Analysis
   - AI reviews the XLeap-generated report and extracts:
     - Key themes, insights, and contradictions.
     - Gaps or missing perspectives that were not fully explored.
     - Suggested next steps and follow-up actions.
   - AI responds to prompts like:
     - "Identify 10 insights humans may have missed."
     - "What trends emerge across different participant comments?"
2. EBS for Group Reflection & Feedback
   - Participants engage in a follow-up brainstorming session to validate AI insights.
   - AI clusters feedback into what worked vs. what didn't.

3. AI for Continuous Improvement
   - AI can compare workshop results over time to track improvement trends.
   - AI suggests new problem-solving frameworks based on evolving challenges.

Conclusion: A Smarter, AI-Augmented Problem-Solving Process

- By combining generative AI and EBS, a small group can:
  - Clearly define problems with AI-assisted framing.
  - Identify root causes with AI-driven analysis and structured brainstorming.
  - Develop and evaluate solutions with AI-enhanced alternative generation and consequence analysis.
  - Follow up efficiently with AI-powered report insights and trend detection.

This approach reduces cognitive biases, accelerates decision-making, and enhances collective intelligence, ultimately leading to more effective problem-solving.

Another way to combine the two technologies is to have ChatGPT analyze the workshop report that is produced by XLeap. A one-day workshop, as I mentioned, typically results in a 30-page written report, which is a quantity of information that would be impossible to capture with a flipchart or whiteboard. I now make it a practice to have ChatGPT review workshop reports and then respond to prompts like: *Identify ten insights in the report that humans would be unlikely to identify.* And then, for each of the insights: *Describe the first-, second-, third-, and fourth-order consequences of this insight.* Many of the responses to these prompts are extraordinarily insightful. To gain a better sense of the potential of querying the electronic brainstorming report, imagine, for example, the insights that might be revealed by applying this process to the report for a one-day workshop devoted to identifying the needs of a company's customers, or the company's strengths, weaknesses, opportunities, and threats (SWOT), or the political, economic, social, technological, legal, and environmental (PESTLE) issues it faces. Or imagine using generative AI to look for insights in a 30-page report produced by a team of scientists or engineers.

Adding Analog and Other Digital Tools

Even more powerful than combining electronic brainstorming and generative AI is to add some number of the analog and other digital tools to the mix. The potential combinations are nearly endless. Examples are listed below:

- *Whiteboards*: Use analog whiteboards to draw a visual representation of the problem or to quickly diagram cause-effect relationships. Make the drawings visible while the participants are brainstorming solutions to the problem.
- *Templates*: Use analog templates (e.g., a *Risk Assessment Template*) to guide breakout groups. Note that using templates in breakout groups can also be implemented digitally with EBS technology.
- *Dialogue Mapping*: Use the dialogue mapping software during deliberations to visually keep track of the issues pertaining to a problem, the different positions the participants are taking on each issue, and the reasons for and against each position.
- *Diagramming*: Use a diagramming tool (e.g., *Inspiration*) to create a branching issue tree that breaks the problem down into progressively more specific components. Or that breaks an objective down into progressively more specific subobjectives.
- *Risk Assessment:* Use a spreadsheet add on (e.g., *@Risk*) to conduct Monte Carlo simulations that reveal the variance in possible outcomes.
- *System Models:* Use a fuzzy logic modeling tool (e.g. *MentalModeler*) to create semi-quantitative models of a system.
- *Task Planning*: Use a project management tool (e.g., *Trello*) to track projects, tasks, and deadlines.
- *Trend Analysis*: Use a trend analysis tool (e.g., *Futures Platform*) to anticipate risks that might emerge from various trends.
- *Integrated Collaborative Workspace*: In between a series of team meetings pertaining to a project, use an integrated collaborative workspace tool (e.g., *GroveSite*) to maintain a directory of the team members, send emails to them, conduct asynchronous threaded discussions, track the status of follow-up actions, and create a searchable document repository.

Building Better Worlds to Think In

Way back in the Introduction, I noted that both Elon Musk and Jeff Bezos are big believers in making meeting rooms more functional. Here I want to say, "They're right!" It's time to replace traditional conference rooms with more effective spaces for thinking together. Organizations that want to boost the collective intelligence of their teams would do well to design meeting rooms that integrate the floorplans, seating, sensory cues, and analog and digital tools explained in this chapter. Even better is to support teams with the integrated collaborative workspaces I just described and with other digital tools for interacting remotely between face-to-face meetings. Whether you are designing physical or virtual meeting rooms, remember what Andy Clark had to say about the idea of an *extended mind* that loops through the technologies that augment our intelligence and his observation that throughout history man has engaged in the "culturally transmitted process of designer-environment construction: the *process of deliberately building better worlds to think in*" (italics mine).[50] As I explain in the next chapter, at no other time in history has there been a greater need to build better worlds in which to think together.

Summary

In this chapter, we looked at the *platforms* upon which a cognitively diverse group of *people* can execute their chosen problem-solving *processes*. There are analog and digital platforms. Especially effective, in my experience, is dialogue mapping and combining electronic brainstorming and generative AI. There are multiple ways to complement this combination with other analog and digital tools. All this takes us closer to Doyle and Strauss's far-sighted vision of sophisticated centers for problem-solving and decision-making.

Notes

1 Michael Doyle and David Strauss, *How to Make Meetings Work* (New York, NY: Jove Books, 1976), 197–200.
2 Scott Dorrley and Scott Witthoft, *Make Space: How to Set the Stage for Creative Collaboration* (Hoboken, NJ: John Wiley & Sons, 2012), 5.
3 Michael Schrage, *No More Teams! Mastering the Dynamics of Creative Collaboration* (New York, NY: Currency Doubleday, 1989), 124–127.
4 Patricia Fierro-Newton, "How Ceiling Height Influences Creativity and Focus," *NeuroTectura*, December 26, 2024, https://neurotectura.com/2024/12/26/how-ceiling-height-influences-creativity-and-focus/
5 Jim Determan, Mary Anne Akers, Tom Albright, Bill Browning, Catherine Martin-Funlop, Paul Archibald, and Valerie Caruolo, "The Impact of Biophilic Learning Spaces on Student Success," chrome-extension://efaidnbmnnnibpcajpcglclefindmkaj/https://cgdarch.com/wp-content/uploads/2019/12/The-Impact-of-Biophilic-Learning-Spaces-on-Student-Success.pdf
6 Ian Ritchie (Ed.), *Neuro Architecture: Designing with the Mind in Mind* (Oxford, UK: John Wiley & Sons, 2020), 113.
7 Anjan Chatterjee, "How the Brain Responds to Architecture," *Psychology Today*, February 26, 2020, https://www.psychologytoday.com/us/blog/

brain-behavior-and-beauty/202002/how-the-brain-responds-architecture?utm_source=chatgpt.com

8 Wikipedia Contributors, "Health Effects of Sunlight Exposure," in *Wikipedia, the Free Encyclopedia*, downloaded January 1, 2025, https://en.wikipedia.org/wiki/Health_effects_of_sunlight_exposure?utm_source=chatgpt.com

9 "Transforming Spaces, Transforming Minds: The Comprehensive Guide to Neuroarchitecture," *UGreen*, https://ugreen.io/transforming-spaces-transforming-minds-the-comprehensive-guide-to-neuroarchitecture/

10 Annie Murphy Paul, *The Extended Mind: The Power of Thinking Outside the Brain* (Boston, MA: Houghton Mifflin Harcourt, 2021), 134–135.

11 Imagine the sense of fit (or lack of it) felt by the black woman Katherine Johnson, played by Taraji Henson in the movie *Hidden Figures*, doing math in a room filled entirely by white men (made worse by the fact that they all sported the white short-sleeved shirts, thin black ties, and crew cuts of 1960's-era engineers).

12 Katherine E. Eskine, Ashanti E. Anderson, Madeline Sullivan, and Edward J. Golob, "Effects of Music Listening on Creative Cognition and Semantic Memory Retrieval," *Psychology of Music*, November 2018, 1–16.

13 The fourth word is "bath."

14 Marco Mancini, Patrizia Cherubino, Giulia Cartocci, Ana Martinez, Gianluca Borghini, Elena Guastamacchia, Gianluca di Flumeri, Dario Rossi, Enrica Modica, Stefano Menicocci, Viviana Lupo, Arianna Trettel, and Fabio Babiloni, "Forefront Users' Experience Evaluation by Employing Together Virtual Reality and Electroencephalography: A Case Study on Cognitive Effects of Scents," *Brain Science*, February 18, 2021, 1(2), 256, https://doi.org/10.3390/brainsci11020256

15 Margot Bloomstein in Kevin M. Hoffmann, *Meeting Design for Managers, Makers, and Everyone Else* (Brooklyn, NY: Two Waves Books, 2018), 29–31.

16 Margaret Wilson, "Six Views of Embodied Cognition," *Psychonomic Bulletin & Review*, 2002, 9(4), 625–636. This paper discusses how bodily interactions enhance cognitive processing, supporting the idea that physically engaging with a whiteboard improves ideation. Susan Goldin-Meadow, *Hearing Gesture: How Our Hands Help Us Think* (Cambridge, MA: Harvard University Press, 2003). The author explains how gestural activity, including writing and spatial structuring, supports cognitive processing and recall.

17 David Kirsh, "Thinking with External Representations," *AI & Society*, 2010, 25, 441–454, https://doi.org/10.1007/s00146-010-0272-8. Kirsh explores how external representations, such as whiteboards, facilitate faster and more flexible problem-solving. Don Norman, *The Design of Everyday Things* (New York, NY: Basic Books, 2013). Norman's work on usability and affordances supports the idea that direct manipulation, such as writing on an analog board, is faster and more intuitive than interacting with digital interfaces.

18 Ask yourself this: Would your board of directors or management team do a better job of thinking together if one of the walls in the boardroom was made into a whiteboard? If your answer is "Yes," why haven't you done it?

19 Scott Dorley and Scott Witthoft, *Make Space: How to Set the Stage for Creative Collaboration* (Hoboken, NJ: John Wiley & Sons, 2012), 28–29.

20 OpenAI, Response to "Imagine that you are a meeting facilitator. It is a good meeting practice to give the breakout group participants templates to follow so that all the breakout groups can make apples-to-apples comparisons when they reconvene. Describe the format of five hypothetical templates." *ChatGPT-4o*, 2025.

21 OpenAI, Response to "Describe the comparative advantages of digital tools (e.g., diagramming software) over analog tools (e.g., whiteboards)." *ChatGPT-4o*, 2025.
22 Sometimes a reason and an argument are said to be the same thing. I prefer to distinguish them by saying that a reason is part of an argument that consists of a position (conclusion) and a reason. The distinction clarifies the meaning of the term *reasoning*, which is the process whereby one draws conclusions (positions) based on reasons.
23 A dialogue map is a great way to visualize the way a cognitively diverse group contributes and combines their different chunks of knowledge (pieces of the puzzle), that is, the sub-topics, issues, positions, and reasons.
24 Jeff Conklin, *Dialogue Mapping: Building Shared Understanding of Wicked Problems* (Hoboken, NJ: John Wiley & Sons, 2006).
25 OpenAI, Response to "Read the foregoing text. Then explain how generative AI could be used to augment dialogue mapping." *ChatGPT-4o*, 2025.
26 OpenAI, Response to "Evaluate your answer to determine the degree to which the current capabilities of generative AI can support your responses." *ChatGPT-4o*, 2025.
27 Darleen M. DeRosa, Carter L. Smith, and Donald A. Hantula, "The Medium Matters: Mining the Long-Promised Merit of Group Interaction in Creative Idea Generation Tasks in a Meta-Analysis of the Electronic Group Brainstorming Literature," *Computers in Human Behavior*, 2007, 23, 1549–1581.
28 Wikipedia Contributors, "Linus Pauling," in *Wikipedia, the Free Encyclopedia*, January 26, 2025, retrieved 17:09, February 5, 2025, https://en.wikipedia.org/w/index.php?title=Linus_Pauling&oldid=1271910124
29 In 2001, after reading about EBS in Michael Schrage's earlier-cited book *No More Teams! Mastering the Dynamics of Creative Collaboration*, I toured the 40-seat EBS facility at the University of Arizona's business school.
30 See, for example, James Phoenix and Mike Taylor, *Prompt Engineering for Generative AI: Future-proof Inputs for Reliable AI Outputs* (Boston, MA: O'Reilly Media, 2024); Gilbert Mizrahi, *Unlocking the Secrets of Prompt Engineering: Master the Art of Creative Language Generation to Accelerate Your Journey from Novice to Pro* (Birmingham, UK: Packt Publishing, 2023).
31 You can sign up for his newsletter here: https://almosttimely.substack.com/
32 You can download a summary of the framework here: https://www.trustinsights.ai/insights/instant-insights/instant-insights-trust-insights-rappel-ai-prompt-framework/. Make sure to watch the video in which Penn explains his framework here: https://www.youtube.com/watch?v=F8VARHirkhs
33 OpenAI, Response to "Generate a detailed explanation of the things it is important for a user to know to obtain good responses to prompts in ChatGPT." *ChatGPT-4o*, 2025.
34 OpenAI, Response to "Read the foregoing text pertaining to universal semantic relationships. Then tell me if instructing a generative AI model to consider the relationships when responding to a prompt would cause it to generate a better response and, if so, why. Provide an example that pertains to a social problem. Then tell me how to write a prompt that contains an instruction for you to consider universal semantic relationships." *ChatGPT-4o*, 2025.
35 OpenAI, Response to "Tell me this. What is the value of instructing a generative AI tool like ChatGPT to employ the concept of semantic pointers when responding to a prompt? How would you suggest that the prompt be phrased?" *ChatGPT-4o*, 2025.

36 OpenAI, Response to "Tell me this. What is the value of instructing a generative AI tool like ChatGPT to employ concepts from cognitive linguistics theory. How would you suggest that the prompt be phrased?" *ChatGPT-4o*, 2025.
37 OpenAI, Response to "In other prompts, I asked you to explain the value of instructing generative AI to consider semantic pointer theory and cognitive linguistic theory when generating a response to a prompt. Are there other linguistic or cognitive theories that will improve generative AI's responses? Include an example of the way each of the theories might be used in a prompt that pertains to identifying the causes of an undesired state or ways to act on a cause to transform it into the cause of a desired state." *ChatGPT-4o*, 2025.
38 OpenAI, Response to "What are some optimized prompt templates that leverage the subject-predicate core of language?" *ChatGPT-4o*, 2025.
39 Here, the term "questions" is used to refer to both questions and instructions.
40 OpenAI, Response to "List 20 reasons why nonprofit organizations have a difficult time retaining volunteers. Yes. Consider item #2. List 20 ways for a nonprofit organization to communicate with its volunteers in a way that will enable it to retain them. Combine three of the foregoing solutions to create a solution that is superior to any one of the solutions alone." *ChatGPT-4o*, 2025.
41 OpenAI, Response to "I entered a series of prompts in the foregoing conversation. Describe three examples of a series of prompts that a group might enter, such as, for example, the series of prompts a team of scientists might ask to understand the what and why of some phenomenon." *ChatGPT-4o*, 2025.
42 OpenAI, Response to "Read the foregoing text. Then generate an example of the process described in the text." *ChatGPT-4o*, 2025.
43 Edward Y. Chang, *LLM Collaborative Intelligence: The Path to Artificial General Intelligence* (Stanford, CA: Edward Chang, 2024), 45.
44 I asked ChatGPT how many fields of study there are. It said, "If we count broad academic disciplines (~100–300), university specializations (~1,500), and interdisciplinary/emerging fields (thousands), AI can process knowledge across at least 10,000–100,000 named fields and subfields."
45 Edward Y. Chang, *LLM Collaborative Intelligence: The Path to Artificial General Intelligence* (Stanford, CA: Edward Chang, 2024), 119.
46 U.S. Secretary of Defense Donald Rumsfeld popularized the following distinctions. *Known knowns* are things we know we know. *Known unknowns* are things that we know we don't know. *Unknown knowns* are things we think we don't know but actually do. *Unknown unknowns* are things that we don't know that we don't know.
47 Edward Y. Chang, *LLM Collaborative Intelligence: The Path to Artificial General Intelligence* (Stanford, CA: Edward Chang, 2024), 45.
48 OpenAI, Response to "Read the foregoing text. Then create a hypothetical conversation between GPT-A and GPT-B pertaining to a business topic." *ChatGPT-4o*, 2025.
49 OpenAI, Response to "How can generative AI and electronic brainstorming be combined to help a small group carry out the problem-solving process?" *ChatGPT-4o*, 2025.
50 Andy Clark, *Natural-Born Cyborgs: Minds, Technologies, and the Future of Human Intelligence* (New York, NY: Oxford University Press, 2003), 78.

Chapter 5

Postlude

Complex Problems Require Hybrid Intelligence

Putting it as concisely as possible, the message of this book is this. The collective intelligence of a small problem-solving group is increased by assembling the right *people*, equipping them with the right *processes*, and executing the processes on the right *platforms*. Adding generative AI to the mix creates a *hybrid intelligence* that is smarter than the *collective intelligence* of the group or the *artificial intelligence* of generative AI alone.

Most books on group problem-solving start by saying that our problems have become so complex that they require multi-disciplinary group to solve them. I'm going to end by saying it. First by revisiting the definition of a *problem* given in Chapter 1, then by defining a *complex problem*, then by asking ChatGPT if the number and complexity of complex problems are growing, and finally by emphasizing the value of creating a hybrid intelligence to solve the problems.

I said in Chapter 1 that a *problem* exists when there is an undesired effect (state) and the problem solver lacks the knowledge required to transform it into a desired effect (state). Unlike exercises, problems do not come preformulated, do not have a single correct solution, do not always remain solved, frequently require a multi-disciplinary team to solve them, and become progressively better defined during the problem-solving process. *Problem-solving* is defined as the process of coming to know the causes (there's usually more than one) of the undesired effect and ways to act on the causes to transform them into the causes of the desired effect. Determining how to act on a cause involves first thinking of alternative ways of acting on it (diverging), then selecting one of the ways as best (converging). This idea is illustrated in Figure 1.1 and again in Figure 3.6 and once again in Figure 5.1 so that you don't have to page back to find one of the other two figures.

A *complex* thing, such as a human body, a rocket, or a social system, consists of a diverse array of interacting parts. *Complexity* refers to the

DOI: 10.4324/9781003654407-6

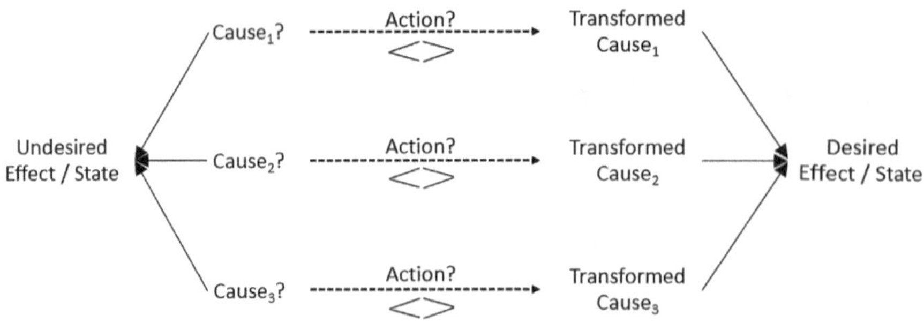

Figure 5.1 A *problem* exists when there is an undesired effect (or state) and the problem solver lacks the knowledge required to transform the undesired effect into the desired effect (or state). *Problem-solving* is thinking of ways to act on the causes of the undesired effect (or state) to transform them into the causes of the desired effect (or state).

degree of interconnectivity and interdependence of the parts and the resulting unpredictability of the thing's properties (qualities, behaviors, capabilities). Thus, we can say that a *complex problem* is an undesired effect that has a diverse array of interacting causes. The complexity of a problem grows as the degree of interconnectivity and interdependence of the causes grows, making the emergent properties of the undesired effect harder to predict.

Diagnosing and acting on a problem with a diverse array of causes requires a cognitively diverse team. For example, a rocket malfunction (the undesired effect) might be caused by mechanical issues, software errors, material defects, structural weaknesses, or human error. Diagnosing and acting on the causes will require some combination of aerospace, structural, propulsion, avionics, systems, software, ground control, materials, or quality control engineers. And a complex social problem, such as community's homelessness problem, will likely require a multi-disciplinary team of mental health, employment, addiction, law enforcement, and other kinds of professionals to solve it.

Now let's turn to the number of complex problems in the world. Is the number of complex problems and their degree of complexity growing, as many authors claim? I turned to ChatGPT for an answer.[1] Here is what it had to say.

Prompt

I have defined a complex problem as set forth in the foregoing text. Is the number of complex problems and their degree of complexity growing? If so, explain why and give examples.

ChatGPT's Response

Yes, the number of complex problems and their degree of complexity are growing. Several interrelated factors contribute to this trend, including technological advancements, globalization, increasing interconnectivity, and accelerating change. Below, I outline the reasons and provide examples.

1. *Increasing Interconnectivity and Interdependence*

- The modern world is more interconnected than ever, with digital networks, supply chains, and global governance structures linking diverse systems.
- Interdependence means that local disturbances can propagate through complex systems, creating emergent problems that are difficult to predict and control.

Example: The 2008 financial crisis was triggered by failures in the subprime mortgage market but quickly escalated into a global economic meltdown due to interdependencies in financial markets, banking systems, and trade networks.

2. *Technological Acceleration and Disruptions*

- Rapid technological progress introduces new capabilities but also new vulnerabilities and unintended consequences.
- The increasing complexity of technology itself creates new failure points that are difficult to anticipate.

Example: AI-driven automation improves efficiency but disrupts job markets, creates ethical dilemmas (e.g., bias in decision-making), and raises risks related to cybersecurity and misinformation.

3. *Expanding Scale and Scope of Human Activity*

- As societies become more advanced, they engage in larger and more ambitious projects that involve numerous stakeholders, increasing the number of variables at play.
- More actors (governments, corporations, individuals) with competing goals create complex negotiation and coordination challenges.

Example: Climate change is a planetary-scale problem caused by industrial emissions, deforestation, and unsustainable practices. Addressing it requires global cooperation, technological innovation, and behavioral change—each with its own interdependent challenges.

4. *Emergent Properties and Unintended Consequences*

- Complex systems exhibit emergent behaviors that cannot always be deduced from their individual components.
- Small changes can lead to disproportionate or nonlinear effects.

Example: Social media was designed to enhance communication but has led to unforeseen problems such as political polarization, misinformation, and mental health crises due to its emergent effects on human behavior and group dynamics.

5. *Acceleration of Change and Reduced Adaptation Time*

- The increasing pace of technological and social change reduces the time available for institutions and individuals to adapt.
- This creates new complex problems before older ones are resolved, leading to cumulative complexity.

Example: The transition to renewable energy is necessary to mitigate climate change, but it disrupts existing energy markets, requires new infrastructure, and creates geopolitical tensions over rare earth minerals.

6. *Increased Data and Information Overload*

- The availability of massive amounts of data makes decision-making more complex, as problem solvers must filter signal from noise.
- More data does not always lead to better solutions; it can create paralysis or biased decision-making.

Example: The COVID-19 pandemic saw an explosion of conflicting data and opinions, making it harder for policymakers to reach consensus on the best course of action.

Conclusion

Yes, both the number and complexity of problems are increasing due to rising interconnectivity, rapid technological advancements, larger-scale human activity, emergent systemic behaviors, and accelerated change. As these factors compound, problems become harder to define, predict, and solve, necessitating interdisciplinary approaches, adaptive strategies, and continuous learning.

ChatGPT's response focuses on problems (undesired states) to which organizations must respond or adapt. To determine the sort of cognitive diversity that might be required to respond to the problems, I followed up with this prompt[2]:

Prompt

It appears that the problems you have described are undesired states of the world to which organizations must respond. Regenerate your response. This time, for each example, also describe what sort of multi-disciplinary (cognitively diverse) team might be assembled to devise a response to the undesired state.

ChatGPT's Response

Yes, the problems described are indeed undesired states of the world that require organizations to respond. Given their complexity, solutions must come from multi-disciplinary teams that bring together different cognitive perspectives, knowledge bases, and problem-solving approaches. Below, I describe each problem along with a suggested team composition for addressing it.

1. *Increasing Interconnectivity and Interdependence*

- Problem: Global financial crises, pandemics, and supply chain disruptions arise from high interdependence among economic, technological, and social systems.
- Example: The 2008 financial crisis was triggered by failures in the subprime mortgage market but quickly escalated into a global economic meltdown due to interdependencies in financial markets, banking systems, and trade networks.
- Cognitively Diverse Team to Respond:

  - Economists—Analyze macroeconomic trends and systemic risk factors.
  - Behavioral Scientists—Study decision-making biases and risk perception in financial markets.
  - Data Scientists—Model market fluctuations and early warning signals.
  - Regulatory Experts—Design policies to stabilize financial systems and prevent future crises.
  - Political Scientists—Advise on global coordination between governments and financial institutions.

2. *Technological Acceleration and Disruptions*

- Problem: Rapid technological development brings efficiency gains but also new vulnerabilities, ethical dilemmas, and unintended societal consequences.
- Example: AI-driven automation improves efficiency but disrupts job markets, creates ethical concerns (e.g., biased algorithms), and raises cybersecurity risks.
- Cognitively Diverse Team to Respond:

    - AI and Machine Learning Experts—Develop fair and explainable AI systems.
    - Ethicists—Ensure AI decisions align with social values and fairness principles.
    - Labor Economists—Assess job displacement risks and propose workforce reskilling strategies.
    - Cybersecurity Specialists—Secure AI systems against hacking and manipulation.
    - Sociologists—Study the societal impact of AI and automation on human relationships and communities.

3. *Expanding Scale and Scope of Human Activity*

- Problem: Large-scale projects (e.g., space colonization, global sustainability initiatives) involve multiple stakeholders with competing interests.
- Example: Climate change is a planetary-scale problem caused by industrial emissions, deforestation, and unsustainable practices, requiring global cooperation.
- Cognitively Diverse Team to Respond:

    - Climate Scientists—Provide data on climate trends and modeling.
    - Energy Engineers—Develop clean energy alternatives to reduce carbon emissions.
    - Economists—Design carbon pricing and economic incentives for sustainability.
    - Policymakers—Negotiate international agreements and enforce regulations.
    - Behavioral Scientists—Create interventions to shift consumer and corporate behavior.

4. *Emergent Properties and Unintended Consequences*

- Problem: Technologies and social systems develop emergent behaviors that are difficult to predict, leading to unforeseen problems.
- Example: Social media was designed to enhance communication but has led to misinformation, political polarization, and mental health crises.
- Cognitively Diverse Team to Respond:

  - Computer Scientists—Improve algorithms to reduce misinformation and harmful content.
  - Media and Communication Experts—Study the effects of digital media on public discourse.
  - Psychologists—Assess the impact of social media on mental health and propose mitigations.
  - Regulatory and Legal Experts—Establish ethical guidelines for content moderation.
  - Civic Engagement Experts—Develop strategies for digital literacy and responsible online behavior.

5. *Acceleration of Change and Reduced Adaptation Time*

- Problem: The increasing speed of technological and social change leaves institutions and individuals struggling to adapt.
- Example: The transition to renewable energy is necessary to mitigate climate change but disrupts existing energy markets, infrastructure, and geopolitical stability.
- Cognitively Diverse Team to Respond:

  - Energy Policy Experts—Develop transition plans that balance economic and environmental concerns.
  - Geopolitical Analysts—Assess risks related to rare earth mineral supply chains.
  - Industrial Engineers—Innovate new energy storage and grid solutions.
  - Economists—Evaluate market incentives for renewable energy adoption.
  - Community Planners—Ensure fair distribution of renewable energy infrastructure.

6. Increased Data and Information Overload

- Problem: The abundance of data makes decision-making more complex, leading to information overload and confusion.
- Example: The COVID-19 pandemic saw an explosion of conflicting data, making it difficult for policymakers to make informed decisions.
- Cognitively Diverse Team to Respond:
  - Epidemiologists—Interpret public health data and predict disease spread.
  - Data Scientists—Develop real-time dashboards for accurate information tracking.
  - Behavioral Scientists—Understand how people process health information and combat misinformation.
  - Policy Experts—Design clear and effective public health guidelines.
  - Journalists and Science Communicators—Translate complex findings into accessible information for the public.

Conclusion

As the complexity of problems grows, responding to them requires increasingly multi-disciplinary teams that integrate diverse cognitive frameworks. Each field brings different methods of reasoning, tools, and epistemic perspectives, which together can improve the capacity to anticipate, mitigate, and resolve undesired states in the world. Effective problem-solving in a complex world depends on assembling and coordinating these cognitively diverse teams to generate adaptive, innovative, and resilient solutions.

Finally, to round out the examples of complexity, I asked ChatGPT if products and services are becoming more complex, why that might be the case, and to provide examples.[3] It responded in this way:

Prompt

Now I want to examine the need for cognitively diverse teams from another perspective. Is it fair to say that products and services are becoming more complex? If so, describe the reasons why, give examples, and describe the sort of cognitively diverse team that might be assembled to create the products and services.

ChatGPT's Response

Yes, products and services are becoming more complex due to increasing technological advancements, consumer expectations, regulatory requirements, and the interconnected nature of modern economies. Below, I outline the reasons for this increasing complexity, provide examples, and describe the cognitively diverse teams necessary to create and manage such products and services.

1. *Technological Advancements and Integration*

- Reason: Modern products integrate multiple technologies (e.g., AI, IoT, cloud computing, and blockchain) to enhance functionality, automation, and user experience.
- Example: Smartphones now function as communication devices, digital wallets, health monitors, and entertainment hubs. They incorporate AI-driven personal assistants, biometric security, and real-time cloud synchronization.
- Cognitively Diverse Team for Smartphone Development:

    - Hardware Engineers—Design high-performance processors, sensors, and materials.
    - Software Developers—Create operating systems, apps, and AI-driven assistants.
    - Cybersecurity Experts—Protect data privacy and enhance encryption methods.
    - UX/UI Designers—Optimize the user interface and experience.
    - Behavioral Scientists—Study human-device interaction and optimize engagement.

2. *Customization and Personalization Expectations*

- Reason: Consumers expect products and services tailored to their specific needs, requiring sophisticated data collection and real-time adaptation.
- Example: Streaming Services like Netflix use AI algorithms to recommend personalized content based on user preferences and behavior.
- Cognitively Diverse Team for Streaming Service Development:

    - Data Scientists—Develop recommendation algorithms and analyze viewing patterns.
    - Psychologists—Study consumer preferences and attention span.

- Content Creators—Produce engaging and culturally diverse content.
- Cloud Engineers—Optimize storage and streaming capabilities.
- Legal Experts—Navigate copyright and content distribution rights.

3. *Regulatory and Ethical Considerations*

- Reason: Increasing legal scrutiny (e.g., data privacy laws like GDPR) and ethical concerns (e.g., AI bias) make product development more complex.
- Example: Autonomous Vehicles require compliance with traffic regulations, ethical decision-making frameworks (who does a self-driving car protect in an accident?), and cybersecurity measures.
- Cognitively Diverse Team for Autonomous Vehicle Development:

  - AI and Robotics Experts—Build perception and decision-making systems.
  - Automotive Engineers—Design reliable mechanical and electrical components.
  - Ethicists—Establish decision-making principles for AI-driven safety.
  - Regulatory Specialists—Ensure compliance with global transportation laws.
  - Cybersecurity Professionals—Protect vehicles from hacking threats.

4. *Rising Interconnectivity and System Dependencies*

- Reason: Many products and services rely on interconnected ecosystems (e.g., smart homes, digital banking, and supply chains), making their design more complex.
- Example: Smart Homes integrate IoT devices, AI assistants, and cloud services to control lighting, security, and energy usage seamlessly.
- Cognitively Diverse Team for Smart Home Development:

  - IoT Engineers—Design connected home devices (e.g., smart thermostats).
  - Software Developers—Ensure interoperability across platforms.

- Data Privacy Experts—Secure user data from unauthorized access.
- Architects and Urban Planners—Design smart home infrastructure.
- Sociologists—Assess the impact of automation on daily life.

5. *Demand for Sustainable and Circular Economy Models*

- Reason: Environmental concerns push companies to develop eco-friendly products with minimal waste and resource consumption.
- Example: Electric Vehicles (EVs) are replacing traditional combustion-engine cars to reduce carbon emissions, but they require sustainable battery production and recycling solutions.
- Cognitively Diverse Team for EV Development:

  - Battery Chemists—Develop longer-lasting, recyclable batteries.
  - Mechanical Engineers—Design lightweight, efficient car structures.
  - Energy Policy Experts—Advocate for infrastructure and incentives.
  - Economists—Evaluate pricing and market penetration strategies.
  - Environmental Scientists—Assess lifecycle impact and recycling methods.

6. *The Rise of the Experience Economy*

- Reason: Consumers value experiences over ownership, leading to business models based on access, membership, and immersive interactions.
- Example: Virtual Reality (VR) Entertainment offers interactive gaming, virtual tourism, and simulated training experiences.
- Cognitively Diverse Team for VR Development:

  - VR Developers—Build immersive 3D environments and interactive content.
  - Neuroscientists—Study cognitive responses to virtual stimuli.
  - Gamification Experts—Design engagement-driven interactions.
  - Storytellers and Narrative Designers—Create compelling user experiences.
  - Ergonomics Experts—Ensure comfortable and accessible device use.

Conclusion

The growing complexity of products and services arises from technological convergence, personalization demands, regulatory challenges, system interconnectivity, sustainability imperatives, and shifting consumer expectations. Addressing these complexities requires assembling cognitively diverse teams that integrate expertise from multiple domains, ensuring holistic, innovative, and adaptive solutions. As products and services become more multifaceted, organizations must embrace interdisciplinary collaboration to navigate uncertainty, anticipate emergent challenges, and create meaningful, high-impact innovations.

Considering the growing number and complexity of the problems to which organizations must respond and the rising complexity of the products and services they must design and produce, it simply stands to reason that organizations must become better at thinking together, which is to say, better at combining collective intelligence and artificial intelligence to solve complex problems. To do this, as summarized in the following bullet points and depicted in Figure 5.2, they must:

- become adept at assembling cognitively diverse groups of *people* that engage in functional meeting behaviors and follow a collaboration strategy;
- equip them with meeting, group, and problem-solving *processes* that guide and stimulate their thinking;
- provide them with analogical and digital *platforms* for executing the processes; and
- learn to use *generative AI* to augment the people, processes, and platforms.

This book has described each of these factors in detail, including numerous ways that generative AI can be used to augment each factor. I hope it will help your organization to solve the complex problems it faces.

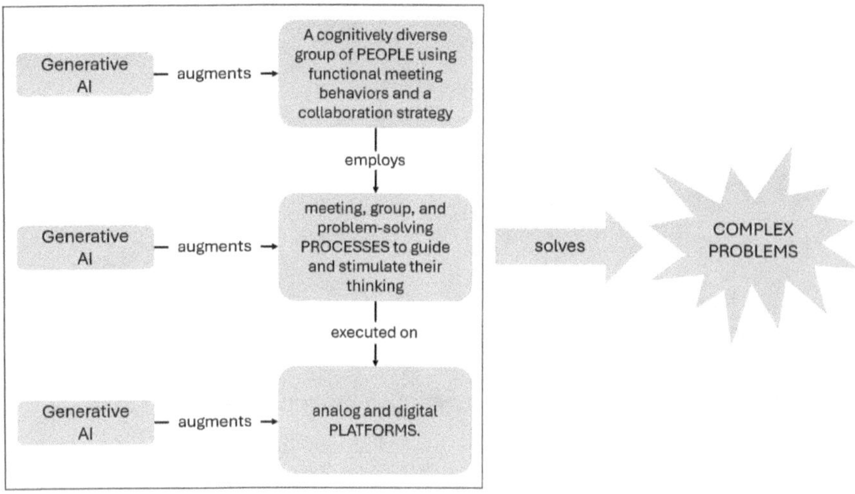

Figure 5.2 A cognitively diverse group of *people* using meeting, group, and task *processes* executed on analog and digital *platforms*, all augmented by generative AI, solves complex problems.

Notes

1 OpenAI, Response to "I have defined a complex problem as set forth in the foregoing text. Are the number of complex problems and their degree of complexity growing? If so, explain why and give examples." *ChatGPT-4o*, 2025.

2 OpenAI, Response to "It appears that the problems you have described are undesired states of the world to which organizations must respond. Regenerate your response. This time, for each example, also describe what sort of multi-disciplinary (cognitively diverse) team might be assembled to devise a response to the undesired state. If so, why?" *ChatGPT-4o*, 2025.

3 OpenAI, Response to "Now I want to examine the need for cognitively diverse teams from another perspective. Is it fair to say that products and services are becoming more complex? If so, describe the reasons why, give examples, and describe the sort of cognitively diverse team that might be assembled to create the products and services. If so, why?" *ChatGPT-4o*, 2025.

Index

Note: Page numbers in *italic* indicate a figure on the corresponding page.

FSC
www.fsc.org
MIX
Papier | Fördert gute Waldnutzung
FSC® C083411

Kolibri 360 GmbH
Ferdinand-Jühlke-Straße 7
99095 Erfurt, Deutschland
produktsicherheit@kolibri360.de